HANDS OFF MY GUN

Defeating the Plot to Disarm America

DANA LOESCH

**CENTER
STREET**

New York Boston Nashville

Center Street
Hachette Book Group
1290 Avenue of the Americas
New York, NY 10104

www.CenterStreet.com

Printed in the United States of America

RRD-C

First edition: October 2014

10 9 8 7 6 5 4 3 2 1

Center Street is a division of Hachette Book Group, Inc.
The Center Street name and logo are trademarks of Hachette Book Group, Inc.

The Hachette Speakers Bureau provides a wide range of authors for speaking events. To find out more, go to www.HachetteSpeakersBureau.com or call (866) 376-6591.

The publisher is not responsible for websites (or their content) that are not owned by the publisher.

Library of Congress Cataloging-in-Publication Data

Loesch, Dana.
  Hands off my gun : defeating the plot to disarm America / Dana Loesch. — First edition.
      pages cm
  Summary: "How many people in America today are truly well versed in the history of the Second Amendment, and why and how it was included in the Bill of Rights? Dana Loesch gives her views on all that and much more, thanks to the research she offers in HANDS OFF MY GUN. Fearless and fiery conservative talk show host, blogger, and TV commentator, Loesch digs deep into past, present, and future facts, attitudes, and actions regarding gun rights. HANDS OFF MY GUN is filled with research and detail. In addition to explaining why the Founding Fathers insisted on including the right to bear arms in the Bill of Rights, Loesch argues that "gun control" regulations throughout history have been used to keep minority populations under control. She also contends that current arguments in favor of gun control are primarily based on emotions and fear. This narrative is a must-read for every committed Second Amendment supporter. Dana Loesch is a determined and fierce advocate for those rights and shouts out with confidence: hands off my gun!"—Provided by publisher.
  Includes bibliographical references and index.
  ISBN 978-1-4555-8434-5 (hardback) — ISBN 978-1-4789-8275-3 (audio download) — ISBN 978-1-4789-5758-4 (audio book) 1. Gun control—United States. 2. Firearms ownership—United States. 3. Firearms owners—Civil rights—United States. I. Title.
  HV7436.L64 2014
  323.4'3—dc23
                                      2014027970

For Chris, Liam, and Ewan, truth isn't mean, it's truth.

In memory of Howard Scaggs and Chip Gerdes. Rolltide.

———————

Acknowledgments

Psalm 106:1. Psalm 144:1. Matthew 26:52–54.

Before anything, thanks be to God.

Thank you to my husband, Chris, for being my biggest champion and greatest supporter. Who knew that two former goth kids with a love for M.A.C. would turn out like this? This is all the more fun with you riding shotgun. I love you.

Thank you to my sons Liam and Ewan, who encourage me and remind me why I fight for truth. I don't want rights that we have known for so long be foreign ideas to you in the future. When you fight, have fun. This country is too amazing to not be a happy warrior.

Thank you to my mother, Gale, for being a real-life Julia Sugarbaker. That's where the fire comes from. Now people know where I get it. To my father, Robert, for making me believe that lawn mowers were more dangerous than the .38 in your nightstand after accidentally running over all our cordless phones with your riding mower when I was a teenager.

To my in-laws Danny and Gale, who pray nonstop and it shows. Thank you for helping to instill a love of the shooting sports into your grandsons and for buying them their first rifles.

To my grandparents Howard and Beulah, I miss you. Thank you for making me feel safe as a kid and for letting me know that no matter how mean life could be, I could always find refuge in your little house on the side of the hill. I will see you again someday.

To our amazing, ridiculously large southern Missouri families, even though half of you will hate this book, we're blood and I love you and that's all that matters. To the ones who agree with it, HIGH FIVE. You just made the fancy Christmas card list this year!

To our Lou crew friends, you have been there from the very beginning, back when I freelanced on the side and faked using cloth diapers to make mommy friends. Even though some of you have never even fired a gun, I know you'll have this on your bookshelf just because I wrote it. Kung Pow Meow, ladies.

Acknowledgments

Thank you, Chip Gerdes, for being a happy warrior. We miss you. Your funeral was the funeral scene from Burton's *Big Fish*. Such friends are rare and your absence is felt every day.

To Jimi Pirtle, you are an amazing friend. I'm still holding you to your promise of a sixer of Ski. To the Krutas, ChowSTL, and Gateway Grassroots, thank you for your friendship.

To George Hiltzik, I'm sorry that I thought you were trolling me when you first called. Fortunately, I called you back and am I ever so glad that I did. Thank you for everything these past few years.

To Glenn Beck, thank you for being the sort of boss who is as inspired by the people who work for him as they are by him. The results are magic. Thank you for this new platform at TheBlaze. I'm home.

To Eric Kayira, words are insufficient here. You're family now. This means you have to vote Republican. (Just kidding!)

To the late Andrew Breitbart, you told me once "let me be your rodeo clown" at a time when the heat was excruciatingly hot. Your loyalty to others, and your vision and dedication to truth, inspired their loyalty to you. It is glaringly missed.

To Jim Hoft, I'll never forget our 2 a.m. flyer drop around the city or any of the other frillion or so escapades we've gone on in the past seven or so years. You are such a talented friend and I'm proud to know you. Also proud to know Andrew Marcus and Jeremy Segal, the Chicago contingent of our ride-or-die crew.

To Ben and Breeanne Howe, we are blessed and strengthened by your friendship.

To Keith Urbahn, Matt Latimer, and the Javelin team, it is a joy working with you and I'm not just saying that because you have the best Christmas swag in Washington. To my amazing, wonderful editor Kate Hartson at Center Street.

Thank you: Michelle Malkin, Ted and Shemane Nugent, Sean Hannity, David Limbaugh, Mark Levin, Megyn Kelly, Glenn Reynolds, John Lott, Michael Savage, Virginia Grace, and Joel Cheatwood.

To Jeff Allen, Kevin Conrey, Harley "Kane" Lightle, and my flagship team at Emmis and KFTK 97.1 FM Talk. To Jamie Allman, Mike Paradiso, Rich McFadden, and Greg Edger at Radio America. To my programming directors at our affiliates across the country. To Tony Katz, Crane Durham, Marc Cox, Stacy Washington, Stephen Yates, Ann Coulter, Steven Crowder, Gary and Shelli Eaton, and Peter Kinder.

To Joel, Stan, and the team at Top Gun Shooting Sports in Arnold, Missouri. And to Jon, Grady Powell, Jared Ogden, and the crew at Asymmetric Solutions.

Contents

Introduction

When I was a little girl, my grandpa took me out in his backyard. He showed me how to shoot food cans with a BB gun, then he graduated me to playing with my male cousin's little green army men. He was obviously the kind of person who Barack Obama had in mind when he famously and derisively mocked gun owners and other rural Americans as "bitter" "clingers." Talking about visiting small-town Americans as if he were on some kind of safari, the elitist Harvard-trained community organizer, believing he was talking to donors in a private setting, confided his total contempt. "It's not surprising then they get bitter," he said. "They cling to guns or religion or antipathy toward people who aren't like them."

Well, I guess you could say my grandpa was an OBC, an Original Bitter Clinger. The man thought bankers were crooks, doctors were quacks, and that the only things you could count on in life were God, family, and a shotgun. He probably wouldn't care much for Barack Obama—not, as Obama apparently assumed, because anyone who disagreed with him was a racist. Instead, it was because the president lacks what my grandpa had in abundance: common sense. Obama organized communities—whatever that means. My grandpa actually lived in a community, and my visits there really changed my life.

Their little bolthole in the Ozarks was a sanctuary for a kid like me. The nearest supermarket was forty-five minutes away. If you needed beer or cheese in a pinch, the Mini Mart had you mostly covered; otherwise you killed it, milked it, caught it yourself, or distilled it in a bathtub. My grandparents ate everything they killed—raccoon, squirrel, fish, deer, turkey—and were grateful for nature's bounty. They kept goats and harvested fresh eggs from their chickens most mornings. Grandpa would take his grandsons hunting with him and bring back whatever they killed, then let us granddaughters watch him skin and clean it in the backyard. One time he made me hold a squirrel's legs while he pulled the fur off.

When I stayed with my grandparents during the falls and winters, I loved to curl up with blankets by their wood-heated stove. That often meant I'd wake up with whatever Grandpa killed last night carefully laid out as a joke beside me, their lifeless eyes staring straight into mine.

Nothing my grandpa killed ever went to waste. That's how bitter clingers work in a community: They live in harmony with nature because they rely on nature to provide and sustain them. Hunting out of season or thinning a herd too much meant destabilization. Bitter clingers are conservationists, not environmentalists. They don't need bureaucrats in plush offices in Washington lecturing them about how to protect the land; the land is essential to their way of life.

My grandparents always had some of us grandkids staying with them. Bless them, they were never left to their own devices, and I'm not sure they would have known what to do if they ever were alone. They had a few bedrooms in their tiny house, but it didn't matter: The youngest grandkids would all somehow find their way into Grandma and Grandpa's bed and they slept there, much like a little kid crowds their bed with stuffed animals. As a result, Grandpa was always falling out of his own bed or some kid was falling and getting stuck between the mattress and the wall.

One summer night I slept in their bed with my younger cousin as the cool valley breeze blew through the window, rustling through the curtains. The chorus of frogs and crickets outside was broken by the sound of someone sobbing and running up my grandparents' gravel drive. The storm door slammed and there was commotion. I learned at a young age that you hear more if you pretend to be asleep, so I did just that when Grandma rushed down the hall to check on us before hurrying back down the dark hall toward the light of the living room. The late-night visitor was their daughter, my aunt, clad in nothing but nightclothes. She had been assaulted by her estranged husband. In between sobs, she told them that she had escaped after her husband tried to take a knife to her throat. When he had gone for his gun, she managed to flee. As she sat in her parents' house, shaking, she was terrified that he'd come for her. Grandma called "the law," but in a rural county such as these parts, "the law" could be miles and miles away. While Grandma dialed it in, Grandpa silently strode into their bedroom. His every step rang simultaneously with anger and with careful purpose. He quietly opened his glass-and-wood gun case, removed his shotgun, and strode back through the living room. From there he went right out to the front porch, sat on the swing, and cocked it.

As I listened to him rock rhythmically, creaking back and forth in that swing, I never felt safer in my life. I fell into a sound sleep.

I later learned that Grandpa sat on that porch swing until a deputy arrived nearly forty minutes after Grandma's call. People were expected to be able to take care of their own, with prejudice. I didn't know it at the time—it was really the only world I knew—but the Ozarks were different. It was a place different from other parts of the country where you cannot be prevailed upon to do anything without the aid or permission of the government. Where my family is from, it never occurred to us to outsource our self-defense to a distant law enforcement entity that had huge rural counties to cover with just a few deputies. It also never occurred to me that our grandparents' or parents' firearms were toys with which we could play. We knew what firearms were and that you can't unpull a trigger; we were taught that lesson from the very first moment we could walk. Guns aren't toys. The lesson about guns was so ingrained in our communities that people had them in gun racks in their pickups, without any fear that a child might grab one. That was unheard-of. My grandpa's own handcrafted gun case didn't have a lock and was used more to display his collection than to keep them locked away. Our parents taught us not to touch a hot stove, not to run into the street, not to play with guns. Most important, we were taught a respect for life.

"You don't put your finger on this unless you're fixin' to kill something," my Grandpa once sternly told me as I trained the barrel of my cousin's BB gun on a He-Man action figure. When we moved to the city I was shocked at how many of my friends weren't taught this. My mom kept a loaded .38 revolver in her nightstand; I knew it was there, and I knew that I was to never mess with it except as my last hope of defense. I mentioned it once to a girlfriend during a sleepover. She was shocked and wanted to see it.

"No," I told her. My family also taught me respect for privacy. "My mother will ask you to leave." And that was the end of that.

Living in St. Louis, I didn't need to hunt for my own food, since supermarkets were minutes away. We had a few guns in the house for security, but that was the extent of it.

It wasn't until I got active in politics that my life and the lives of my children were threatened that I got angry. Kids can tell when their parents are afraid. They can sense when their safety isn't assured. I never wanted my family to have that feeling. I wanted my children to feel as secure as I did that night at my grandparents's house, with my grandpa keeping watch on the porch, creaking away on his porch swing all night long.

HOW I LEARNED TO FIGHT BACK

I began blogging on politics in 2001, under a pretentiously ridiculous handle, "Catalyst." I was twenty years old, struggling prematurely through a midlife crisis, and working out my political evolution online. I created a website with some friends and wrote about politics and pop culture. It received a fair amount of traffic and made the lists of various promoters, publishers, and PR flaks who constantly sent me materials. We covered music, interviewed some A-level indie artists, attended screenings, and penned film reviews; we wrote about politics with an unaffiliated, libertarian-infused, independent conservative perspective.

By the time I had my first child, as most mothers would understand, I didn't have the energy to keep up with the site anymore. Plus many of my friends were getting married and moving away, so it didn't make sense to continue. But I learned a lot during my stint as a web publisher. During my time as Catalyst, I experienced how nasty the Internet can be when empowered anonymous nobodies sitting in their bedrooms and hating the world think they can spit fire at you with no accountability. But that didn't turn me off to the Internet. Despite this, or maybe because of it, the Internet felt like the Wild West. I could give as good as I got. I loved it. My voice grew stronger because of it.

When I had my second son in 2004, I began a new site called *Mamalogues*, and chronicled what it was to be a young mother who never set out for the idyllic family life I had created. Readership grew. I pitched the site as a weekly column for the daily paper; it was accepted and over time it became one of the most popular columns on their website. I suppose I could have just written about vanilla-wafer, noncontroversial things like where to get the best deals on diapers, but that wasn't really my style. I was never someone who was afraid to stir things up. Readers were aghast when I wrote a column in support of public breastfeeding, but nothing matched the complaints that flooded into the paper when I penned another column about how I was a mother and a gun owner and kept firearms in my home, where my children lived and slept.

Judging from the contempt leveled down on me, you would have thought that I was forcing them to embrace my lifestyle and demanding that they themselves purchase a gun and give a rifle to each of their toddlers for Christmas. Suddenly I wasn't edgy and provocative. I was—*quelle horreur!*—controversial. As a result, my editors advised me to tone down my "bluntness"— the very quality, of course, that they originally found appealing. I knew what was happening. These guys were bending to the pressure from within the paper and from the outside community—a platoon of little old blue-haired liberals who formed a significant segment of their readership. Even though I had won an award from the paper's rival, an alternative weekly, for best column in the city, my own paper dropped me from print.

The official narrative offered to their readers was that we had gone our separate ways, but the actual narrative was that I was too often covering issues through a conservative lens. The column on firearms was the final straw. My departure created a big controversy in the local media; the alternative weekly, gleeful that they had dirt on their competitor, wrote a piece on the fallout and later put me on the cover of their publication, dressed as a revolutionary soldier in period uniform. Next, I was invited to appear on a local radio program in St. Louis, and from that I was given my own Sunday night broadcast (I am now nationally syndicated through weekday afternoons) where I kicked off the tea party movement in St. Louis; one of the first tea party rallies was held in the cold February of 2009. To a lot of fashionable people on the coasts of America, the tea party was another group of bitter clingers who dared to petition and—gasp!—demonstrate against their government without anybody's permission. I felt right at home. The tea party movement restored my faith in the American political system.

That summer in 2009, everything changed for me, though, in the parking lot in a St. Louis suburb where Democrat congressman Russ Carnahan was holding a town hall meeting with his constituents. Until the formation of the tea party, congressional town halls were expected to be boring affairs where one or two people show up to air hyperpersonal grievances. The congressman puts on a show caring for their issue and gets his picture in the paper shaking the hand of Grandma Voter before sealing himself back into his Washington bubble. That was before the tea party.

During that hot summer congressional town halls became the places to be, where scores of angry citizens gave their tone-deaf government what for after Washington policies led to a deep recession while they spent taxpayer dollars on a billion-dollar bailout of their buddies on Wall Street and in the auto industry. People were hot with rage, and rightly so. This being America, there were also clever entrepreneurs onsite who were trying to make a living selling T-shirts and other paraphernalia to tea party crowds that had gathered. In St. Louis, the Democrats didn't like that, and neither did their left-wing allies.

Because Kenneth Gladney was a traveling vendor who matched his wares to his audience, he was profiled by the Service Employees' International Union (SEIU) as a black conservative. The union thugs didn't take kindly to his presence at the Carnahan town hall selling Gadsden flags to scores of tea party attendees; Carnahan volunteers were caught on tape mocking him and calling him "black man." This didn't seem to be a new tactic for the labor unions. Since these were a group of liberals, it long had been OK for them to be racists. But this time I was at this event—and so were citizen journalists with cameras; as everyone was leaving the town hall, SEIU thugs ratcheted things up a notch. They attacked Gladney, even as cameras rolled. Yet because this was Democrat-rich St. Louis, a proud union town, the blue-collar attackers got off scot-free.

I worked to bring attention to this story. I covered it on air, wrote about it on my website, canvassed my Twitter stream with links to video, conducted interviews with Gladney and the various witnesses on the scene. I worked with others to identify and contact everyone in the parking lot who witnessed the assault.

Greta Van Susteren at Fox News was the first national reporter in America to pick up this story. I had been in my car, in the parking lot of the school where Carnahan's town hall was held, about to leave for an appearance on Fox when the Gladney incident went down. I had already been planning to go on the show for another purpose, but as soon as I was miked and in the chair, I informed her producer of the breaking news situation. They wanted video as soon as I could get them any, which I did in time for their broadcast the next evening.

After my appearance on Greta came Fox News's Bill O'Reilly. And then conservative commentator and friend Andrew Breitbart emailed me in half CAPSLOCK to ask for footage and updates as SEIU fought and disputed the allegations. Andrew plastered his popular Breitbart website with updates and declared war on the media outlets that were ignoring the story. (Most of them.) Meanwhile, progressives put Gladney in their crosshairs—along with the few of us helping to bring his story to national attention.

It was during this time that the emails started. I had a public e-mail address on my flagship station's site, KFTK 97.1 FM Talk. Before long that address was barraged with nasty e-mails and threats. Having been a commentator for a while now, I was used to this sort of response; the hot hatred had roughed up my skin and made me a bit tougher than I had any reason to be as a mother of two children. They failed to get the reaction that they wanted, so the calls began. People would cuss me out on-air. They would call and say horrible things to my call screener. They left nasty messages for my programming director. This was having no effect; the meaner they got, the harder I pushed.

After that people started following me. I was followed to the grocery store, to Walgreens, to work. My husband was followed and guys would sit outside his building, watching him whenever he entered or exited.

I pushed on—out of anger, out of spite, out of pure punk rock defiance. I was born for the storm and loved to fight. I thrived.

That is, until I received one more e-mail, which stopped me cold. One of the regular haters asked me how my kids were. He informed me that they knew where I lived, and that my kids might not be OK when I got home. As I looked down at those words, I was not a revolutionary anymore, or a catalyst, or a tea partier. I was not a cheerful warrior. I was a mom. I froze. The station deemed this e-mail had gone too far and involved the police.

"You need a handgun," said one detective.

"You need to get your CCW" [concealed-carry weapon]," said another, a cop who later became the chief of St. Louis City Police. "We can't be there all the time."

I went home after my show that day, grabbed my kids, and sat in the lower level of my husband's business, a former icehouse turned recording facility where the walls were four feet thick with concrete and brick. I felt untouchable in there. I was so stupid, I told myself. I decommissioned my parenting blog, privatized photos of my kids on my Flickr account, and thought about stopping what I was doing entirely. If I had to risk my family's well-being, it wasn't worth it. Almost as if it were in response to my inner monologue, my friend Chip called.

"Dana-doo," he said slowly, "you stay right where you are.

The Wolf is here. I've got your back. I'mma call you back in a few. Stay right by your phone."

The word was spreading on Twitter that I had received threats while I was on air that day. Less than a minute after I hung up with Chip, my phone rang again. It was Andrew Breitbart, calling me for the first time.

"THESE BASTARDS," he raved into the phone in place of "*hello.*" "THESE INSUFFERABLE BASTARDS. The safest place for you is in the light. The spotlight. Do not let these people throw you off from covering what is happening. Dana, if they can make you run away from it, it will establish a precedent. Then they can run anyone off. We will get through this." Then he hung up. At that moment, I knew he was right. But I really wasn't thinking about precedents.

Chip called back minutes later. That evening I had a dear friend of Chip's, a veteran, a member of special ops, sitting outside my house to bring me peace of mind. Chip also had me drive out to the countryside to meet a guy who would teach me krav maga, the hand-to-hand combat techniques taught in Israel. He also arranged for me to meet with Laura Clark, a security expert and an author, for several months. Clark took us through situational awareness, surveillance detection courses, and taught me the basics of self defense. She accompanied me to a few events, including Sen. Claire McCaskill's town hall at Jefferson College in the summer of 2009, where a group of men in purple SEIU shirts glared at me for a full hour and gave Clark cause for concern.

"Don't ever show them that you are afraid," Clark advised me. "Fear is their tactic. Defeat it."

I went out and bought a handgun. Though I grew up with

rifles, handguns were new to me. So I practiced. I got to know my firearm and shoot it well. I went for my CCW. I bought more handguns. While Andrew Breitbart worked to help elevate my story, I received a sense of confidence from the widespread public support I received. Chip worked to bring me peace of mind and a confidence in the security of my family. The efforts were effective. Probably more than my liberal provocateurs ever hoped. Scratch that. Definitely more than the left ever hoped.

As the days progressed, as I mulled over what these thugs had threatened to do to me, what they did do to a black man they didn't like, how they used my love for my kids to keep me silent, I became enraged. It was a white-hot anger, a fire, that rose from my gut and seared my throat. Through that rage I became hyperfocused on the Gladney story. Instead of cowering before organized thuggery, I got louder. My words grew into sharp instruments. I pushed back twice as hard at every attempt to intimidate me. I was infuriated by the manifest hypocrisy in the media and by the so-called civil rights activists who didn't have the time of day for a black conservative beaten by white liberals. I showed up to a protest outside of the NAACP's office with Gladney and others and I screamed for an Al Sharpton march to counter the injustice. The illustrious reverend, a shepherd of the flock, a man supposedly of God who I personally believe reaps money off the backs of the minorities he hustles into the hurt-and-rescue tactics of the grievance industry. I once asked him after we appeared on *Real Time with Bill Maher* together whether or not he could name any black tea party members or black conservatives running for office. I named a few, including Cedra Crenshaw and Antoine Members of Illinois. Sharpton brushed them off. He hadn't heard of them, he said, "and that's only a couple."

"It's a shame you don't know their names," I retorted.

When Sharpton isn't seemingly inciting riots leading to the incineration of fashion marts in Harlem, he's playing fake reverend with Jesse Jackson, also a fake reverend. Whenever a black liberal is offended, the Wonder Reverends are first on the scene, though this concern isn't equally extended to black conservatives, or even black Americans who may not be conservative per se, but were profiled as such because they sold a Gadsden flag to an elderly white woman in a St. Louis suburb. Sadly and predictably, they were nowhere to be found for Kenneth Gladney. Gladney wasn't the right kind of black American—at least, so said the head of the St. Louis chapter of the NAACP on a tape now widely available on the Internet, when he blasted Gladney as an "Uncle Tom" for selling Gadsden flags. I brought the story to the attention of Bill O'Reilly, who had the St. Louis NAACP leader on his show a day following one of my appearances, and the leader doubled down on the sentiment.

I called out the labor bosses by name along with their professional rent-a-thugs who showed up to fill audiences at Democrat events. The fear morphed into an indignant fury aided by the fact that unlike three months ago, this time I could protect myself. As the months progressed, my training led to the development of instinct. I walked to the parking lot from my radio station with confidence. I attended rallies with confidence, knowing that I could protect myself. I'll be damned if anyone ever makes me live in fear or feel victimized again.

Finally, the thugs went away. The bullies lost. This, I learned, is how you counter bullies. Never allow them to make you afraid. You fight back.

What all of this means to say is that I take gun rights very personally. I view it as a threat to my and my family's well-being whenever anyone seeks to erode or take away my Second Amendment civil liberty. The people screeching about disarming someone like me, a mother trying to protect her family—and make no mistake, that's exactly what they are doing—do not face what I face. They have not been threatened by their fellow citizens as I have been threatened simply for expressing a political thought contrary to their own. These individuals find their security by hiring private security or, if in office, security at taxpayer expense. I don't have such a luxury. These individuals also may find security in outsourcing their protection, such as depending upon the local police or a guard at the door of their secured apartment buildings. I do not find security that way. I trust no one but myself and my husband when it comes to keeping my family safe. I'll call 911, but until law enforcement arrives, I and my husband will hold down the fort. Perhaps I learned that from my grandfather, his shotgun laid across his lap as he gently swayed on the front porch swing. It's what I know and I think it's what millions of Americans who grew up in "flyover country" know. It's what infuriates us when empty-headed liberals or community activists or elitist politicians mocking God and guns tell us that we don't have a right to defend ourselves.

Once again I'm facing bullies; this time it's the anti–Second Amendment gun control lobby. They wear designer suits;

they're driven in chauffeured SUVs; they'll go on MSNBC and flash their whitened smiles and explain how more women should be left to the devices of brutes who would ravage them "for the children," as the talking point goes. I'm not fooled, though. These white-collar gun control thugs are a criminal's best friend. They may not rob or rape you themselves, but they aid in making it possible. See, without their help, criminals would have far less vulnerable prey.

———

Among the most notorious anti–Second Amendment advocates are former New York City mayor (and kazillionaire) Michael Bloomberg, his dwindling Mayors Against Illegal Guns, and their associated group, Moms Demand Action for Gun Sense in America. (They couldn't pick a name that didn't sound like a porno title?) Unlike the tea partiers these people mock, these are anything but grassroots groups that sprouted up from Middle America. The Moms Demand group, for example, is fronted by a professional Fortune 500 PR exec whose campaign involves bringing around a minivan (when a chauffeured SUV with tinted windows isn't available) driven by supposed soccer moms who want to disarm America. When I guest-co-hosted "*The View*" in 2014, Shannon Watts's group frantically tried to get me booted from the show, launching mass e-mails, Facebook petitions, and a Twitter campaign. They called me "Nancy Lanza," the mother of serial killer Adam Lanza, as if I was somehow responsible for the 2013 murder of children at Sandy Hook Elementary School. They claimed that I was paid by the firearms and accessories manufacturer Magpul, because a reporter and I rode in a rented chopper with a Magpul sticker on it for fifteen minutes while at a rally on behalf of my friend Kelly Maher's Coloradan grassroots group Compass Colorado. Even if I had been a Magpul employee or paid by Magpul—which I wasn't— so what?

Second Amendment supporters turned out in droves to counter the hateful push from the Moms Demand crowd. When I walked into makeup at the *View* studios in New York, the fight was one of the first things Whoopi Goldberg brought up.

"Why are so many people angry that you're here?" Whoopi asked me. She described how people were cluttering up her Twitter timeline screeching about guns. Jenny McCarthy agreed.

"Just the wrong way to go about that," McCarthy said, shaking her head at the Moms Demands group.

As before, whenever I'm confronted with a bully I take them head-on. I invited Shannon Watts, the Moms Demand PR exec honcho, onto my show on TheBlaze. I offered to pick her up from the airport, fly her to Dallas, drive her to our studios, feed her, do her makeup and hair, and have a fair conversation with her, before having her driven back to the airport to fly home. All she had to do was pack, breathe, and walk through two doors—hers and ours. Literally. That's it. She chose to ignore this invitation. Her pricey Washington-based PR firm, Berlin Rosen, sent me a mass publicity request concerning one of their initiatives, and once again I offered airtime. My replies went unanswered. Instead, Watts prefers to subtweet me on Twitter— that is, passive-aggressively attack me without having the guts to put my Twitter handle in her tweets so that I could see it and respond directly. I don't subtweet. I'll fly to your protest with cameras.

This is why I'm writing this book. The past few years saw an unprecedented push by anti–Second Amendment groups and politicians to restrict our civil liberties. The media and gun-grabbing progressives have put taking our guns from us at the top of their agenda. To do this they vilify us as murderers and argue that we're complicit in mass shootings, which are by definition the acts of the criminally insane. They defame us as those who don't respect life. They portray us as careless accomplices to acts of unbelievable horror.

Truth is, I got tired of making the same defenses over and over to people who refuse to listen to or even research online the simplest fact in making an argument. I got tired of hearing people like Mike Bloomberg bleat out ridiculous claims about firearm ownership and victimizing the innocent for the acts of criminals. I have known victims. I know what it's like to be targeted. I too have lived in fear.

As I did when my family was threatened, I'm pushing back. I hope other readers will join me. This book will cover every square inch of the gun control debate. This book will beat your progressive friend upside the head with facts. I hope you'll consider giving him or her a copy. They need to read this. We all do. This book will challenge those who may be well-intentioned, but are uneducated about what our gun rights really mean, where they originate, and what the statistics actually say.

Anti–Second Amendment advocates don't want you to read this book. Make doing so an act of resistance.

CHAPTER 1

The Tragedy Caucus

"Never let a good crisis go to waste."
—RAHM EMANUEL

December 14, 2012, was a day of horror and heartbreak. In the tiny town of Newtown, Connecticut, a twenty-year-old lunatic named Adam Lanza walked into Sandy Hook Elementary School and murdered twenty-six people. Twenty of his victims were in the first grade.

I was live on the radio as Lanza's shooting spree unfolded, and it was one of the most difficult broadcasts of my entire career. I have children myself and, as a parent, you see your child in every other child. I watched children fleeing from the school, single file, on my in-studio monitor. They were the same ages as my boys. Those children could have been my children. One of the students was wearing a button-down shirt that looked like the button-down belonging to my oldest son. The emotion was hard to choke back. I had a duty as a broadcaster when all I really wanted to be was a scared and angry mother. When you learn about children whose lives were cruelly cut short, you think about how precious and fragile are the lives of your own children. I fell asleep that night in my youngest son's bed, my arms wrapped tightly around him. I didn't for a moment think that I was to blame for this horrible tragedy. Or that our Founding Fathers were. Or the National Rifle Association, as loudly and publicly claimed by many gun control advocates. Or that anyone else who supported the Second Amendment to the United States Constitution had blood on their hands.

Within hours of the shooting, a despicable woman named Nouel Alba claimed on Facebook to be the aunt of a six-year-old victim at Sandy Hook and later asked for money to pay for funeral expenses. In fact, Alba had no relation to the shooting victim she said was her nephew, and she never gave a nickel of the money she received to the victim's family. After an investigation, she was later charged with fraud and sentenced to eight months in prison.

Like Alba, many gun grabbers saw the Newtown tragedy as an opportunity to exploit people. Some of them even unabashedly used the word *exploit* to describe their intentions. But instead of trying to exploit dead children in order to take people's money, the Tragedy Caucus wanted to exploit this tragedy as a tactic to take away law-abiding citizens' guns. They immediately saw Newtown as an opportunity to score political points and push their anti–Second Amendment agenda onto a grieving nation.

The use of children to scare people into submission has a storied history among demagogues. Throughout World War II, Adolf Hitler surrounded himself with children to demonstrate support for his brutal policies. As did Joseph Stalin, while he consolidated iron control of the Soviet Union and other nations in Eastern Europe and threw his opponents into gulags. Prior to the start of the war in Iraq in 1990, Saddam Hussein met with children from Western countries in an obvious attempt to make them hostages should the United States attack. The intention of the children's presence was to offset the brutality of their leader in the perception of the public. Gun control advocates do this to suggest that if you disagree with their desire to abolish the Second Amendment, then you must not value the lives of these children. None of this is meant to compare gun control zealots in America to Hitler and Stalin. While both Hitler and Stalin believe in disarmed populaces, modern-day gun control advocates freely admit that they want to exploit the deaths of children to achieve political goals that the country would otherwise oppose. As an example, in the July issue of *Rolling Stone*, Tim Dickinson wrote:

3. Politicize Disaster, Unabashedly

This may make some progressives queasy. But if you don't have the stomach for hardball politics, just accept that you're going to be steamrolled by the NRA—which shamelessly stokes the emotional power of national tragedies like 9/11, Katrina, and Superstorm Sandy to convince Americans that social collapse is around the corner, and you really should be buying that AR-15.

This isn't complicated: Making a political issue of the tiny coffins of dead children in the wake of a school shooting isn't just a thing that helps pass strong gun control, it's practically the only thing in the last quarter century that's moved the needle on anti-gun-violence laws.

It's interesting: Maybe if abortions were done with so-called "assault weapons," progressives would finally be OK with firearms.

Just hours after Adam Lanza's first bullet was fired, Mayor Michael Bloomberg urged the president to "send a bill to Congress to fix this problem." Because Congress could legislate away evil and madness, you see. He added, "We need immediate action." While parents were in shock and police were still stationed at their homes to protect families' privacy, New York congressman Jerry Nadler took to cable news and told MSNBC, "I think we will be there if the president exploits it."

Nadler wasn't alone in wanting to "exploit" the death of children. That same day, New Jersey senator Frank Lautenberg proclaimed, "Americans are sick and tired of these attacks on our children and neighbors and they are sick and tired of nothing being done in Washington to stop the bloodshed. If we do not take action to address gun violence, shooting tragedies like this will continue." New York's senator Chuck Schumer—never one to pass up the opportunity to grandstand in front of a television camera to admire the sound of his own voice—said, "Perhaps an awful tragedy like this will bring us together so we can do what it takes to prevent this horror from being repeated again."

Just two days later, California senator Dianne Feinstein made it clear what Schumer meant by "bring us together." She proposed to ban so-called "assault weapons," a made-up kittens-and-dandelions term used by people who have no understanding of firearms. "Assault weapon" has come to define any long gun that is black with lots of "stuff" stuck on it. Handguns are not included, although one you affix a silencer on a gun, grabbers think it makes it "shootier" and then you get into "assault-y" territory.

A brief special comment about Dianne Feinstein. The eighty-year-old California Democrat has been a crusader against the

Second Amendment to the Constitution since she was elected to the United States Senate. Most recent, as noted, was her crusade against "assault weapons." But she's made no secret about her stance against guns in general. The irony is that it was a gun that likely made her a senator in the first place.

In late 1978, San Francisco supervisor Harvey Milk, the first openly gay man elected to public office in California, was assassinated by a fellow supervisor, Dan White. Carrying a .38 revolver and ten rounds of ammunition, he had evaded the building's metal detectors by climbing in through a window. In the attack, Mayor George Moscone also was killed, leaving the president of the San Francisco Board of Supervisors, Dianne Feinstein, in line to succeed Moscone as mayor.

The shooting understandably had a profound effect on her. As it would on anyone on the scene of such a violent crime. "When you come from where I've come from and what you've seen, when you found a dead body and put your finger in bullet holes, you really realize the impact of weapons," she said on CNN in 2013. "I remember it, actually, as if it was yesterday."

Undoubtedly, Feinstein believes that had stricter gun control laws been passed in California, Harvey Milk and Mayor Mascone wouldn't have been killed. But that's assuming that Supervisor Dan White would follow the law. White was a troubled man who'd resigned his job and then wanted to be reinstated. He was not likely to be deterred from killing his intended victims because of any gun control law. He could have stolen a gun, or used a knife, or planted a bomb. Who knows what goes on in a troubled person's mind? Milk is one of many examples of why people, gay Americans in particular, shouldn't be disarmed. You could argue instead that Harvey Milk and the mayor might have survived had they been armed with guns of their own. Just like Dianne Feinstein was. Yes, that's right. Four years after the killing of Milk, she carried a .38 special in her purse. She had purchased the gun in the 1970s after a terrorist group shot out windows at her house. "I know the urge to arm yourself, because that's what I did," Feinstein once said. "I was trained in firearms. I walked to the hospital when my husband was sick. I carried a concealed weapon and I made the determination if somebody was going to try and take me out, I was going to take them with me."

You might consider Feinstein hypocritical, which she was, but it's not surprising. Members of Congress always think the laws don't apply to them. So I guess the lesson is: Gun control laws should apply to everyone except to Dianne Feinstein.

Accustomed to leading from behind, Barack Obama waited three whole days after the Sandy Hook tragedy before joining the Tragedy Caucus, but on December 17, 2012, he came out swinging. The stage he chose for his latest act of launching an initiative to take away Americans's freedoms? A prayer service. Yes, while moms and dads were mourning murdered loves ones, Barack Obama was practically standing on top of the coffins with his insincere grin and his teleprompter, ready to realize his lifelong dream of disarming any American who opposes him.

"We can't tolerate this anymore," he said, referring to the massacre, as if there were a tradition in the United States of widespread tolerance toward deranged lunatics who commit mass murder. "These tragedies must end. And to end them, we must change." *We* must change? We had nothing to do with this.

By then, I'd seen four years of Obama's idea of "change," and I wasn't holding hope for what would come next. "In the coming weeks," he vowed, "I will use whatever power this office holds to engage my fellow citizens—from law enforcement to mental health professionals to parents and educators—in an effort aimed at preventing more tragedies like this. Because what choice do we have? We can't accept events like this as routine. Are we really prepared to say that we're powerless in the face of such carnage, that the politics are too hard? Are we prepared to say that such violence visited on our children year after year after year is somehow the price of our freedom?"

Obama never used the terms "gun control" or "background checks" or "assault weapons," but behind his lofty rhetoric was a clear message: Guns are to blame for Newtown, and I'm coming after them. The president chose a prayer service as the vehicle from which to launch a political campaign. You couldn't disagree with President Obama at a prayer service because that would be un-Christian. That campaign was couched in kinder, gentler veneer than Michael Douglas's more direct proclamation at the end of Aaron Sorkin's *The American President*, but Obama's message was the same as the fictional President Andrew Shephard: "You cannot address crime prevention without getting rid of assault weapons and handguns. I consider them a threat to national security, and I will go door to door if I have to, but I'm gonna convince Americans that I'm right, and I'm gonna get the guns!"

I watched Obama's speech live and was outraged. I'm known for wearing my emotions on my sleeve, especially concerning life and liberty, and my thoughts exploded onto Twitter. "He just politicized a prayer service," I tweeted. It was nothing more than a reasonable statement of the obvious. In another tweet, I wrote, "This is really in poor taste. It's a prayer service. In front of the families. They need consolation, not your politics, Mr. President."

My tweets were accurate and restrained. What I really felt like saying was what Joseph Welch had once said to a different bully out to exploit innocent people in order to score cheap political points: "Have you no sense of decency, sir? At long last, have you left no sense of decency?" While I thought my tweets were obvious observations conveyed in a relatively restrained manner, gun grabbers disagreed. One individual, who I'm sure gets lots of dates, called me a "crazy cunt," tweeting "@DLoesch believes Pres was wrong to speak of taking action so other massacres may be prevented elsewhere. Go blow the NRA bitch!" Others were just as adorable:

"That is a disgusting picture on your twitter wall. And you dare criticize the President. You are a merchant of evil," Tweeted @desertcronenm (I had a photo of myself at the range with an AR-15 on my Twitter page months before Newtown).

"What a pathetic crock of sh!t you are! How many children do you have? #heartless," another by the handle @arendabdoory tweeted.

Progressives were aghast that I reasonably observed that the president had politicized a prayer service. Democrats have done it before; they turned Paul Wellstone's wake into a party pep rally.

"I'M YOUR HUCKLEBERRY"

It's hard to expect discourse more civil and thoughtful from anti–Second Amendment advocates on Twitter, but I expected better from my old sparring partner, Piers Morgan. Alas, I was soon to be disappointed. Over the course of several appearances on the British host's CNN show after the Newtown shooting, I pointed out several facts that often go overlooked in the debate over how many more restrictions on gun owners America needs. "Piers," I pleaded, much in the same way a mother pleads with a baby to eat, "we have gun laws already on the books. Most of the proposals are simply redundant." I asked, "Why are we paying individuals to go and essentially waste taxpayer dollars to argue laws that we already have on the books? Laws which either aren't enforced or criminals don't obey them simply because that's what criminal don't do? Criminals are called criminals because they don't follow the law." I also pointed out that Adam Lanza "did try to purchase a firearm. And Connecticut's gun laws prohibited him from doing that...But, you know, again, he stole firearms, he committed a crime to obtain a firearm which he then used illegally." Morgan and other anti–Second Amendment flat earthers do not understand the concept of evil people not following the laws. In their crazy-headed worldview, if only they could ban guns, then bad guys would throw up their hands and say, "Well, you got me. I was going to steal a revolver, but I don't want to break the law." People hell-bent on enacting mass murder aren't going to be deterred by a gun law, especially if they're not going to be deterred by the laws prohibiting multiple murders. Between illegally possessing a firearm and mass murder, mass murder is worse. It's kinda tops in terms of crimes one can commit.

During further conversations, Morgan and I talked about the common denominator for recent mass shootings—young men, estranged from society, on psychotropic drugs, some with little supervision. I told Morgan, "Every single one of them are on psychotropic drugs and yet we have little to no conversation about this at all whatsoever. And certainly I think that there need to be some reforms done to the mental health community in that particular area to address this."

Morgan needs to talk over his guests like a solar-powered calculator needs sunlight to function, but I thought that over the course of several shows, we had both been able to represent our own side and give as good as we got. Even when he responded to my comments by saying, "It makes me sick when I hear people say that kind of stuff," and throwing a wad of paper at me, I didn't take it personally because he threw like a girl. After all, he is entitled to a bit of hyperbole. It comes with the territory in politics.

Then one day Piers Morgan banned me from his show. CNN brass have never been fans of mine, because I was too uncomfortably and unabashedly conservative for them when I was a contributor. They could barely tolerate me as a guest, because heaven forbid someone doesn't verbally fellate Karl Marx during their time in the talk box.

My ban from Morgan's show—which proved only temporary, and I'd always kept in contact with his amazing and likely long-suffering staff—was a textbook case of liberal hypocrisy on gun control. It began in early May 2013, when I noted on Twitter that some friends and I had enjoyed some time at my favorite gun range. It was all (obviously) legal and all harmless, but Piers Morgan took issue. In response to my first tweet—"Took a crew of friends to my home range where we fired all manner of rifles, pistols, and yes, some fully auto. #Merica"—Morgan mockingly tweeted, "Yee-haw!" And when I posted a picture of my AR-15 rifle, which was one of the guns I'd shot at the range, Morgan wrote, "The assault rifle used at Aurora Sandy Hook."

When I replied, "@piersmorgan And everyone safe with all these rifles in the hands of law-abiding citizens!" Morgan replied, "Like Mrs Lanza?"

I was stunned. Mrs. Lanza had failed to properly and safely secure her guns. Her son Adam was a homicidal maniac. What exactly was Piers Morgan saying about me and my family? So I asked.

Me: "@piersmorgan Are you calling me Nancy Lanza?"

Morgan: "No. But she was a law-abiding, gun-loving, AR-15 owning citizen like you"

Me: "@piersmorgan So you're saying my son is a crazy murderer and I don't properly store my guns?"

Morgan: "No @DLoesch—I'm saying Adam Lanza and his mother were both 'law-abiding citizens' with a house full of guns. Then he shot up a school."

Me: "So because Adam Lanza's mom had a certain rifle, anyone else who owns this rifle is involved in shooting up schools, says @piersmorgan."

I was flabbergasted that despite his protestations, Piers Morgan was making a direct comparison between me and Adam Lanza's mother, just because we both owned a popular, legal rifle. Jeffery Dahmer and Piers Morgan both wore shoes, so is Piers going to lure men to his apartment and eat them? He fired off one last tweet that claimed, among other things, that "the Lanzas were law-abiding citizens." Cold-blooded killers who murder elementary school students do not count as "law-abiding citizens," but we had reached the point of diminishing returns in the argument. When a policy debate begins with a personal attack, it lacks any potential to be a serious and thoughtful discussion.

The Twitter battles between Morgan and me escalated later that same month after the horrific murder of a British soldier named Lee Rigby, who was beheaded by terrorists in South London. The soldier was killed near the Royal Artillery Barracks by an Islamic extremist wielding a machete and proclaiming, "We swear by Almighty Allah we will never stop fighting you. The only reasons we have done this is because Muslims are dying every day. This British soldier is an eye for an eye and a tooth for tooth. We apologize that women had to see this today but in our lands our women have to see the same. You people will never be safe."[1]

Anti–Second Amendment advocates are always blaming the NRA for high-profile murders, so I tweeted, "Was the guy with the machete a member of the NRA? Asking for a friend." My point, obvious to anyone not blinded by left-wing ideology, was that the British soldier was killed with a machete, rather than a gun. This was not a tragedy liberals could blame on the NRA. None of these mass murderers were members of the NRA. This wasn't a tragedy that could have been prevented with gun control. In fact, Britain has some of the toughest gun control laws in the world. If gun control laws really make crime go away, Lee Rigby would still be alive.

Piers Morgan responded to my tweet with outrage. He wrote, "You think the beheading of a soldier is something to be glib about???"

I cannot understand what made Morgan bleat out that response. He supports the gun laws that disarmed Rigby. Was he just bored and looking for a fight? Or was this man truly so obtuse that he didn't even realize it was his ideology of disarmament that was being mocked? No bipedal sentient human being would arrive at the conclusion that I was mocking one of Britain's finest (Rigby, not Morgan). If I wanted to be "glib" and mock a soldier, I'd ask Piers Morgan how to do it. He holds the record for endangering lives with doctored images of soldiers and Iraqi prisoners and was harshly denounced by his country's own military leaders for endangering their lives and mission. In 2004, he was fired from his post as editor of Britain's *Daily Mirror* after he published doctored photos that misleadingly showed British soldiers abusing Iraqi prisoners. The act directly endangered the lives of British troops still serving overseas.

To borrow a phrase from the gun control wars, I stood my ground. I tweeted, "As opposed to you calling me Nancy Lanza because I stood up for 2A rights? Get real, @piersmorgan."

I was of course referring to the earlier instance on Twitter when Piers Morgan had made a fool of himself by comparing me to Sandy Hook shooter Adam Lanza's mother, Nancy. But Morgan was determined to look as silly now as he had earlier in the month. "No @DLoesch," he tweeted, "there is a time to shut up with stupid political wisecracks, and this is one of those times. Show some bloody respect."

By this point, I had had enough. Apparently, only gun control advocates, and not opponents, are allowed to mention gun control after a tragedy. "That's rich coming from you, @piersmorgan," I shot back. "You stood on the graves of children and attacked my family. Get some consistency." Later, referring to my belief that the British soldier who was attacked should have been allowed to carry a weapon to protect himself, I wrote, "Yes, heaven forbid I think soldiers should at all times be able to protect themselves and point out what happens when PC intervenes." What happened to Rigby happened at Fort Hood: Nidal Hassan carried out his own jihad against our soldiers killing thirteen and injuring thirty-two.

I can only guess it was my belief that the otherwise defenseless should be allowed to protect themselves from machete-wielding Islamic terrorists that got me banned from Piers Morgan's show, because the next thing he wrote was, "Can't stomach @DLoesch goading Brits with her outrageous tweeting re beheaded soldier story. Unfollowed, and banned from my show."

"Classic," I replied, "@piersmorgan bans me from a show no one watches." I later added, "Even after he danced on the graves of children and said my children would grow up to be murderers, I was respectful to @piersmorgan …Speaking of 'goading,' @piersmorgan falsely implied my comment was otherwise and inadvertently sent a wave of death and rape threats my way."

I also couldn't resist noting that Morgan didn't have any right to sit on a high horse and condemn other journalists. I tweeted, "Maybe instead of mocking the disarmament ideology that creates victims, I should have Photoshopped soldier pics, right @piersmorgan ?"

Morgan's enthusiasm for attacking me is instructive: They show that there are no limits to gun grabbers' hatred for the Second Amendment. They will make any accusation, no matter how baseless, and demonstrate massive insensitivity by exploiting the most awful tragedies The fact that Piers Morgan's show was unceremoniously canceled by CNN and his eminence relegated to obscure tweets about British soccer teams shows that there wasn't much of an audience for his lectures night after night about how lawful gun owners like me and millions of Americans are responsible for tragedies like Sandy Hook. Interestingly, Morgan's ban didn't stick. Over a year later I was invited back onto his program in its final weeks, as both his producer and my producer from TheBlaze are friends. I was invited with one caveat: I was not to bring up the Photoshopping of soldier photos or hacked phones. I considered it a win.

The anti–Second Amendment advocates' willingness to exploit children was on display a month after the Newtown shooting when Barack Obama and Joe Biden spoke in the South Court Auditorium of the Eisenhower Executive Office Building. The audience included some of the families of the children murdered at Newtown, and behind Obama and Biden were four children who had written letters to the White House about gun violence. The visual message was clear: If you don't support gun control, you don't care about the death of kids like these kids behind me and the grief of parents like these parents we've invited to the White House today. As Rush Limbaugh correctly said, "Obama uses kids as human shields. The Democrats use kids as human shields. He brings these kids supposedly who wrote letters to the White House after Newtown, bring them up there to present a picture of support among the children."

The spoken message was just as heavy-handed and exploitative as the visuals. "I know for the families who are here that time is not measured in days," Joe Biden said, "but it's measured in minutes, in seconds, since you received that news." The point was made, but Biden kept going. "Another minute without your daughter. Another minute without your son. Another minute without your wife. Another minute without your mom." While

33

the vice president's emotional appeal was understandable, the message was that innocent Americans should expose themselves because a lunatic with an irresponsible mother caused a tragedy. There exist mothers who don't want to be punished and have their right to carry stripped from them because another parent's poor choices resulted in the unthinkable. Stripping mothers like me of our 2A rights only maliciously indicts us as coconspirators in a tragedy we didn't commit and places our own families at greater risk because we lack the equal means to protect them.

When Obama spoke, he called on Congress to pass a slew of progressives' all-time favorite anti–Second Amendment proposals, such as expanded background checks, a ban on so-called "military-style assault weapons," and a ban on "high-capacity magazines" (which are actually standard-capacity magazines).

This stuff was, by then, par for the course. Anti–Second Amendment advocates have used their special-interest money, phony polling data, and willingness to exploit tragedies to lobby for such laws for many years. But Obama didn't stop there. After the latest attempt at abridging the Second Amendment failed congressionally (Feinstein's resuscitated "Assault Weapons Ban" legislation) He announced "twenty-three executive actions" he would take, and the White House later laid out just what those actions would involve:

1. "Issue a Presidential Memorandum to require federal agencies to make relevant data available to the federal background check system."
2. "Address unnecessary legal barriers, particularly relating to the Health Insurance Portability and Account-

ability Act, that may prevent states from making information available to the background check system."

3. "Improve incentives for states to share information with the background check system."

4. "Direct the Attorney General to review categories of individuals prohibited from having a gun to make sure dangerous people are not slipping through the cracks."

5. "Propose rulemaking to give law enforcement the ability to run a full background check on an individual before returning a seized gun."

6. "Publish a letter from ATF to federally licensed gun dealers providing guidance on how to run background checks for private sellers."

7. "Launch a national safe and responsible gun ownership campaign."

8. "Review safety standards for gun locks and gun safes (Consumer Product Safety Commission)."

9. "Issue a Presidential Memorandum to require federal law enforcement to trace guns recovered in criminal investigations."

10. "Release a DOJ report analyzing information on lost and stolen guns and make it widely available to law enforcement."

11. "Nominate an ATF director."

12. "Provide law enforcement, first responders, and school officials with proper training for active shooter situations."

13. "Maximize enforcement efforts to prevent gun violence and prosecute gun crime."

14. "Issue a Presidential Memorandum directing the Centers for Disease Control to research the causes and prevention of gun violence."

15. "Direct the Attorney General to issue a report on the availability and most effective use of new gun safety technologies and challenge the private sector to develop innovative technologies."

16. "Clarify that the Affordable Care Act does not prohibit doctors asking their patients about guns in their homes."

17. "Release a letter to health care providers clarifying that no federal law prohibits them from reporting threats of violence to law enforcement authorities."

18. "Provide incentives for schools to hire school resource officers."

19. "Develop model emergency response plans for schools, houses of worship and institutions of higher education."

20. "Release a letter to state health officials clarifying the scope of mental health services that Medicaid plans must cover."

21. "Finalize regulations clarifying essential health benefits and parity requirements within ACA exchanges."

22. "Commit to finalizing mental health parity regulations."

23. "Launch a national dialogue led by Secretaries [Kathleen] Sebelius and [Arne] Duncan on mental health."

These executive actions were half "scratching an itch" and half an attempt at yet another abridgment. Numbers 16 and 22 stuck out the most to me. The first encourages doctors to ask about guns in the home, as if the inanimate object transfers mental instability to its owner, and the vague reference to regulations concerning sharing mental health assessments. A first step at reducing the difficulty of adjudication? Some of Obama's steps post-Newtown even ended up vindicating the beliefs of folks who support the Second Amendment. For example, after Obama issued his "presidential memorandum directing the Centers for Disease Control to research the causes and prevention of gun violence," the CDC came back with a report showing that gun control doesn't work.

But even if some of the executive actions seemed benign, the exploitative manner in which Obama announced them was disturbing. Obama's use of the children onstage was a way to insulate himself from any criticism involving his executive decisions. It was propaganda, pure and simple. Obama quoted the kids's letters, as if crime control policy and the nuances of constitutional rights are best understood by five-year-olds. "I think there should be some changes," wrote one. "We should learn from what happened at Sandy Hook…I feel really bad."

Such sentiments are heartfelt, and such compassion and civic-mindedness deserve to be nurtured as children grow and mature and learn. Those sentiments do not, however, deserve to be exploited on national television or treated as guidance for making public policy. When Jimmy Carter implied in his debate with Ronald Reagan days before the 1980 election that he was taking foreign policy advice from his thirteen-year-old daughter ("I had a discussion with my daughter, Amy, the other day before I came here to ask her what the most important issue was.

She said she thought the control of nuclear weaponry."), Carter was roundly and justifiably mocked.

Of course, Obama wasn't really using children as policy advisors. He was using them as props. And in doing so, he was following in a long line of tragedy junkies who exploit children and high-profile murder victims to push their agenda on America. President Bill Clinton waited less than a week after the shootings at Columbine in 1999 before introducing laws prohibiting the sale of private weapons at gun shows. The legislation fortunately never made it through the Republican House of Representatives, but that wasn't the case after Gian Luigi Ferri killed eight people and wounded six others in a San Francisco law office in 1993. Bill Clinton used family members of the victims as props when he pushed, successfully, for a ban on so-called assault weapons, which Clinton ridiculously called "weapons of mass destruction." (The ban expired after ten years, and it has not been renewed.)

If there's any defense of the Clintons and Obamas and Bloombergs of the world, it's that they simply can't help themselves. Liberals believe that our Second Amendment rights are what perpetuate horrific massacres like those at Sandy Hook and Columbine. They believe that if firearm ownership were illegal, then Adam Lanza wouldn't have murdered anyone.

But where have many of the mass tragedies occurred? Virginia Tech. Aurora, Colorado. Schools. And what do these locations have in common? They are designated "gun-free" zones. As Glenn Harlan Reynolds wrote in *USA Today*, "One of the interesting characteristics of mass shootings is that they generally occur in places where firearms are banned: malls, schools, etc. That was the finding of a famous 1999 study by John Lott of the

University of Maryland and William Landes of the University of Chicago, and it appears to have been borne out by experience since then as well."

Why are progressives unable to recognize that their gun control was already in place? Guns were already forbidden. I am still waiting for someone to explain how more laws like a gun-free school zone, in a state with some of the most stringent gun control laws in the country, would have prevented the actions of Adam Lanza, a man whose intent was to violate the law on that terrible day.

The twenty-year-old Lanza could not have legally obtained the firearms he used, because it is illegal in Connecticut to purchase or possess a firearm under the age of twenty-one. Because he couldn't legally obtain a gun, Lanza stole his mother's firearms. Theft is a crime. That is not a failure of gun laws; it is a failure of personal responsibility. What will more redundant laws do when the laws already in effect fail to stop a criminal— who, by the very definition of the word, has no intention of following the law anyway? More laws for criminals to not follow? Does the left expect criminals and madmen who already don't follow the laws on the books to suddenly become law-abiding citizens because progressives pass new anti-gun laws?

It's instructive to consider that Chicago's homicides exceeded 436 in 2012. I'd say that's pretty high for a place that previously banned guns. I'd like for anti-2A advocates to explain how it is people are dying from gunshots in Chicago when the city explicitly banned firearms.[2] I would also like to know where the absence of outrage is from the left: Three Sandy Hooks take place every month in Chicago, the progressive model for gun control. Sometimes it seems like gun grabbers care a lot more about white children from Connecticut than black youth in inner-city Chicago.

If anything, the fact that so many mass shootings occurred in "gun-free" zones suggests that it's time we start allowing potential victims to arm themselves so they won't be defenseless against madmen who chose to flout the law. Guns are neither good nor bad. Motive is. Intent is. Character is. Inanimate objects have no such qualities. Let's not risk more lives by pretending that gun control works.

And yet a year after Sandy Hook, the Democrats and the Obama administration went right on cooking up ways to exploit the tragedy on its anniversary. As the news outlet *Politico* reported,

> *Officials from the White House Office of Public Engagement, which reports to senior Obama aide Valerie Jarrett, are now carrying the administration's gun control efforts. OPE officials hold a regular meeting with the major gun control groups known as the Gun Violence Table. The weekly sessions often include OPE Director Paulette Aniskoff or official Paul Monteiro along with representatives from Mayors Against Illegal Guns, the Brady Campaign to Prevent Gun Violence, Moms Demand Action, the Center for American Progress, Organizing for Action and Americans for Responsible Solutions. The groups are coordinating a November lobbying effort and planning events to commemorate the first anniversary of the Newtown, Conn., massacre last December.*

Some vultures never learn.

Chapter 2

Obama's War on Guns

We're a nation that believes in the Second Amendment. And I believe in the Second Amendment.

—Barack Obama, Lie #1,245

Politicians say a lot of things to get elected. This is the courting period. When it's discovered that the politician du jour was dishonest and broke his or her promises, the Washington, D.C., political class calls this "spin." Out in real America, where promises still mean something and words count, we call it lying. The first greatest lie ever told is that the devil doesn't exist. The second greatest lie is any Democrat saying that they're for the Second Amendment. It is the oft-repeated refrain of our current president, usually declared on the eve of an election, that he supports the Second Amendment. After his "If you like your doctor, you can keep your doctor," right up there with George Bush's "Read my lips" and Bill Clinton's "I did not have sexual relations with that woman" is the whopper by Barack Obama expressing his belief in the Second Amendment. But whether or not he believes the Second Amendment exists, doesn't necessarily mean he thinks it should exist. Democrats can claim that they believe in

Second Amendment rights (Allison Grimes in Kentucky is one such politician) but who are they going to vote for as majority leader? As Speaker of the House? A gun-grabbing Democrat who believes that gun control constitutes a commonsense solution.

Barack Obama has spent two decades of his public life advocating for radical anti–Second Amendment zealots' most extreme anti-gun policies. In his five years in the Oval Office, he has surrounded himself with anti-gun radicals and empowered them to defy federal law and risk innocent lives in pursuit of their agenda of destroying the Second Amendment. He has wealthy, Second Amendment–hating allies right along with him. Through their unified campaign for power and their efforts to impose a vision of a nearly gun-free American on an unwilling nation, they have insulted gun owners, lied to them, impugned their motives, and accused them of spreading misinformation—a case of the pot calling the kettle black, if ever there was one.

The "Audacity of Deception" campaign began in 1996, when an obscure community organizer named Barack Obama first ran for the Illinois State Senate. When he was asked in a candidate questionnaire if he supported state legislation to "ban the manufacture, sale, and possession of assault weapons," he replied, "Yes."

A word on "assault weapons": They are a myth. The phrase "assault weapons" is a poll-tested, make-believe unicorn term used to demonize certain kinds of semiautomatic rifles by conflating them with their military-issued model relatives, which are virtually illegal. There is no "assault weapons" section of a gun shop. No one walks into a Walmart and asks, "Excuse me, but can you point me to an assault weapon, please?" If the goal is to sound like the most unintelligent person in the room when it comes to the subject of civilian-use firearms, by all means, use the term "assault weapon." What "assault weapons" actually are is a term commonly given to rifles that are black and have scary-looking, cosmetic components attached, which anti–Second Amendment advocates believe magically and dramatically alter the original function of the rifle to make it "shootier" once affixed. The fact that the rifle is black means the bullets come out faster than if the rifle is pink, too. (Earlier we spoke about the racist roots of gun control, and apparently this extends to the guns themselves.) I once had someone tell me (in a swiftly deleted comment once mockery ensued) that the scope on a rifle was a grenade launcher. Watching anti-gun progressives try to describe firearms is exactly like watching a baby sit on the floor with a shape sorter and try to force the square shape through the round hole.

In fact, these rifles are less dangerous than semiautomatic handguns—which the Supreme Court held constitutionally protected in *District of Columbia v. Heller*—because these rifles, unlike handguns, can't be easily concealed. The fact that the rifle is semiautomatic merely means that it fires one bullet with every squeeze of the trigger—as opposed to an automatic rifle, which fires multiple rounds with a single squeeze of the trigger. Only flat-earther, remedially literate anti–Second Amendment advocates with an irrational hatred of regular guns bordering on bigotry would call a semiautomatic rifle an "assault weapon."

On the same 1996 questionnaire, when Obama was asked if he supported "mandatory waiting periods, with background checks, to purchase guns," he again answered, "Yes." That position was even more extreme than the final version of the Brady gun control law enacted by a Democratic Congress in 1993 and signed by a Democratic president, Bill Clinton. The Brady Law called for waiting periods to be replaced by instant background checks in 1998. Despite the passage of this law, certain anti-gun advocates like Moms Demand leader Shannon Troughton-Watts believe that background checks don't exist.

Those two opinions—opposition to semiautomatic rifles and support for waiting periods—were early signs that Barack Obama was no friend of the Second Amendment, but they were nothing compared to the third answer he gave on the same questionnaire. He was asked if he supported a law to "ban the manufacture, sale, and possession of handguns." With no explanation for why such a drastic ban was justified or how it would be constitutional, Barack Obama simply answered, "Yes."

The depth of the hostility to the Second Amendment revealed by that answer is staggering—and dangerous. There are approximately 114 million handguns possessed by civilians in the United States.[1] As the Supreme Court has declared, "the inherent right of self-defense has been central to the Second Amendment right." A ban on handguns, like the ban favored by Barack Obama circa 1996, would amount "to a prohibition of an entire class of 'arms' that is overwhelmingly chosen by American society for that lawful purpose" of self-defense. Because banning handguns even in the home, "where the need for defense of self, family, and property is most acute," would deny Americans "the most preferred firearm in the nation to 'keep' and use for protection of one's home and family," banning handguns "would fail constitutional muster." In short, according to the Supreme Court, a ban on handguns would render "the Second Amendment extinct."

Yet, in Barack Obama's America, the government not only can but should outlaw 114 million handguns, deprive Americans of their quintessential weapons of self-defense in the home, and make the Second Amendment "extinct." That is quite a policy from a man who pretends to, in his words, "believe in the Second Amendment."

OBAMA: THE EARLY ANTI-GUN YEARS

After he was first elected to office in 1996, Obama spent eight years in the Illinois State Senate, where he was unabashed in his opposition to the Second Amendment. He boasted of his support for "a package of bills to limit individual Illinoisans to purchasing one handgun a month; require all promoters and sellers at firearms shows to carry a state license; allow civil liability for death or injuries caused by handguns; and require [Firearm Owner Identification] applicants to apply in person."

Barack Obama's support for "liability for death or injuries caused by handguns" is worth a moment of consideration. Call me old-fashioned, but I believe that when a cold-blooded killer shoots an innocent person, it's the fault of the killer, not the person who makes the gun. We don't blame utensils for making people fat, as the saying goes. Barack Obama, however, disagrees, because the concept of personal responsibility eludes him. Instead, he believes in lawyers and lawsuits and big, fat jury awards because the people in the trial lawyer racket are his friends. This sort of thinking is why criminals who are injured breaking into your home can sue you in some states, because your home should not be a dangerous and inhospitable place for someone who wants to steal from or rape you. It's victim shaming.

Fortunately, a bipartisan coalition in Congress passed a federal law in 2005 invalidating state laws that would otherwise allow these lawsuits against gun makers when criminals use their products for unlawful purposes. Among the people invalidating the state anti-gun laws were fifty-nine Democratic House members and fifteen Democratic Senators, including die-hard liberals like Jay Rockefeller, Robert Byrd, and Herb Kohl—all of whom hated guns less than Barack Obama.

Eight years later, when Obama was running for the U.S. Senate and had to appeal to rural Illinois voters, he was a little cagier about his dream of banning each and every one of America's 114 million handguns. He recognized that gun control was unpopular on a national level and wanted to minimize his support for it in exchange for electability. While advocating "reasonable restrictions on the sale and possession of handguns," he said that "a complete ban on handguns is not politically practicable." Think for a moment about what he didn't say. He didn't say, "Banning handguns would be unconstitutional." He didn't say, "Millions of law-abiding, decent Americans own handguns for self-defense." He didn't even repudiate his prior support for a ban on all handguns. Instead, he merely said, in effect, "I'd like to ban handguns. We can't pass a bill to do it today. Maybe someday." As soon as we subvert that pesky Constitution.

———

After Obama made it to the United States Senate, he continued his advocacy against the Second Amendment. One of his most telling votes came in support of a proposal by the late, not-so-great Massachusetts senator Edward M. Kennedy, who wanted to expand the definition of "armor-piercing" bullets.

In an effort to take cop-killer ammunition off the streets, Congress long ago banned the sale, manufacture, and import of armor-piercing bullets for handguns. But the revered Ted Kennedy—who knew a thing or two about killing people, though with a car, not a gun—wanted to go further. He wanted to redefine "armor-piercing" bullets and give the attorney general the authority to regulate a wider range of ammunition. The new definition would have been broad enough to cover one of the most common rounds used for deer hunting—the .30-30.

The ammunition Kennedy's law would have covered has been used for over a hundred years, but that didn't stop Barack Obama from voting with the "Liberal Lion" and his radical anti-hunting proposal. Of course, Kennedy claimed he didn't want to cover hunting ammunition. But as constitutional scholar David Kopel explained, "The plain language of the bill, and not Senator Kennedy's floor statements, were what would be enacted into law. If there were ever a judicial challenge to ban particular rifle ammunition, a court might well find that the language of the statute, along with judicial deference to agency interpretation of the statute, meant there was no need to look to legislative history."

If Obama's policy positions weren't enough to show his contempt for gun-owning Americans, his rhetoric during his presidential campaign in 2008 showed how he felt about men and women who believe it's their God-given right to own a gun for self-defense, target shooting, and hunting. Speaking of blue-collar workers in towns that have lost industrial jobs, candidate Obama said, "They get bitter, they cling to guns or religion or antipathy to people who aren't like them or anti-immigrant sentiment or anti-trade sentiment as a way to explain their frustrations." There you have it: In Obama's mind, guns are only for bitter, frustrated bigots who aren't as enlightened as he is and can't afford to outsource their family's security. You know you've gone too far when even Hillary Clinton is like, "Whoa, dude."

Caught on tape saying such ridiculous, bigoted things, Obama apologized. Well, sort of. "I said something everybody knows is true, which is there are a whole bunch of folks in small towns in Pennsylvania, in towns right here in Indiana, in my hometown in Illinois, who are bitter," he said. "So I said when you're bitter, you turn to what you can count on. So people vote about guns, or they take comfort from their faith and their family and their community. Now, I didn't say it as well as I should have. If I worded things in a way that made people offended, I deeply regret that." Which, if you think about it, really wasn't an apology at all.

It's no wonder that as soon as Barack Obama made it to the White House, he made prospective employees answer the question, "Do you or any members of your immediate family own a gun?"[2] (If they admitted to being one of the "bitter" Americans who "cling to guns," I doubt it was counted as a reason to hire them.) And it's no wonder that Obama surrounded himself with anti-gun staffers and Cabinet secretaries.

Let's take a quick look at some of those appointees.

Two of Obama's highest-ranking White House staffers were

regulatory czar Cass Sunstein and Chief of Staff Rahm Emanuel. Sunstein, who is a liberal law professor at Harvard Law School when he's not in Washington finding new ways to regulate Americans, is on the record as supporting a ban on all sports hunting. "We ought to ban hunting, I suggest, if there isn't a purpose other than sport and fun," he said. "That should be against the law. It's time now."

Emanuel is no less extreme. While working in Bill Clinton's White House, he helped pass the assault weapons ban. Later, as mayor of Chicago, Emanuel pushed for taxes on ammunition and a statewide handgun registry. Under his plan, every Illinois handgun owner would have to pay $65 to register a handgun, would need to reregister every five years for a $25 fee, and would be guilty of a felony for possessing an unregistered handgun.

Mayor Emanuel also wrote to two of Chicago's biggest banks suggesting that they not lend money to two gun manufacturing companies. As Second Amendment defender Ted Cruz said in a subsequent letter to those banks, "Both of your companies do considerable business in the City of Chicago, and you may be understandably concerned that there are risks to refusing to comply with the demands of a politician who has earned the nickname, 'The Godfather.'" He then added, "In Texas, we have a more modest view of government. We do not accept the notion that government officials should behave as bullies, trying to harass or pressure private companies into enlisting in a political lobbying campaign."

Obama's Cabinet is no less gun-hating than his White House staff. To lead the Department of Homeland Security, Obama tapped Janet Napolitano. As governor of Arizona, she vetoed a bill that would have allowed Arizonans to display a gun in self-defense when confronted by a criminal and a bill that would have made concealed-carry permits valid for life. Once in office in Washington, Napolitano gutted an important program to protect air travelers from a repeat of September 11. Whereas the Bush administration had signed into law a bipartisan bill to fund firearms training for commercial airline pilots—so that they can carry a weapon and fight off attempts to rush the cockpit by the likes of the 9/11 hijackers—Napolitano's Homeland Security Department and the Obama administration proposed a 50 percent cut in the program's already meager funding. Ten thousand pilots were trained after the law was passed in 2002, but the program is now so poorly funded that no new federal flight deck officers are being trained. Napolitano refused to privatize airline security, which would make government-funded training for pilots a responsibility of the airlines, who would likely do a better job than the United States government would ever do.

Consider also Obama's secretary of state: Hillary Clinton, a lifelong enemy of the Second Amendment. Like Obama, she opposed a federal law to prohibit lawsuits against gun manufacturers, and she has supported gun control at almost every opportunity. "I stand in support of…commonsense legislation to license everyone who wishes to purchase a gun," Clinton said in 2000. "I also believe that every new handgun sale or transfer should be registered in a national registry." A few years later, she proposed limiting handgun purchases to one per month and raising the legal age for handgun ownership to twenty-one—because, according to Hillary, you can be drafted into the defense of your country with a gun at age eighteen (unless you dodge the draft like her husband), but you shouldn't be allowed to defend your home, your life, and your loved ones with a handgun until you're twenty-one. Hillary is all about protecting young people, unless they're interns in her husband's White House. She's all about protecting women, unless they are Second Amendment supporters, in which case she accuses them of "terrorizing" people with their basic support of 2A.

After Obama put Hillary Clinton in charge at Foggy Bottom, she didn't disappoint her gun-grabbing boss. One of her most liberty-threatening decisions was reversing the U.S. government's opposition to the United Nations Arms Trade Treaty. Even though the treaty has the admirable goal of "eradicat[ing] the illicit trade in conventional arms and to prevent their diversion to the illicit market"—and who could be against that?—the devil is in the details. The treaty requires signatories to regulate "small arms and light weapons." That means it requires Second Amendment–violating restrictions on guns that are in common use in America. Its Fifth Article commands signatories to "establish and maintain a national control system," including a "national control list." That means a national gun registry, so Washington can keep track of who's armed. Even worse, the treaty requires the United States to "provide its national control list to the Secretariat, which shall make it available to other State parties." Not only will Obama and his left-wing bureaucrats know which Americans are armed; other, unfriendly nations will know, too.

The U.N. Arms Trade Treaty doesn't even recognize the right of ordinary citizens to use guns in self-defense. It says it is "mindful"—whatever that means—of the "legitimate trade and lawful ownership" of guns for "recreational, cultural, historical, and sporting activities." But as former U.N. ambassador John

Bolton and constitutional law professor John Yoo wrote in a *Wall Street Journal* op-ed, there's "not a word" in the treaty "about the right to possess guns for a broader individual right of self-defense."

As Bolton and Yoo observe, there's something devious about how gun control advocates plan to use the treaty. Gun grabbers "will use these provisions to argue that the U.S. must enact measures such as a national gun registry, licenses for guns and ammunition sales, universal background checks, and even a ban of certain weapons." Because the Obama administration believes treaties allow them to regulate conduct that the Constitution otherwise leaves to the states to regulate, the U.N. Arms Trade Treaty "thus provides the Obama administration with an end run around Congress to reach these gun-control holy grails."

Back in 2001, John Bolton had told a United Nations conference, on behalf of the Bush administration, "We do not support measures that prohibit civilian possession of small arms…The United States will not join consensus on a final document that contains measures abrogating the constitutional right to bear arms." But in 2010, the Obama administration's undersecretary for arms control said, "We will work between now and the U.N. Conference in 2012 to negotiate a legally binding arms trade treaty…We have made that fundamental policy commitment." Three years later, Clinton's successor at the State Department, John Kerry, signed the treaty—making Congress the only obstacle left to the ratification of this empowerment of international bureaucrats and this threat to every American's constitutional rights.

Perhaps no Obama appointee is more hostile to the Second Amendment than his lawless attorney general, Eric Holder. In 1995, Holder said, "We need to…brainwash people into thinking about guns in a vastly different way." When Holder took the reins at the Justice Department, he likely hoped a scheme code-named "Fast and Furious" would be an effective way to accomplish that brainwashing.

In a shocking abuse of power, Holder's Justice Department armed Mexican drug lords with American-made weapons, possibly in an attempt to build a political case for a national gun registry. In fact, Michael Bloomberg's Mayors Against Illegal Guns issued a report in 2010 in which they tried to blame gun trafficking across the U.S.-Mexico border on our gun laws. The Obama administration forced firearms dealers in the Southwest to sell rifles to suspicious straw purchasers. The straw purchasers in turn sold the guns to Mexican drug cartels. The supposed plan was for the Department of Justice (DOJ) to track the guns, but the guns ended up being used in hundreds of murders, including the killing of a U.S. Border Patrol agent.

Extensive evidence suggests that this Fast and Furious operation was more than just a gun-tracking scheme gone awry. E-mails indicate the operation was part of a plan to build political support for gun control in America. In a July 2010 e-mail, a U.S. attorney in Arizona—who had once been instrumental in passing Bill Clinton's 1994 gun ban—wrote, "Some of these weapons bought by these clowns in Arizona have been directly traced to murders of elected officials in Mexico by the cartels, so Katy-bar-the-door when we unveil this baby." In July 2010, an ATF agent named Mark Chait sent an e-mail to the ATF agent in charge of "Fast and Furious," Bill Newell. It said,

"Bill, can you see if these guns were all purchased from the same [licensed gun dealer] and at one time? We are looking at anecdotal cases to support a demand letter on long-gun sales." Six months later, Chait e-mailed Newell again: "Bill—well done yesterday...In light of our request for Demand letter 3, this case could be a strong supporting factor if we can determine how many multiple sales of long guns occurred during the course of this case."

Here's the translation of those e-mails. "Demand Letter 3" requires gun dealers to register certain sales of semiautomatic rifles. In April 2011, the Department of Justice sent "Demand Letter 3" to dealers in four border-states: New Mexico, Arizona, Texas, and California. As the National Rifle Association has explained, "This reporting scheme would create a registry of owners of many of today's most popular rifles—firearms owned by millions of Americans for self-defense, hunting and other lawful purposes."

Of course, registering guns is a longtime obsession of gun grabbers like Obama and Holder. But it's shocking that they would arm violent drug lords in order to justify such a registry. In doing so, they likely took heed of then-Obama chief of staff Rahm Emanuel's favorite phrase, "You never want a serious crisis to go to waste." "Very clearly," said Representative Darrell Issa of California, "they've made a crisis and they're using this crisis to somehow take away or limit people's Second Amendment rights."

Sen. Charles Grassley of Iowa agrees. "There's plenty of evidence," he said, "showing that this administration planned to use the tragedies of 'Fast and Furious' as rationale to further their goals of a long gun reporting requirement." The evidence

Grassley was referring to might be even more overwhelming if Eric Holder had not chosen to withhold from Congress more than seventy thousand pages of documents in the Department of Justice's "Fast and Furious" file.

In response to the outcry over Obama and Holder's egregious abuse of power, the administration doubled down. The head of the Bureau of Alcohol, Tobacco, Firearms and Explosives (ATF) attempted to chill whistleblowers by ominously proclaiming that "if you make poor choices, that if you don't abide by the rules, that if you don't respect the chain of command, if you don't find the appropriate way to raise your concerns to your leadership, there will be consequences."

For his part, Holder defied Congress, refused to turn over subpoenaed documents related to Fast and Furious, and became the first sitting Cabinet official to be held in criminal contempt by Congress. Nearly every Republican and seventeen Democrats voted for the contempt resolution, which authorized congressional leaders to submit a criminal referral seeking charges against the man ironically responsible for enforcing America's laws. Unfortunately, until we have in office an attorney general interested in enforcing existing gun laws instead of breaking them himself, nothing will ever come of this.

In explaining his historic vote, House Speaker John Boehner said that the "House needs to know how this happened, and it's our constitutional duty to find out…No Justice Department is above the law, and no Justice Department is above the Constitution."

Florida congressman Dennis Ross explained, "In the real world Americans are expected to comply with subpoenas. Is the attorney general any different? No, he is not…The attorney general can stonewall all he wants. The attorney general can misremember all he wants. But whether he likes it or not, today responsibility will land on his desk."

Texas's Ted Poe was even more direct: "Even the attorney general cannot evade the law. [It's] time for America to find out the truth... [It's] time for a little transparency. Today is judgment day. That's just the way it is."

Unfortunately, despite Congress's attempts to investigate the Fast and Furious operation, the American people are still largely in the dark about many of the details concerning what happened, why it happened, and who knew it was happening. That's mainly because of the media's failure to hold Obama and the anti-gun Justice Department accountable. When Mitt Romney tried to talk about the scandal in a presidential debate in 2012—"the greatest failure we've had with regards to gun violence, in some respects," he said, "is what is known as Fast and Furious, which was a program under this administration...where thousands of automatic and AK-47-type weapons were given to people that ultimately gave them to drug lords"—CNN's Candy Crowley immediately changed the subject. Obama never once had to explain the death of a Border Patrol agent or the deaths of hundreds of Mexicans shot by drug dealers armed by the United States Justice Department.

Obama did, however, have something to say about gun control in that debate moderated by CNN's Crowley. He endorsed "seeing if we can get an assault weapons ban reintroduced," defending his position by misleadingly saying that "weapons that were designed for soldiers in war theaters don't belong on our streets." Except soldiers don't carry civilian semiauto rifles. They don't carry AR-15s; they carry fully auto M4s. Just because a civilian rifle is styled in the manner of a military rifle doesn't mean it has the same mechanisms or capabilities.

By the time of the 2012 debates, then, Obama had demonstrated a lifelong animosity to guns. An animosity that became an obsession. He had voiced support for the prohibition against all handguns. He had dismissed gun owners as "bitter" bigots who "cling to guns." He had given us the Fast and Furious operation, with its bloody aftermath and scandalous cover-up. But even still, none of this amounted to the anti-gun crusade he would wage in his second term—because until the votes were counted in November 2012, Obama wasn't willing to risk his reelection.

"After my election," he infamously told Russia's president Dmitry Medvedev in March 2012, "I have more flexibility." And although he wasn't talking about gun control at the time, he made similar statements to gun grabbers about his secret plans to take away Americans' guns. Obama told the chair of the Brady Campaign, Sarah Brady, "I just want you to know that we are working on [gun control]...We have to go through a few processes, but under the radar."

Obama sent similar signals during his first term to anti-gun zealot Carolyn McCarthy. "I have spoken to the president [about guns]," Congresswoman McCarthy said, "and it's just going to be when that opportunity comes forward that we're going to be able to go forward."

For Barack Obama, that opportunity appeared to present itself when a horrific tragedy in Newtown, Connecticut, brought a nation to tears. For most Americans, it was a time for grief and prayer. But for Obama, it seemed a time for playing on people's emotions and introducing gun-control measures on an unwilling nation at a remembrance ceremony. As the next chapter shows, Obama and his fellow gun grabbers abided by the cynical adage propounded by Rahm Emanuel: They didn't allow a serious crisis to go to waste."

Chapter 3

The Anti-Gun Lobby

If someone has a gun and is trying to kill you, it would be reasonable to shoot back with your own gun.

—THE FOURTEENTH DALAI LAMA

The bus was black. It had few windows. Splashed on its side, against a map of the United States, was the bus tour's name: *No More Names*. Beside the map were the words *The National Drive to Reduce Gun Violence*. Listed below was the obligatory website—www.nomorenames.com.

Embarking on a twenty-five-state, one-hundred-day tour, the black bus began its tour in Newtown, Connecticut. Of course. It was six months to the day since a deranged shooter had murdered children, and gun grabbers weren't finished exploiting the tragedy.

"At every stop along the way," said an affiliated website, "gun violence survivors, family members, and community members will come together to read the names of people who have been murdered with guns and to rally for comprehensive and enforceable background checks legislation."

Well, sort of. That was how the tour started. But it was

59

long before, in a sense, that the wheels started coming off the bus.

The first problem was attendance. Normally, grassroots rallies try to encourage participation from the grass roots. They conduct highly sophisticated advance work like announcing the location of a rally. And the time.

For some bizarre reason "No More Names" was determined to keep those minor details a secret for as long as possible. They were worried that if the public had advance notice about the time and place of the bus stops, the public might show up. *All* the public. Including the part of the public that believes Americans have the right to keep and bear arms.

What would happen, the bus tour's planners asked themselves, if the gun owners outnumbered the gun grabbers? What if they showed up with signs saying things like "Don't Tread on Me" or "The Second Amendment: America's Original Homeland Security" or "I'll Keep My Guns, Money, Freedom, and God: You Can Keep the 'Change'"? The optics would be horrible. And the optics—the backdrop, the images, the concept—were the whole point. This wasn't a bus tour. It was a traveling photo-op designed for local news stations in twenty-five states.

The *Washington Examiner*'s David Codrea hit the nail on the head when he reported: "What this looks like is calculated willing media exploitation—get the bus tour on the local news, get a lot of exposure from friendly 'Authorized Journalists' on friendly turf to create the impression of widespread grassroots support—and then move on, doing it in a way to minimize the chances of the opposition having time to mount an effective counter-protest." It's very Sun Tzu: Create the perception of numbers.

So, the bus tour would be a relatively stealthy operation, even if it guaranteed that the grassroots citizens would have a hard time hearing about the grassroots rally.

The second problem was the inclusion of certain names in the "No More Names" lists to be read at every (sparsely attended) event. To be sure, many of the names belonged to innocent victims whose lives were tragically cut short by violent criminals—though their deaths strike me as no more tragic than those murder victims excluded from the list because they were killed by other weapons. To ring every ounce of exploitation out of the names and make the scene as dramatic as possible for local news stations, the readers stated not only the names of the deceased but the dates and locations, as well as a common refrain: "killed by a gun."

At one of the first stops, in Concord, New Hampshire, a strange thing happened. As the crowd listened respectfully to the names of people shot since Sandy Hook, they heard a surprising name. The name was familiar to everyone who lost a loved one at the Boston Marathon bombing. It was known to everyone in Boston whose life was upended by the bombing. It was heard by the millions of Americans who watched television footage of the bombing, the search for the perpetrators, and the dramatic arrest of the violent Muslim radical hiding in a Watertown resident's boat.

The name announced in Concord as a "victim of gun violence" was Tamerlan Tsarnaev.

Attendees immediately recognized Tsarnaev as the older of the two brothers who murdered an MIT police officer and exploded a bomb near the finish line of the 2013 Boston Marathon. He was killed during a shootout with the police several nights after his bomb marred, maimed, and otherwise injured nearly three hundred people and killed Martin William Richard, Lu Lingzi, and Krystle Marie Campbell. Martin Richard was eight years old.

As soon as the "No More Names" tour proclaimed that Tsarnaev was a "victim of gun violence," audience members shouted back in protest, "He's a terrorist!"

If those appalled by a tribute to Tsarnaev in the "No More Names" tour had known the identities of other names announced that day and at other rallies, they would have had even more to shout about. One in twelve were crime suspects killed in self-defense by citizens or police.

Was the inclusion of so many violent thugs on the "No More Names" list a sneaky way of inflating the number of names? The bus tour claims it wasn't. Tsarnaev "was absolutely not a victim, his name should have been deleted before the list was provided to a family member for reading and his name should never have been read," said a spokesman. "It was a mistake, it should not have happened and we sincerely apologize." The bus tour's organizers claimed they copied the list from one that the liberal website *Slate* had compiled of gun victims. So, assuming the inclusion of murderers like Tsarnaev was an accident, it was a case of the blind leading the blind.

THE FACE OF GUN CONTROL

The man behind the disastrous "No More Names" bus tour was New York mayor Michael Bloomberg, and when the bus tour paid tribute to the Boston Marathon bomber, more than a few people thought Bloomberg's mistake was indicative of a larger problem. "Bloomberg's apology is disingenuous at best," said New York state assemblyman Kieran Lalor. "He has been misleading the American people to score political points. A quick look at the list would have revealed there were many criminals on it. It included a man shot by police while threatening to kill a two-year-old girl he had snatched from her mother in a parking lot. This is a group that doesn't distinguish between a gun being used to save a kidnapped child and the victim of a crime. They're just concerned about making a political statement."

Bloomberg funds and runs a gun-hating group called Mayors Against Illegal Guns. It was founded in 2006, but it wasn't until the shooting at Sandy Hook that it started to spread its billionaire-funded wings. I have no idea what an "illegal gun" is. These guns are just "dreamers."

Before Sandy Hook, the Brady Campaign to Prevent Gun Violence was America's most famous and famously successful gun control group (if we exclude the Ku Klux Klan's unsurpassed record of successfully grabbing guns from African-Americans in the aftermath of the Civil War). The Brady Campaign brought us the Brady Bill, which imposed a waiting period and background check on the purchase of a gun, and the so-called assault weapons ban in Bill Clinton's 1994 Crime Bill.

The Brady Campaign benefited from its namesake. A former Republican, Jim Brady was the anti-2A progressive's ideal spokesman because he was a victim. Brady, the White House press secretary under President Reagan, was shot in an assassination attempt on Reagan by the deranged John Hinckley. He survived and made gun control a personal crusade.

Ultimately, the Brady Campaign's limited successes were

undermined by two mighty obstacles: the American people and the United States Constitution. The Brady Law's waiting period was eliminated in 1998 by the Republican majority elected in part for its opposition to the Brady Campaign's signature accomplishments. In addition, the Supreme Court in *Printz v. United States* struck down as unconstitutional the law's infringement on states' rights. And the assault weapons ban expired after ten years, when, in 2004, there was far from sufficient support from the American people to renew it.

Two years after the expiration of the assault weapons ban, Bloomberg created Mayors Against Illegal Guns. It didn't have a compelling namesake, like the Brady Campaign did, but it had something with the potential to be more powerful and important: Michael Bloomberg's bank account and the catty, competitive demeanor of its staff.

The thinking of Bloomberg—who is one of the world's one hundred richest people—was simple. It went something like this: "I like gun control, and if I spend enough of my billions, I'll make Americans like gun control. At the very least, I'll use my money to bully the people's representatives into ignoring their pro-gun constituents and doing what I want."

Bloomberg has, of course, grown accustomed to making people do what he wants. When he wanted people in New York City to eat fewer trans fats, he banned them. When he wanted people to drink less soda, he banned Big Gulp–size fountain drinks in every place but supermarkets (he lacked the authority to ban them inside the stores). When he wanted people to smoke less, he banned cigarettes in public places. Bloomberg did everything he could to turn New York City into a nanny state with Hizzoner as nanny in chief. And so when he wanted people to have fewer guns, he figured he could just make it so. Bloomberg was like Yul Brynner's Pharaoh in *The Ten Commandments*, who calls out edicts with the order: "So let it be written, so let it be done!"

When Bloomberg founded Mayors Against Illegal Guns in 2006, many mayors were happy to join. After all, who could be for something illegal? It would have made more sense if the group were Mayors Against Illegal Gun Use, or MAIGU, but that extra vowel at the end of the acronym probably wouldn't have fit as nicely on a T-shirt and it sounds like "Magoo." The name itself should have been called into question by anyone with reading comprehension but, alas, this is politics. Bloomberg and his group began to show their true radical colors after the Sandy Hook tragedy in December 2012.

Accustomed to issuing dictatorial fiats over things like horse-drawn carriages, breast-feeding, smoking, and large fountain drinks, Bloomberg demanded that Congress ban semiautomatic rifles (even though they aren't more dangerous than handguns), ban so-called large-capacity magazines (even though they aren't large capacity), and expand background checks. When it quickly became clear that America isn't New York City and that Bloomberg couldn't get everything on his wish list out of America's representatives, he put all his chips on the table in a big bet on background checks. And he even succeeded in getting two senators from pro-gun states to sponsor it.

One of Bloomberg's weapons was an ad he put on the airwaves in Pennsylvania, home of Republican senator Pat Toomey. The freshman senator had challenged the liberal Arlen Specter in the 2004 Republican primary and lost by only about 1.5 percent. In 2009, when he announced his intention to challenge Specter again, Specter switched parties, and Toomey ultimately won the general election in 2010.

Bloomberg's ad in Pennsylvania targeted Toomey directly. "Tell Senator Toomey: Don't protect criminals," it intoned, with ominous music in the background. "Vote to protect gun rights and our families with comprehensive background checks. Demand action now!"

After the ad aired, Senator Toomey caved. He announced his support for more gun control, and he was rewarded with a Bloomberg ad thanking him. "Washington likes to argue," says the ad. "Sen. Pat Toomey wants to get things done. He worked across party lines, leading the fight to take guns out of the hands of criminals. Toomey's idea: Protect our families with comprehensive background checks, so dangerous criminals can't buy guns. Courage and common sense—that's Pat Toomey. Tell him to keep fighting for background checks."

Toomey joined Democratic senator Joe Manchin of West Virginia in drafting a rule requiring background checks for every gun transfer, except transfers between family members. It looked like the big money and hardball tactics of the anti-gun lobby was going to work.

Under the Manchin-Toomey proposal, anyone selling or transferring a gun would have to go to a licensed dealer to get an FBI background check of the recipient. Under this proposal my father-in-law would be a criminal for giving my son, his grandson, a rifle for Christmas. In other words, if a farmer in rural America wanted to give his neighbor a shotgun, he'd have to ask the federal government for permission. The NRA's Wayne LaPierre said, "I just don't think law-abiding people want every gun sale in the country to be under the thumb of the federal government." Here's what Manchin and Toomey don't get: It's irrelevant whether or not private sales are regulated, as there exist laws prohibiting those barred by previous illegal actions or mental instability from owning a firearm, regardless the manner of its acquisition. If you are not legally allowed to own a firearm in your state of residence then you cannot own a firearm, be it gifted or bought on the black market. Considering that most crime committed with illegally used firearms is perpetuated by people with a record of repeat offenses that nullifies their Second Amendment liberty under law, this law would punish only law-abiding Americans. In an effort to remove what they incorrectly perceive as a loophole, lawmakers show that not only are they ignorant about firearms, but also about firearm law.

With a bankroll of $27 billion, Bloomberg vowed to do everything he—and his money—could to force senators to support his precious gun control. What followed was one of the most blatant attempts to use money to influence politics in American history.

Over the course of two weeks in 2013, Bloomberg's Mayors Against Illegal Guns spent $12 million on political ads in thirteen states, urging support for background checks. He hired high-powered image makers like SKDKnickerbocker and Tom Synhorst of the DCI Group. The group's self-professed goal was to "influence the upcoming Senate vote." So much for liberals bemoaning the nexus between big money and political influence.

The ads ran in Arkansas, Indiana, Louisiana, North Carolina, and North Dakota in attempts to bully Democratic senators in those traditionally red states. Ads also ran in Iowa, Maine, New Hampshire, Nevada, and Ohio—hoping to put pressure on Republican senators in states Obama had won. Finally,

Bloomberg's group paid for ads in Arizona and Georgia in the misguided believe that its pro-gun Republican senators would bend to Bloomberg's pressure. (One of Arizona's Republican senators, the anti-2A John McCain, didn't need to be pressured. Bloomberg had him at hello.)

Bloomberg's commercials showed more than the billionaire's hatred of guns; they also showed his comical ignorance of guns—and the ignorance of his allies when it comes to gun safety. "I believe in the Second Amendment," says some Aqua Velvet–esque actor in the commercials who advocates for stricter background checks, "and I'll fight to protect it. But with rights come responsibilities."

The man in the ad had a hipster beard, flannel shirt, hunting cap, and rented pickup truck. Progressives directing the ad went out and bought a Gun Owner dress-up kit featuring the afore-mentioned essentials, because that's what progressives think gun owners look like: hicks sittin' on truck beds. It was even more hysterical upon closer inspection. The actor playing a gun-totin' bitter clinger violated some of the most basic "respon-sibilities" and rules of gun ownership, like pointing the barrel wildly at everything out of frame and not keeping his mani-cured hipster finger off the trigger. Elmer Fudd has more gun sense than this douchebag. The political commercials weren't the only component of Bloomberg's expensive campaign. Ac-cording to *U.S. News and World Report*, the anti-gun group opened "field offices in 10 states; posted multiple job listings for its digital team; stepped up its lobbying efforts in Washing-ton; released new infographics, maps and research on gun sales and background checks; and held a national day against gun violence which it called the 'largest gun violence prevention advocacy event in history.'" It's such a misnomer. In truth, it was advocacy for disarmament.

A spokeswoman for Mayors Against Illegal Guns said, "We work on the weekends...we work day and night." With a vote on gun control expected in the Senate in two weeks, she said, "The next two weeks are incredibly important for us. Everything is on the table."

By mid-April 2013, the gun grabbers were "all in." They'd spent a fortune trying to buy influence in Washington. But when the votes were counted, Wayne LaPierre was proven correct. Americans didn't want "every gun sale in the country to be under the thumb of the federal government." Likely to have fallen well short of sufficient support in the House of Representatives, the Manchin-Toomey proposal didn't even make it that far. It died in the Senate.

That's when Michael Bloomberg got really angry. "Children lost," he said melodramatically. "They are going to die and the criminals won. I think that's the only way to phrase it. This is a disgrace."

Bloomberg started with Kelly Ayotte. The freshman Republican senator from New Hampshire hailed from the Northeast's most conservative state, but Bloomberg figured that because she wasn't from the South or West, her constituents must hate guns as much as he does. At the expense of $2 million, Mayors Against Illegal Guns pummeled Ayotte with attack ads, as did Gabrielle Giffords's Americans for Responsibility. (Like Brady, Giffords is beloved by gun-hating liberals because she is a victim of gun violence. Would either be as revered if they supported law-abiding Americans's 2A rights?)

Bloomberg's ad claimed that 89 percent of people in New

Hampshire supported background checks—a figure that came from a poll Bloomberg had bought and paid for himself. "Eighty-nine percent of New Hampshire supports background checks. But Senator Ayotte voted against them." (Of course, Ayotte didn't vote against "background checks" as a general matter. They are still required from licensed dealers. At issue was whether every exchange of a firearm in America should also be subject to the oversight of the federal government.)

Mayors Against Gun Control also tried to use Bloomberg's billions to punish senators like Republican Jeff Flake and Democrat Mark Pryor. The ad against Pryor featured a woman in tears who had worked for a state party chairman killed by someone illegally using a gun. The ad against Flake was equally heavy-handed. "My son Alex was killed in Aurora, Colorado, shielding his fiancée from a mass murderer with a gun," says Phoenix's Karen Teves in the ad. "We wrote Senator Flake urging him to support background checks. Senator Flake wrote, 'I am truly sorry for your deep loss…Strengthening background checks is something we agree on.'" The ad accused Senator Flake of later voting "against strengthening background checks," and it concluded with a shot at Flake's honesty and integrity: "The issue isn't just background checks. It's keeping your promise. And Senator Flake didn't."

Accusing Jeff Flake of breaking a promise to a grieving mother is pretty serious stuff. If you're going to make that kind of accusation in a thirty-second ad, complete with somber music and a photograph of the mother's dead son, you'd probably want to be sure you have your facts straight. But Mayors Against Illegal Guns derptastically didn't. Flake voted for the Grassley-Cruz amendment, which would have strengthened background checks. As Senator Grassley's office explained, "The Grassley-Cruz proposal would reauthorize and improve the National Instant Criminal Background Check System (NICS), increase resources for prosecutions of gun crime, address mental illness in the criminal justice system, and strengthen criminal law by including straw purchasing and illegal firearm trafficking statutes." The Grassley-Cruz amendment would not, however, put the federal government in charge of all transfers of firearms, including sales between neighbors and friends. It didn't go as far as Manchin-Toomey, and so it didn't go far enough for Mike Bloomberg and Mayors Against Illegal Guns.

The anti-gun lobby's apoplectic reaction to the American people's defeat of Manchin-Toomey rubbed some of its own members the wrong way. Many of them had joined Mayors Against Illegal Guns because they thought, reasonably enough, that the group's purpose was to oppose illegal guns. When the organization launched its crusade against legal guns, legal gun sales, and law-abiding gun owners, many of its members were taken aback.

One of them was Lawrence Morrissey, the mayor of Rockford, Illinois. A midsize town about half way between Chicago and Madison, Wisconsin, Rockford is an ideologically diverse city with a mix of Republicans and Democrats on its city council. Mayor Morrissey is an independent, and after Mayors Against Illegal Guns started throwing around Bloomberg's big money trying to push its left-wing agenda and bully anyone with the guts to defy it, Morrissey dropped out of the group.

"The reason why I joined the group in the first place is because I took the name for what it said—against 'illegal' guns," Morrissey explained. "I thought it was about enforcement of [the] existing gun laws," but "as the original mission swayed, that's when I decided that it was no longer in line with my beliefs."

Silly Lawrence Morrissey—he had taken Mayors Against Illegal Guns at its word. It kind of makes you wonder: When the anti–Second Amendment advocates say they don't really want to ban handguns, and when they say they don't really want to create a national gun registry, should we repeat Mayor Morrissey's mistake and take them at their word?

Another mayor who dropped out of Mayors Against Illegal Guns was Donnalee Lozeau of Nashua, New Hampshire. A turning point for Lozeau was Bloomberg's multi-million-dollar assault against Senator Ayotte after she voted against the Machin-Toomey proposal for background checks. "I said, 'Wait a minute, I don't want to be part of something like that,'" Lozeau explained. "I simply cannot be a part of an organization that chooses this course of action instead of cooperatively working with those that have proven over a lifetime of work their true intentions."

According to Lozeau, "nowhere within the literature of this group was there any indication that there would be campaigns against members of Congress, particularly around issues that were not related to illegal guns." She told Bloomberg's group, "You're Mayors Against Illegal Guns, you're not Mayors for Gun Control."

The real agenda of Mayors Against Illegal Guns was apparent when its director, Mark Glaze, appeared on Chris Matthews's MSNBC show *Hardball*. Even the liberal Matthews was shocked by Glaze's radical view of guns. In Glaze's world, guns should never be used against an aggressor who is not using a gun— even if the aggressor has another deadly weapon.

MARK GLAZE: Very often somebody will come at you. They might want to have a fistfight. They might want to come at you with an ax handle…

CHRIS MATTHEWS: Would you consider the guy with the ax handle armed or not?

MARK GLAZE: Well, not with a gun.

CHRIS MATTHEWS: I'd call him armed. *[Laughter]*

MARK GLAZE: I have a word for him. I grew up in Colorado where my dad was a gun dealer, and a guy who shoots somebody who has anything other than a gun when they could have done something else like talk or fight with their fists…

CHRIS MATTHEWS: How do you talk to a guy with an ax handle?

MARK GLAZE: Well, you fight him. You run away. You deescalate the situation.

And so there you have it. The Mark Glazes and Mike Bloombergs of the world don't want guns to be available, even for self-defense. They would advise a woman not to shoot a rapist if the rapist is threatening her with "only" a knife. They would advise a home owner awakened in the middle of the night by a broken window not to reach for a gun in the nightstand. And if they could have advised fictional DEA Agent Hank Schrader what to do in *Breaking Bad*'s third season, when he was lying wounded in a parking lot and was about to have his skull split by a killer wielding an ax, they would advise him to "deescalate the situation." Heaven forbid a rapist or murderer be physically injured by their prey. On whose side is Bloomberg anyway?

Just as there are no limits to the anti-gun lobby's animosity toward firearms, there is no limit to their hardball tactics. Not only did they run ads trying to punish senators for standing by their principles, they attempted to sabotage the senators' relationships with their supporters. Mayor Bloomberg called on New York donors to cut off donations to the Democratic senators who voted against Manchin-Toomey: Max Baucus, Mark Begich, Heidi Heitkamp, and Mark Pryor.

Bloomberg isn't content to throw around his own money and tell other people what to do with their money. It has been reported that he also may have used taxpayer dollars in connection with his anti-gun crusade.

As the *New York Post* reported, "Mayor Bloomberg is spending city cash and resources on his pet project to toughen U.S. gun laws through his national organization." Bloomberg sent city employee Christopher Kocher "to Nevada as a representative of Mayors Against Illegal Guns to lobby for a bill that enforces background checks on all firearm sales in that state." In an effort to hide the fact that he works for the City of New York—and is paid by the City of New York—Kocher "scrubbed his City Hall e-mail address from the state of Nevada lobbying-registration Web site."

The abuse of taxpayer dollars and government property goes beyond sending a New York City–funded employee to lobby for gun control in Nevada. The *Post*'s sources said staffers for Mayors Against Illegal Guns were "using the ninth floor of the Mayor's Office of Contract Services at 253 Broadway to advance the causes of the mayor's fund." *Politico* also reported that "the group's website is registered to, and handled by, official city government servers and staffers. Domain names for MAIG were registered in 2006 by the New York City Department of Information and Technology, and have remained on official city web servers ever since."

"MAIG has also enticed other mayors to break the law and betray their constituents by paying partial salaries for city employees who are in fact lobbyists for MAIG," reports Jeff Knox of *Shotgun News*. "Cities create new positions, typically providing health benefits and paying a portion of the person's salary, and the 'Coordinator,' who is always a dedicated MAIG operative, lobbies the City Council, state legislature, and governor on behalf of MAIG and their agenda."

MEET THE BLOOMBERG MOMS

Because his Mayors Against Illegal Guns simply wasn't breaking through, Bloomberg created a female-dominate companion group headed up by a Fortune 500 PR executive with decades of experience. Shannon Troughton, who also goes by the name Shannon Watts, is a former staffer for Missouri's late governor, Mel Carnahan, and has worked for Monsanto, Fleishman-Hillard, WellPoint, and more. She went to work for Bloomberg immediately after Sandy Hook.

In February 2014 I was invited to guest-co-host *The View*. As the conservative on the panel, I expected it to be somewhat fiery, but what I did not anticipate was the hysterical, almost envious reaction of Bloomberg's Shannon Troughton-Watts. Immediately after the news was announced Troughton-Watts took to Twitter to condemn *The View* for having as a guest cohost one woman who may think differently from the other four women cohosts. Bloomberg's lobbyist group rallied against my appearance, which was shortly after ABC's *Young Guns* special, which had a decidedly pro-gun-control slant.

"Disappointed @theviewtv having #DanaLoesch on. @JennyMcCarthy @WhoopiGoldberg @SherriEShepherd need #gunsense—I'll watch @TheTalk_CBS," Troughton-Watts tweeted.

She continued with a series:

"#Gunbully #DanaLoesch on @theviewtv on Monday. Will mislead about how guns make women, children safer to make $$. Sad. #momsdemand #gunsense."

Gun lobby and #Magpul pay #DanaLoesch to promote lies about guns—not appropriate guest for @theviewtv

Will tune in to @TheTalk_CBS on Monday to avoid guests on @theviewtv who get $$ from #magpul and spread gun lobby propaganda #momsdemand

"@theviewtv You're going to give another platform to #gunbully online bully no #gunsense Dana Loesch?" Tweeted @jeffe04

More:

"@theviewtv Why would you have a #gunbully like @DLoesch on your show? Paid by the NRA to attack moms for advocating for a safer America." Tweeted @sarahagv

There were scores and scores of tweets from people who called me a bully, said I had no #gunsense, and accused me of being paid by the gun lobby or Magpul or the NRA or all three. This was all in response to the simple announcement that I was going to be guest-co-hosting *The View*. I asked Bloomberg's Shannon Troughton-Watts what she meant by attempting to discredit me in a desperate attempt to deny me a fun, professional opportunity by falsely accusing me of accepting money from a gun manufacturer. The story to which Troughton-Watts linked in her Twitter campaign went to a lefty website that mentioned my appearance at a Colorado rally—which I first wrote about on my own website.

Magpul Industries was formerly headquartered in Colorado but pulled up stakes and split after the Democrat-controlled legislature passed intensely restrictive anti-gun legislation which made many items that Magpul produces—like their standard-capacity magazines—illegal. Magpul figured, why stay in a state that criminalizes its product? So it took its revenue and jobs to another state. Colorado Democrats paid dearly for that abuse of their voters: They lost heavily in the subsequent recall election months later, spearheaded by average Americans angry that Colorado bypassed them by refusing to put restrictions of their Second Amendment liberties to a vote.

Before Magpul left, though, they held a massive rally the weekend before the mag ban kicked into effect. Several state watchdog organizations—including Compass Colorado, run by my friend Kelly Maher—helped organize, numerous city and state elected officials spoke against the gun control legislation and Magpul sold the soon-to-be-banned magazines to eager Coloradans so they would be grandfathered in under the law. I rode in a helicopter Magpul had rented for the occasion, with a Magpul decal on the side, and I gave a speech (I did not receive a dime from Magpul. All travel, lodging, and incidentals were paid for by Compass Colorado.) opposed to the legislation that included the latest crime statistics and a primer on the racist history of gun control. I was proud to have taken part. My friend Kelly Maher, for her part, paid for it through her grassroots group, Compass Colorado. That was it. But it was enough for Bloomberg lobbyist Shannon Troughton-Watts to imply that I was somehow in Magpul's pocket in an effort to hurt Magpul and in an effort to hurt both of us professionally, somehow. The bad news for her is that I wish I was a Magpul employee. They seem to take care of their employees better than Bloomberg takes care of his lobbyists. You'd never see Magpul shove an employee into the spotlight knowing absolutely nothing about the thing they want to ban.

Bloomberg's involvement in Colorado (he spent millions and lost, which we'll cover later) only sold more Magpul products.

The surest way to sell more guns is to rail against them.

Bloomberg Moms' caterwauling had the opposite effect of what they intended. Thousands of regular Americans rallied to my side, even trending an #IStandWithDana sentiment on Twitter. Supporters included Olympic shooter Amanda Furrer, a woman who, unlike the women Bloomberg shoves in front of cameras, actually knows what she's talking about when discussing firearms. When I finally arrived in New York and walked into makeup before the show, the ladies of *The View* greeted me warmly. Despite the disagreements I may have with them on policy, they were gracious and complete professionals, eager to make me feel comfortable at their table. Whoopi Goldberg and Jenny McCarthy were clearly annoyed that their Twitter timelines were filled up with angry women spurred by Bloomberg to nag me off the show.

"It's called *The View* for a reason!" said an exasperated Goldberg loudly.

"Just the wrong way to go about it," McCarthy said.

"Don't tweet to me about it," Goldberg continued. "I don't book the show. But it's called *The View* for a reason. We have all sides."

When your tactics are turning off the likes of the women who should agree with you the most, you're doing it wrong. The show went wonderfully. There was a humorous point at which Barbara Walters asked me if I enjoyed shooting while behind me on their screen a clip of me at the range with my rifle clearly showed that I did. Bloomberg's Fembot lobbying group helped to drum up a lot of publicity for my appearance and tweeted about anything I said all throughout the show. The producers definitely noticed the social media activity, even remarking how much attention this particular show was receiving due to the lobbying efforts against my participation. And why, exactly, were Bloomberg's lobbyists so opposed to my guest-co-hosting *The View*? It's all down to the sexist tactics of Michael Bloomberg, which is why we have Moms Demand.

Michael Bloomberg is using the "war on women" approach to destroy the Second Amendment. He needs the face of the Second Amendment to be a man's. It's hard to defeat a right but it's a lot easier to defeat a right if you give it a face—or a sex. It's why he likes to have Shannon Troughton-Watts as the face of his anti-gun campaign. Bloomberg figures that if he personifies Second Amendment supporters as big, burly men and anti–Second Amendment supporters as vulnerable mothers simply trying to protect their young, then he will finally find the support for gun control that has eluded him and other anti-gun advocates all of these years.

But, in order to do this, he has to disempower women in the eyes of the public. For Bloomberg's shtick to work, he needs to remake the image of a mother into a frightened, helpless creature barely able to shepherd her young through the super-market, much less carry a firearm for her or her family's pro-tection. Women are incapable of protecting themselves—it's the refrain we heard Colorado Democrats tell rape survivors to their faces. It's why Bloomberg ignores the existence of millions of female firearm owners and only pays attention to the men. It's sexism by suppression.

Even worse, he assumes that simply sending out a woman under his banner to rage against guns on television will be enough. He doesn't bother prepping the people he backs fi-nancially. No, instead, he sends out people who claim that any weapon "that fires ten rounds a minute is an assault weapon," as his Moms Demand group did on Twitter in response to me one evening. He sends out the most uninformed and unedu-cated women on the topic of firearms to lecture gun owners—many of whom are women, and our numbers are growing—who know better.

Because now Bloomberg has a women's group, they have the added buffer of maligning anyone who disagrees with them, even on simple fact or policy, as sexist bullies. If Bloomberg had but one educated anti-gun extremist in his harem, that would be a start—but he can't find a knowledgeable, empowered woman who knows about, and how to properly handle, guns and yet who remains afraid of them. They don't exist. Education is the antidote to ignorance. Groups like the Olympic women's shooters team or One Million Moms Against Gun Control, a wonderful group of real grassroots mothers who subsist on their own dime (not $50 million from Bloomberg) make hysterical work of Bloomberg's attempt to cast gun control as a female effort.

Weeks after their small counterprotest at the NRA's convention (discussed later) Moms Demand claimed that one of their members at the rally, a wheelchair-bound victim of gun violence, was spat on at the airport in Indianapolis, the same day that I had flown in and out of the airport on my way to cover the NRA convention. Lefty website *Mother Jones* published this woman's claims, among them: that she was spit on while at the Indianapolis airport, that shadowy men hiding behind her house shot her with a squirt gun before calling her "bitch" for opposing gun rights. I asked *Mother Jones* if they had vetted the woman's account. The airport at Indy was certainly busy that day, and I was there twice on the very day the woman says the spitting incident occurred. Surely there is security footage from the trillion or so cameras there. This is an assault we're discussing. The woman says she shrugged it off and wiped herself off, something I find difficult to believe, considering the way these women react to children who simply eat their Pop Tarts into gun shapes or to me if I post a photo of myself at the range.

I asked because what bothered me is that if it did happen (I lived through the false tea party spitting claims, so forgive my skepticism), then why did no one else there come to her defense? Or even spoke up as witnesses afterward? What an indictment of our society. If such a thing occurred, I'd be the first to go toe to toe with such folks. I find their account tough to swallow considering how many times this group has been caught lying, including about me. Something like this should be easy to prove, and were I Bloomberg, I'd do just that to tarnish my opposition. Claims aren't enough. *Mother Jones*, of course, reacted hysterically when I questioned their integrity, and equated me with a woman hater for not believing the woman's claims without question, as good modern-day "journalists" are supposed to do, apparently. When *Glamour* magazine wrote about the incident I openly questioned the author online asking whether she vetted the piece. She called me a "troll" ("I'm not clicking on your blog, troll") before apologizing for her tone the next day after *Glamour* was besieged via social media. Of course no one vetted the account because the goal was to make the allegation, to plant the seed that gun owners are scary, unsavory male individuals so that it will help inspire full-blown opposition.

Mayors Against Illegal Guns—alternatively titled Extremist Anti-Gun Group That Is Its Own Undoing—and Moms Demand Action for Gun Sense in America were collected and rebranded after the groups failed to make serious traction on their own. In 2014 Everytown for Gun Safety was announced as the parent organization for the two aforementioned groups. No sooner had they announced that former governor Tom Ridge was a board member did he quit Crazytown while throwing some shade at the group in his departing statement to the *Daily Caller*:

"When I signed on as an advisor to Everytown, I looked forward to a thoughtful and provocative discussion about

the toll gun violence takes on Americans," Ridge told the Daily Caller *in a statement, through a spokesman. "After consultation with Everytown, I have decided that I am uncomfortable with their expected electoral work," Ridge said. "Therefore, we have decided that we will pursue this issue in our separate spheres."[1]*

Basically, Tom Ridge just announced that they were all [redacted] crazy. Ridge was counted on to underwrite the legitimacy of the group because none of their other members have any. Ridge wasn't the only one to exit stage right—nearly fifty mayors (yes, fifty!) dropped the group because they discovered that Bloomberg essentially lied to them, that this wasn't about safety or awareness, it was about banning guns, all guns, outright.

While Everytown faded and MAIG descended into madness, Bloomberg put all of his Scrooge McDuck cash into the Moms Demand Action basket. Since they've epically failed at everything they've tried to do and alienated everyone on the left save for the most extremist anti-gun advocates like themselves, and since they had zero legislative successes nationally and few locally, minus states already hostile to 2A, Bloomberg gave them $50 million. Since they couldn't legislate policy, Bloomberg lobbyists decided to do the next best thing and attack...fast food restaurants. Moms Demand has gone after Starbucks, Chipotle, and Sonic. I can't tell if they have unhealthy food habits or are that desperate, perhaps a bit of both, but I can guaran-damn-tee you that the dude making your burrito at Chipotle doesn't care if you're for or against the Second Amendment—just *order your burrito.* Bloomberg's moms haven't scored a single victory as most restaurant owners sigh, roll their eyes, and remind these Franzia fans that they are restaurants, not legislative chambers, please learn to find your state capitol on a map and go there. Aside from Staples (they also targeted office supplies) throwing them out of their headquarters, most restaurants have to pause their day to answer questions like the e-mailed dialogue this listener forwarded to me:

From: Chipotle Support case_activity_track@n-7epvqgrqb2rc3 e1vydlnl1zr8.uy4lnmac.u.apex.salesforce.com
Date: May 22, 2014 at 10:33:06 AM CDT
To: "REDACTED"
Subject: Reply from Chipotle
Reply-To: case_activity_track@n-7epvqgrqb2rc3e1vydlnl1zr8 .uy4lnmac.u.apex.salesforce.com

Yes, that is accurate. This is not a ban.

Sincerely,

Kate

_____

Subject: Reply from Chipotle

Body: Thanks Kate. You understand how this is hard to decipher for me. So when you say you'll continue to comply with local laws, you will technically allow concealed carry where it's allowed in the state, while at the same time encourage people to not do it. Is that accurate?

Sent from my iPhone

When they're not badgering fast food restaurants, Moms Demand is promoting bizarre studies. John Lott's fabulous Crime Prevention Research Center has expertly debunked a number of their claims by analyzing statistics and crime reports. For instance, Troughton-Watts once tweeted "#YesAllWomen are victims of @NRA: 84% of female firearm homicides in 25 countries are in US." The response from the CPRC?

"Moms Demand Action's claim doesn't make much sense as one shouldn't compare the number of homicides since that doesn't account for differences in population size. There are a lot of small population countries. It would make much more sense to compare homicide rates. This figure from the UNODC [United Nations Office On Drugs and Crime] shows that the US has one of the lower female homicide rates in the world. So how does the US compare to other countries in terms of the share of homicides involving females? *While 22.2% of US homicides involve females, that is below the median for all countries of 23.7% and the mean of 24.4%*" [emphasis added].[2]

The Crime Prevention Research Center is a hated clearinghouse (hated by Bloomberg, anyway) of nonemotional analysis focusing particularly on firearms and disputing the sketchy assertions made by people like Bloomberg, who pays for his own push poll so as to present its findings as evidence for his group's wild claims.

THE TRUTH ISN'T MEAN, IT'S TRUTH

On the subject of wild claims, the hallmark of Bloomberg research is to conflate incidents in an effort to boost the number of shootings to make it seem as though lawlessness is the new rule of law with firearms. Case in point: Following the June 2014 shooting at Reynolds High School in Oregon, in which one student was killed and the murderer illegally using a firearm was taken out, Bloomberg's Everytown began pushing the line that "since Newtown there have been 74 school shootings in the United States." They're not counting on anyone to actually look at the seventy-four different examples provided; they just want a sound bite to be regurgitated by networks like CBS (who did indeed). If one closely examines those seventy-four examples, though, what they see is vastly different that what is being peddled as narrative. Reporter Charles C. Johnson did some digging on the map Everytown provided in June 2014. More than half of the incidents listed on their rare (according to FBI crime stats and the CDC study commissioned by the president in 2013) "mass shootings" map were limited to drug or gang violence and weren't even in a school, with a vast number of aggressors not even connected to the school where the crime occurred or occurred nearby. Some examples of incidents that Everytown listed as "mass shootings":

- Hazard Community and Technical College, where an argument broke out in a parking lot and the aggressor shot another party
- A shooting near Morehouse College in Atlanta, which police said "wasn't random"[3]
- A seventeen-year-old gang member who carried a pink pistol to Atlanta's Grady High School and accidentally shot herself in the thigh

- A nineteen-year-old who police suspected wasn't shot on campus in a dispute over a game of dice[4]
- A gang-related shooting involving one victim near, not at, Elizabeth City State University, where the perpetrators were not students[5]
- An argument between two men at Stillman College related to gambling that resulted in one man shooting the other[6]
- An angry ex-husband who shot his wife, an assistant principal of a school, two weeks before school began[7]
- A man at Eastern Florida State College who fired his gun in self-defense[8]
- A suicide at a Maine high school[9]
- One teenage boy who fired shots at another teenage boy in an argument over a girl in a parking lot[10]

Suicides, gang violence, and drug disputes dominate the list. Actual mass shootings remain rare. Rare isn't what helps Bloomberg ban guns, though. He needs to scare parents into believing that mass shootings at schools are real and that their children are going to die unless they ban guns. He can't do it with truth, so he must lie. The goal is to get the talking point to air, and that it's a lie is irrelevant. People can fact-check, but fact-checking is reactive. The narrative is set and the headline is already printed. Repeat the lie often enough, then people will believe it and be fooled into forfeiting their rights to the state.

The story of the small fortune spent by Mayors Against Illegal Guns—some from the bank account of one of the world's one hundred wealthiest people and some of it from the taxpayers who had put that billionaire in the mayor's office—is a story that raises a number of questions, all with the same answer. Why does the anti-gun lobby think it's necessary to spend so much money? Why do they have to lie about people like Senator Jeff Flake? Why did they use the name of their organization to hide their true agenda?

The answer to those questions is simple: Americans don't like what they're selling. Americans don't want more gun control. Americans don't want a national gun registry. And Americans don't believe those being attacked with an ax should toss away their gun and try to "deescalate the situation."

Chapter 4

Flyover Bigotry

My family is from the kind of rural town on which lemonade commercials are based. Kids catch tadpoles and crawdads on gravelly riverbanks; they skip down the holler and run barefoot into the quik mart with gifted change to buy up Slim Jims and Sixlets. There's one restaurant at the center of the tiny, rural town, where the old folk meet in the mornings over strong black coffee and eggs, and the nearest supermarket is thirty minutes away. It's a town where everybody owns livestock, where tea is prepared by placing tea bags inside a big pitcher of sugar water before setting it out on a picnic table in the afternoon sun; where entertainment is bonfires in the woods or camping on the river; where people have tons of ceramic porch geese. When you call the law, it may take a while—and everyone drives a truck with a full gun rack in the back glass. It is truly all of these things. It's also a rural town that would supply a few hundred episodes of *Cops* mostly due to Natty Light–fueled brawls, the fury of which dissipates the next day beginning with the requisite morning handshakes in church.

My grandparents lived in a tiny five-room home in a small

valley on the other side of an old, abandoned mine. I imagine that when the town founders found this craggle in the stone bosom of the Ozarks, they settled upon it because the distance from society outweighed the interest from busybodies who desired to meddle in their business. It's also far enough away from everything and anyone that if the fit hits the shan, you're on your own. The earth is red and rocky and unsuitable for much farming beyond corn and a bit of basic produce. My grandparents kept goats, chickens, and pheasants, apart from my grandpa's dairy cattle on a pasture a few miles away. Grandpa hunted for most everything else until supermarkets came near to town, which coincided with my youngest aunt's entry into high school, the timing of which her angsty teenaged self was thankful for. My grandparents's gun cabinet was kept in their bedroom. Where I'm from, people don't have "safes," they have wooden cabinets with etched glass front doors, where instruments of protection and means to provide meat for your family take pride of place as display. Another way to look at it: It's a fancy way to store metal middle fingers to Michael Bloomberg and the anti-gun lobby.

A lot of folks make their own cabinets; my uncle made my grandfather's for him. The cabinet was always unlocked, with kids running everywhere at all times, and not once was there a single accident in Grandma and Grandpa's house. Despite the best efforts of wealthy New Yorkers to cast rural gun owners as bitter clingers and straw gnawers whose children teethe on gun barrels, we never even gave a thought to touching anything in Grandpa's gun cabinet, just as we didn't raid Grandma's jewelry box or rummage through their prescription medications. For one thing, we were brought up to respect the private property and privacy of others. Every person in my family makes what I call an "eagle face"—a stone cold glare and narrowing of the eyes—and 99 percent of the time that was all it took to send a message about bad behavior.

Secondly, we knew what guns could do. We knew that the blood-stained tarp in the back of Grandpa's old truck wasn't stained from grape juice. For people who love science, the left is clueless about it whenever the subject of guns arises. My cousins and I knew how to behave around firearms because we learned by example: We saw how our elders behaved around and with firearms. My grandpa and uncles didn't play around with their guns. The only times we saw them shoot was for target practice; otherwise, their work with their guns was done out in the woods with the animals they hunted and brought home for us to eat. Sometimes after Grandpa got a deer I'd go to the backyard where he'd hang it up, stand on the picnic table, and look in its glassy, empty eyes. It was the look of death. When the trigger of a gun is pulled a sacrifice is made, be it for sustenance or, God forbid, to save a life. It's always a trade, though; this we knew at a young age.

My grandpa once saw me standing on the picnic table staring at one of his deer, and he walked over and put his old, leathered arm around my little shoulders. "Do you know how that deer got in that way?" he asked? I shook my head no. "He looked down my barrel," he said, staring right into my eyes. "He looked down my barrel and I squeezed my trigger." He made the motion with his hand and index finger. He motioned to the deer. "That's what happens when you squeeze a trigger." Sometimes Grandpa and my uncles would round up the hound dogs and take the younger boys out at night to hunt raccoon. Grandpa could never get all his granddaughters to shut up and stop giggling, so we weren't the best hunters at that age. We girls would pile into Grandma and Grandpa's tiny living room in front of the old woodstove to sleep. Out of all the animals they hunted, raccoons were my least favorite, because to me they all looked like tiny, lovable bandits. "Tasty-as-hell bandits," a cousin once said to me in response.

I'm sure anti–Second Amendment advocates would be sad to learn that my family and their neighbors didn't shoot up their town, or any town, or that none of my cousins shot themselves or anyone else. People didn't rob each other, no one was carjacked, no one tried to rape anyone, all because of the simple fact that they were raised right and everyone was armed. It was a real community, not one where people outsourced everything to the government because doing so was easier than investing the time themselves. They voluntarily depended on one another for everything from elderly care to watching out for the kids playing in the field behind the school. They were aware; they were plugged in; they the willing spirit of a volunteer.

When you go to a rural town the first thing you see is everyone's chin is up, not tucked into their chest thumbing on a phone. A child growing up on a farm or the child of a family who hunts receives no better lesson on the value of life that what can be seen in their own backyard. My family taught my cousins and me how to behave around firearms—just as they taught us not to run out into the street and not to talk to strangers—because they believed in being proactive to protect us and prevent accidents from occurring. Why would any other parent not do the same?

BITTER CLINGERS

During a 2008 fund-raiser in tony San Francisco, then junior senator Barack Obama delved into the psyche of small-town America, via small-town Pennsylvania. I mentioned this quote earlier in the book, because it's so offensive and yet also so educational about how leftists think that it's worth reading in full:

> *You go into these small towns in Pennsylvania and, like a lot of small towns in the Midwest, the jobs have been gone now for 25 years and nothing's replaced them. And they fell through the Clinton Administration, and the Bush Administration, and each successive administration has said that somehow these communities are gonna regenerate and they have not. And it's not surprising then they get bitter, they cling to guns or religion or antipathy to people who aren't like them or anti-immigrant sentiment or anti-trade sentiment as a way to explain their frustrations.*

That's the view progressives have of Middle America, yes? We're collectively the bitter, bastard child of the coasts, and we use our guns, faith, and racism as Linus blankets to soothe our insecurities because of George W. BUSH, obviously. We all sit around and eat corn from a shared tooth and every person, down to the babies, fashions their hair into a Kentucky Waterfall/ Camaro crash helmet/mullet. *Bitter* isn't the word I would use to describe the region in which I was born and raised. These people aren't bitter, and President Obama doesn't know the Midwest. He grew up the entitled grandson of a bank vice president with a well-educated, globe-trotting mother, and he attended private and Ivy League schools. He's the first president I've seen ever pictured with an inability to properly shoulder a shotgun. He grew up in a city with the toughest anti-gun laws in the country (where only criminals have guns and the innocents have to pray that the police arrive before they bleed to death). The only church he's ever attended is where an angry racist screamed about white America creating AIDS to kill black people. No wonder he has such a low opinion of middle America. No wonder he has such a low opinion of the Second Amendment. I don't begrudge him or anyone a lack of experience or knowledge about firearms. I am, however, critical of these same people with their lack of experience and knowledge on the subject lecturing those of us with the experience and knowledge about this civil liberty.

Interestingly, according to data from the U.S. Census Bureau and FBI crime reports, the states with the highest levels of gun ownership do not have the highest homicide rates. For comparison, Illinois, which has some of the strictest gun regulations in the country, has nearly three times the gun-related deaths as Alabama, a state which has a roughly 30 percent higher firearm ownership rate.[1] When states began enacting nondiscretionary concealed-carry laws in the early 1990s, violent crime and murder rates plummeted.[2] States that did not implement concealed-carry laws saw a violent crime rate at 81 percent higher than states that did issue concealed-carry permits. The same applies to murder rates: States that did not allow for concealed-carry saw a 127 percent higher murder rate.[3]

Former governor Zell Miller of Georgia instigated the

modern-day, state-by-state concealed-carry issue by implementing the law in his state in 1976. Murder, assault, rape, and other violent crimes dropped. A few other states—Indiana, Maine, Washington, the Dakotas, and Vermont—already had shall-issue laws (Vermont had no licensing at all and to this day has laxer gun laws than perceptually-freer states like Texas), but these garnered no headlines. No one began paying attention until Florida in 1987 passed concealed-carry and anti–Second Amendment advocates predicted that the state would turn red—not from politics, but from a bloodbath. They were almost sad when it never came to pass; in fact, according to FBI crime data, crime began to drop when the law was passed. Florida's homicide rate was previously 36 percent above the national average, and it fell to 4 percent below that average after the passage of concealed-carry.[4] According to the Florida Department of Justice, only .02 percent of all concealed-carry permit holders in Florida were involved in a crime.

The Florida Model, as it came to be known, began to pick up steam. Suddenly it wasn't just flyover country that carried.

My home state of Missouri passed concealed-carry in 2003. I used to live in downtown St. Louis. I could see the Arch from my backyard. I'd sit outside on warm summer nights and smell the barley and hops in the air from the brewery several blocks away. I love my hometown city, but I'm also aware of the realities of living in it: You carry in St. Louis. My cousin Nathan lived three doors down from us and was robbed at gunpoint one night in our neighborhood. A friend who worked with my husband was robbed at gunpoint a year before that in a city parking lot across the street from our block. The "knockout game" was born in my city, where young men hit men and women in the head, seriously injuring them, and run off, all for the fun of it. One of the attacks occurred right in front of the city mayor.

The current police chief, who has been slowly cozying up to anti–Second Amendment groups (it helps the image in a progressive town) once told me to get a handgun because they (the police) "can't be everywhere." This was after my station talked with local law enforcement after I received a rash of threats following the Kenneth Gladney beating (mentioned in the Introduction). It's so very different from rural America, where being a bored bureaucrat isn't an industry and people are left alone. I felt safe getting gas alone at the pump farthest from the attendant at night in my family's rural Missouri hometown. I feel safer. Some of it is lifestyle and a different emphasis on mortality, but a lot of it is that everyone assumes everyone else is armed because, in my experience, they usually are armed. As I said, I love my city, but I won't walk around it unarmed. Not surprisingly, the states with the highest gun-related deaths also have the most restrictive laws concerning gun rights. According to the 2012 FBI Uniform Crime Reports, California took the crown for most murders—1,879—with 1,304 of those being firearm related. Alabama ranks ninth on the list of states with highest gun ownership yet had one murder by firearm—a handgun—that year. By comparison, California, which ranks in the top ten of most restrictive gun laws in the country had 899 murders related to handguns, 38 related to rifles, and 52 related to shotguns.[5]

In fact, the states with the most Second Amendment freedom consistently saw fewer murders. Wyoming was ranked as the state with the highest gun ownership in 2007, which, following anti–Second Amendment logic, would mean that the prevalence of guns equates to an equal amount of murders. Wrong. Wyoming had one of the lowest murder rates total, and only seven murders related to firearms: two by handgun, two by rifle, two by shotgun, one listed as "Firearms (type unknown).[6] "You don't need any Michael Bloomberg Violence Policy Voxs plaining for this—the data speaks for itself.

Now that the numbers were failing them, the anti–Second Amendment lobby, with their catered rallies and NY-plated, chauffeured SUVs, needed to find a way to stem this expansion of what they view as flyover "gun culture." A poorly researched and poorly written piece appeared in the *New York Times* in March 2013 attempting to hype a decline in gun ownership, never mind that background checks due to gun purchases have increased. Newsbusters measured how long it took the paper to mention that it's virtually impossible to measure gun ownership in the United States and that gun sales have actually increased. (Twelve. It took them twelve paragraphs. Talk about burying a lead.) The paper also declined to include women as the fastest-growing gun-owning demo, a spike first noted by CBS in 2011.

Flyover is spreading. People in cities realize that they can have the same protection and peace of mind as their rural brethren. Some are even waging a war to get those rights back, as in the case of Otis McDonald (*McDonald v. Chicago*), who fought the urban Chicago machine so he could carry a handgun and protect himself in his neighborhood, where robbery is rampant. It's no surprise that when Chicago finally implemented concealed-carry, their crime rate plummeted. Within the first three months the city saw a 9 percent drop in murder and 55 fewer murders in 2013 than in 2012, along with 90 fewer shootings and 119 fewer shooting victims. *Huffington Post* also reported that crime was down by 25 percent from 2013.[7] It's far from being as safe as some of the rural towns where my family lives, but it's a start.

ANTI-GUN AND ANTI-SCIENCE

Anti–Second Amendment advocates profess to love science while demonizing people of faith, but you'd never know this by their arguments. Bloomberg PR exec/mom Shannon Watts-Troughton once told me via Twitter that "an assault weapon enables humans to shoot 10 rounds in one minute. @blueelephant69: @shannonrwatts @DLoesch."

What in flat-earthing hell is this?

I can throw ten bowling balls a minute, I have assault arms, ban them.

By her estimation, "assault weapons" are any firearms that can shoot ten rounds per minute, which is every firearm. Even a bolt action rifle can shoot ten rounds per minute. That leaves us with old-timey cannons, trebuchets, and similar hurling devices, muskets (perhaps, if everything isn't measured and ready), oh, and the preferred weapons of choice for individuals who live in totalitarian, anti-gun rights states: rocks and sticks. During the Arab spring in 2011, Yemeni protesters got creative with their self-defense accoutrements with one man famously taping bread to his head as a helmet while furiously throwing rocks at state forces. (Bread Helmet Man quickly became a meme thereafter.) Considering we can fire off those projectiles at faster than ten per minute, anti-2A advocates would ban those, too. Any firearm from the past 150-plus years would be banned according to this arbitrary measure. At least Bloomberg, through Shannon Troughton-Watts, is honest: Anti–Second Amendment advocates believe in far more than simple restriction—they want all firearms banned.

Anti–Second Amendment advocates also do not know how firearms work. This is probably why they immediately think that any gun that is black and has rails and a scope is a supercalafragalisticexpialaassault weapon capable of firing one frillion rounds per second. One of these gun geniuses once told me that select fire capability meant that the individual operating the firearm could select to fire it or not. Once, for my self-titled television show on TheBlaze, I brought my own AR-15 and my youngest son's AR-15–styled BB gun in for a pop quiz. I showed both on camera and asked viewers to use Facebook, Twitter, and e-mail, and let me know which was which. I also posted a photo of the two guns on Instagram and asked the same. All my fly-over folks knew immediately. "Well, you've got a Magpul p-mag on the one on the right, so that one is the real one," or "the mag on the left is shorter, so that's the BB gun, plus I can tell that's an Aim scope on the other one." Anti-gun advocates simply accused me of owning two "assault weapons." I know, it was a trick question. Both rifles were black.

Honestly, it kills brain cells without the benefit of alcohol trying to make sense of these people. While once on Piers Morgan's now-defunct show (complaining about Americans and their gun rights for an hour five times a week isn't enticing to viewers, apparently) I had to use my "assault lighter"—a candle lighter styled in the fashion of an AR-15, to demonstrate how semi- and fully automatic firearms work. According to anti-2A advocates, the weight of a single person's gaze upon a firearm is enough to squeeze the trigger and slaughter trillions.

Some anti-2A advocates (who simultaneously lecture people of faith) themselves have faith that firearms are magical creatures who discriminately creep around wealthy white schools and neighborhoods to shoot up people. When this happens in places like Chicago or Detroit it's called "gangs" or "drug-related violence," but everywhere else it's called "an epidemic" of inanimate objects causing destruction.

Anti–Second Amendment advocates also believe that inanimate objects like firearms are inherently evil, forged in the fires of Mordor each with the ability to transfer its evil to its possessor. Behaviors such as abuse, drugs, alcohol, or an individual's true nature are immediately discounted. All it takes for an angelic child to turn into a wee demon is for the child to look upon a firearm and *voila!* The "Children of the Corn" theme plays and the transformation is finished. Nothing of what they believe is based in science or supported by statistics; it's all raw, emotional, prejudicial hoplophobia.

Before we moved to a different state, I had an acquaintance in a playgroup who had grown up on the west coast. She confided that she wasn't entirely comfortable with my sons playing with brightly colored water pistols.

"Do you think they're going to magically turn into real guns?" I joked in response after she encouraged her son to play with a different toy.

"They just don't exist in our home," she said matter-of-factly.

"They still exist out in the real world," I replied. "Maybe you choose not to talk about them in your home, but that doesn't erase their existence out in the rest of the world."

She was opposed even to the mere idea of teaching her children firearm safety. There was no need, she argued, because her children were never going to be around them. She couldn't differentiate between firearm education and firearm ownership. I wasn't telling her to go out and buy a gun, but she recoiled from increasing her knowledge about guns, as if the action would make a gun appear in her hand. I stopped short of reminding her that accidental gun deaths related to children are the result of either improper or no education, or improper or irresponsible storage—and are extremely rare and grotesquely outnumbered by child deaths from drowning, abuse, and other non-firearm-related variables.[8]

Education is the antidote to ignorance. There was a time when people used to believe this. My mother didn't even own a gun when my family members began teaching me the dos and don'ts of firearms. I was taught for my own safety and for the safety of children around me. The more I knew about firearms, the less curious I became. Knowledge fed that curiosity and cultivated an understanding of what those inanimate objects could do with the wrong will. My family also raised my cousins and me with the knowledge that respect for life and use of firearms are not mutually exclusive things.

These people who claim that guns are nothing more than a psychological crutch for the weak willed have never had to hunt for their food or rely upon them for safety. With the time and money Bloomberg groups spend demonizing peaceful, law-abiding mom-and-dad gun owners, they could have promoted real gun safety. Bloomberg's $50 million to shout down dissent on Second Amendment issues could have gone toward putting a safe in every American home or teaching children about proper behavior with and around firearms. He could have donated to Project Child Safe, a wonderful program created by the National Shooting Sports Foundation, which gives away free gun locks in gun safety kits through partners in every state. Over thirty-six million safety kits have been distributed through partnerships with law enforcement agencies in all fifty states. Unfortunately, $90 million was cut from their funding by the Obama administration in 2009; since that time the NSSF covered the financial loss themselves. Steve Sanetti of the NSSF told me on my radio program in July 2014 that Project Child Safe had reached out to Bloomberg for assistance as Bloomberg claimed to promote gun safety, but Bloomberg never responded. Instead, his money has gone to support a warped idea of "safety," which is to incite furor and violence. To recap: It was gun control advocates who turned their backs on a national gun safety program that provided gun locks. Not the gun industry.

When One Million Moms Against Gun Control—a real grassroots group of moms across the country who pay their own way—was featured on MSNBC, Shannon Watts-Troughton went ballistic, repetitively tweeting and posting on Facebook about and to these moms, trying to goad progressives into attack mode. As a result, violent commentary flooded the One Million Moms Against Gun Control's Facebook page. Read one: "Now I've heard everything stupid in this world, hope your kids shot [sic] each other on the face and you enjoy it, as one of you said 'The killing of children is the price we pay to keep our guns.'" Apparently, inspiring threats against law-abiding Second Amendment moms is Michael Bloomberg's idea of "safety."

Most of these anti-gun bigots—and I don't use that word lightly—are locked up in Tupperware-fresh urbia, and everything from their food to the security of the family is outsourced. They stick signs in the front of their homes warning would-be criminals that an automated system will call someone with guns to come and stop them midway through their act of atrocity. The closest they'll get to killing their own meat is buying prepackaged deer sausage at the supermarket. Everything is convenient and within reach. Perhaps that's why many of them feel that rural Americans and their firearms are anachronistic.

More than just for self-defense, the Second Amendment is also the teeth against domestic tyranny, the epitome of big government, as well as tyranny abroad (the Founders' own remarks on how to deal with tyranny are more strident than the simple exercise of this civil liberty). The firearm is a tool of an individual, and in an era where individualism is suspect, it's viewed with contempt. Individuals can protect themselves and their families and provide food for their families without the need for government intervention. Therein lies the problem: As long as Americans have their Second Amendment civil liberty, those who seek to envelop them completely in the web of excessive government will always fail.

Chapter 5

Guns for Them, But Not for You

> I actually hate guns.
> —MILLIONAIRE ACTION FILM STAR
> (AND HYPOCRITE) MATT DAMON

NBC News reporter David Gregory was on a tear. Lecturing the NRA president—and the rest of the world—on the need for gun restrictions, the D.C. media darling and host of NBC's boring Sunday morning gabfest, *Meet the Press*, Gregory displayed a thirty-round magazine during an interview. This was a violation of District of Columbia law, which specifically makes it illegal to own, transfer, or sell "high-capacity ammunition."

Conservatives demanded the Mr. Gregory, a proponent of strict gun control laws, be arrested and charged for his clear violation of the laws he supports. Instead the District of Columbia's attorney general, Irv Nathan, gave Gregory a pass:

> *Having carefully reviewed all of the facts and circumstances of this matter, as it does in every case involving firearms-related offenses or any other potential violation of D.C. law within our criminal jurisdiction, OAG has determined to exercise its prosecutorial discretion to decline to bring criminal*

charges against Mr. Gregory, who has no criminal record, or any other NBC employee based on the events associated with the December 23, 2012 broadcast.

What irked people even more was the attorney general admitted that NBC had willfully violated D.C. law. As he noted:

No specific intent is required for this violation, and ignorance of the law or even confusion about it is no defense. We therefore did not rely in making our judgment on the feeble and unsatisfactory efforts that NBC made to determine whether or not it was lawful to possess, display and broadcast this large capacity magazine as a means of fostering the public policy debate. Although there appears to have been some misinformation provided initially, NBC was clearly and timely advised by an MPD employee that its plans to exhibit on the broadcast a high capacity-magazine would violate D.C. law.

David Gregory gets a pass, but not Mark Witaschek.

Witaschek was the subject of not one but two raids on his home by D.C. police. The second time that police raided Witaschek's home, they did so with a SWAT team and even pulled his terrified teenage son out of the shower. They found inoperable muzzleloader bullets (replicas, not live ammunition, no primer) and an inoperable shotgun shell, a tchotchke from a hunting trip. Witaschek, in compliance with D.C. laws, kept his guns out of D.C. and at a family member's home in Virginia. It wasn't good enough for the courts, who tangled him up in a two-year court battle that he fought on principle but eventually lost. As punishment, the court forced him to register as a gun offender, even though he never had a firearm in the city. Witaschek is listed as a "gun offender"—not to be confused with "sex offender," though that's exactly the intent: to draw some sort of correlation, to make possession of a common firearm seem as perverse as sexual offenses. If only Mark Witaschek got the break that David Gregory received.

So the left's standard is this: Gun control laws should be enforced against minorities, Republican politicians, Republican women seeking to defend themselves, and anyone in support of Second Amendment rights. But gun control laws should not be imposed against liberal media outlets. That makes perfect sense, doesn't it?

Consider as well the utter hypocrisy of other celebrities on guns. Which brings me to my favorite empty-headed hoplophobe, Piers Morgan. Outside of Piers Morgan's home is a sign strategically positioned in the front of his property by the walkway. Its bold red-and-white typeface is a warning to all passersby: "Protected By Armed Response Security Systems." James O'Keefe of Project Veritas discovered the sign as he sought signatures for a petition seeking to rid Hollywood films of all firearms. He took a photo of the sign and asked Morgan via Twitter "Hey, @piersmorgan, can you explain these signs on your Beverly Hills property?" Morgan could not, so he ignored it.

While Morgan snores soundly in his bed, he has a security firm keep watch with a firearm and rush to Morgan's defense if Morgan finds himself under threat. This way Morgan can pretend that he's against firearms when, really, he's just outsourced his gun. He is a royalist: He believes that commoners shouldn't possess firearms, especially Americans. It's the ultimate hypocrisy: Progressives view firearms as only situationally evil. They're evil in the hands of anyone other than themselves or their security firms. Don't tell that to their progressive brethren: Jared Loughner posted videos of himself on YouTube burning the American flag; his favorite books reportedly included *Mein Kampf* and *The Communist Manifesto*; his classmate Caitie Parker tweeted in the aftermath of Loughner's crime: "As I knew him he was left wing, quite liberal." Virginia Tech murderer Seung-Hui Cho sent a twenty-three-page manifesto to news media in which he railed against Christians and wealthy people. Clay Duke, the man who in 2010 opened fire during a school board meeting, railed against rich people on Facebook and posted links to his favorite sites, including Media Matters and other far-left websites. James Von Brunn, the man who shot up the U.S. Holocaust Memorial in 2009, hated Fox News and conservative media, and was anti-Semitic, according to the *Huffington Post*. James Jay Lee, the ecoterrorist who took hostages at the Discovery Channel headquarters in 2010, claimed he was inspired by Al Gore's documentary *An Inconvenient Truth*.[1] Despite this and more, the media always tries to paint these murderers without any regard for life as tea partiers.

During a December 2012 press conference, their first after the Sandy Hook massacre, the NRA announced its National School Safety Shield program. Headed by Asa Hutchinson, of the Drug Enforcement Administration and the Department of Homeland Security, the program is designed to train schools in security protocols as well as arm and train qualified security personnel, depending upon the wishes of district parents. The reasoning is that only good guys with guns can stop bad guys with guns.

Tragedy glutton Michael Moore was apoplectic. Schools should employ magic or hire wizards to deter criminal attacks with nonlethal lightning bolts—or perhaps develop a course which teaches students to freeze bullets mid-trajectory like Neo from *The Matrix*. At least, this was the suggestion, because Michael Moore definitely did not want armed security in schools. He tweeted on December 21, 2012:

Armed guards in schools? Hmmmm...Oh! That's why the 2 armed guards that were at Columbine HS that day were able to prevent the 15 deaths?

Moore disqualifies that more lives were saved than lost because Dylan Klebold and Eric Harris shot and killed twelve. More students may have been tragically lost had good guys with guns not arrived on scene. In writing for *Examiner.com*, blogger Victor Medina explains:

Deputy Gardner was notified of the shooting by a custodian within three minutes of the first shot, and had to drive around the campus to enter the parking lot where the shooting took place. It took him two minutes to arrive. He confronted the shooters in the parking lot, about five minutes after the first shot was fired. Deputy Gardner exchanged fire with Harris and Klebold, which stopped the pair from firing at students. Gardner's actions allow teacher Patti Nielson and student Brian Anderson (who were both shot at and injured) to escape and survive.

Even though Deputy Gardner exchanged shots with the pair, he was over 60 yards away, and the two ducked into the school without being hit. Gardner called for backup on his radio before taking a position outside as more officers arrived. Gardner did not follow the pair, as he helped dozens of fleeing students coming from the building.

Later, Gardner again exchanged gunfire with the pair as they shot from windows into the parking lot. He then saved the lives of 15 students in the line of fire as they hid behind a car. One at a time, he escorted them from cover to safety. About 45 minutes after the shooting began, both Harris and Klebold killed themselves in the school library. All of their victims were killed within the first 15 minutes of the shooting.

The contention that Gardner's presence did not make a difference is not supported by the facts. He not only briefly stopped their assault on students, he made it possible for an untold number of students to escape the cafeteria and get to safety.[2]

In essence, Michael Moore is OK with the nation's school children having less protection than he has himself.

One of Moore's former bodyguards, Patrick Burk, got himself into a bit of trouble in 2005 when he tried to carry a .40-caliber Mauser pistol on his flight to Los Angeles. Bizarrely, in what perhaps was the only time that the left ever zealously defended the Second Amendment, far-left website Democratic Underground posted what they claimed was a letter from Gavin de Becker Associates in a heated defense of Burk's Second Amendment rights (the original link to the de Becker website has since disappeared):

The headline indicates that Patrick Burk was arrested on an "airport gun charge." He was not. The charge involves having a firearm without a New York City License to carry it. On that note, Patrick Burk was not carrying a weapon on his person (only locked in his baggage), and the police do not allege that he was carrying a weapon on his person, as your story implies.

Suddenly, it's OK to carry a gun. It was locked in his baggage. The left was angry that Fox reported Burk as Moore's bodyguard, when, in fact, he absolutely was his former bodyguard (oooh, scoreboard!). On December 18, 2012, at 1:22 p.m., Moore tweeted, "Guns are for hunters…and cowards." I imagine that there are worse words to describe anti-gun men who outsource their gun to a "coward"—besides describing them as blind to irony. The bigger question of course, is who'd want to waste their time with Michael Moore? His movies are terrible, to be sure, but he's a joke to all, not a threat to anyone.

"'Cold Dead Hand' is abt u heartless motherf%ckers unwilling 2 bend 4 the safety of our kids. Sorry if you're offended," tweeted Jim Carrey, mall rat style, as he advertised his rehashed Fire Marshall Bill take on Charlton Heston in a video mocking Second Amendment supporters. Carrey believes in the Second Amendment, all right, just only for those who can afford to pay someone else to carry a gun for them. Carrey tweeted on March 25, 2012:

G'morning! Hope you're enjoying Cold Dead Hand. FYI, my bodyguard doesn't have a hundred rounds in his clip. I wish u all a bullet free day! ;^}

His bodyguard. What if you wanted to be your own body-guard? According to Jim Carrey, you're a "motherf%cker." What about eighty-six-year-old Louise Howard of Tennessee who faced down a home invasion with her firearm?[3] Or the fifteen-year-old who defended himself and his twelve-year-old sister from a home invader using an—gasp—AR-15? All "mother-f%ckers," right, Jim Carrey?

A few days after a teenaged skateboarder shot and killed two people at a mall in Maryland, Katy Perry tweeted:

> Is anyone else really sad about the constant stream of shoot-ings and how normal it's becoming to see these headlines on a weekly basis?
>
> Scared to go to school? Scared to go to the mall? Scared to go to the movies? Me too. When will there be ACTUAL change? How many more?!
>
> You and I both know this is getting embarrassing...MY heart goes out to ALL the victims and their families this week. I pray for change.

I'm not sure of what "change" Perry desires, but it does seem a lot easier not to be at risk when you've a security team to carry your guns for you.

As Sen. Rand Paul once put it, "Many rich Hollywood celebri-ties have armed guards with them at all times and many regular people who live in a poor neighborhood, who have a business in a poor neighborhood and a neighborhood that may have higher crime—those people have to suffer the vicissitudes of violent crime without protection sometimes because of gun control laws."

These celebrities should practice the sermons they preach. Let them walk among the masses without any armed gunmen in sunglasses accompanying him. Let's see how they like it if they carried baseball bats or, to be even safer, butter knives. Maybe they could follow the University of Colorado's rules on self-defense: urinate on themselves or vomit if they feel like they're in danger. Let them play roulette with their family's safety as they wait out the twenty-minute average response time to 911 while home invaders make their way to their children's bedrooms. If it's good enough for us, it's good enough for them, right?

Former New York City mayor Michael Bloomberg took it a step further, collecting a gaggle of celebrities to create his "Celebrities Demand a Plan" (the DemandAPlan.org URL now redirects to the Everytown website). Then came the predictable black-and-white, soft-lighting video PSA, where the P stands for "propaganda," featuring the likes of Beyoncé, Jason Bateman (you killed me, Michael Bluth), Christina Applegate, Jennifer Garner, Jessica Alba, Jamie Foxx, Jeremy Renner, and a host of other celebs reading lines about massacres committed with illegally possessed and illegally used firearms. Then they started the demands for a plan. A plan for what? They never actually say:

How many more? How many more? How many more colleges? How many more classrooms? How many more movie theaters? How many more houses of faith? How many more shopping malls? How many more street corners? How many more? How many more? Enough! Enough! Enough! Enough! Demand a plan. Right now. As a mom. As a dad. As a friend. As a husband. As a wife. As an American. As an Ameri-

can. As an American. As a human being. For the children of Sandy Hook. Demand a plan. No more lists of names. It's not too soon. It's too late. Now is the time. Before we all know someone who loves someone on that list. No more lists. No more 'who they might have been.' No more 'if we'd just done something yesterday.' It's time. We can do better than this. We can do better than this. It's time. It's time. It's time for our leaders to act. Demand a plan. Right now. Right now. You—demand it! Enough! Enough! Enough! Enough!

Demand a plan! What kind of plan? We don't know! Just demand one! The video, combined with the Bloomberg involvement, suggests the eradication of firearms. No evil ever existed in this world until firearms were introduced. Firearms, the original sin. At least, that's the suggestion.

While denying you your right to self-protection, have any of the above examples offered to pay for your security? To the left, the only valuable lives are those lives that can afford the king's ransom of private, personal, armed protection. It's the ultimate class warfare from real 1 percenters. If only middle-class Americans could afford the posh, private security of million-dollar comics like Carrey or editor turned Photoshop aficionado turned pundit like Piers Morgan or the celebrities in this PSA. Does Lady Gaga have armed security at her concerts? She was more than happy to pose naked with an M4—two, in fact—for a promo photo. Jeremy Renner glorified guns in *The Bourne Legacy* (among other films), in which he handled Nemesis Arms' Vanquish. I'm sure the guns on the security seen escorting Beyoncé in various paparazzi photos are simply toys. Jamie Foxx wasn't glorifying gun violence in *Django Unchained* at all, I'm sure. I'd like to know when actor and celebrated gun hater Matt Damon is going to return the blood money he's made starring in films *The Bourne Identity* and *The Bourne Ultimatum*. Not to mention his star turn in the anti-American, anti-CIA, anti-military film *The Green Zone*. Isn't Mr. Damon part of the problem, too? Not to mention America-hating Danny Glover, of the *Lethal Weapon* films, and Richard Donner, who made millions directing Glover in those very pictures, along with other films centering on gun violence, such as *Conspiracy Theory*.

We could go on and on about Hollywood hypocrisy, so why don't we? There's Susan Sarandon, one of the loudest brayers against gun rights. Yet she starred in a movie, *Thelma and Louise*, in which her character shoots and kills a man threatening to rape Thelma. Guns for women's self-defense? I guess only in movies.

NBC's Bob Costas—when he is not out praising Vladimir Putin at the Olympics—is railing against the dangerous gun culture of America, perpetuated by (cue low piano keys) the villainous NRA. When it was pointed out to Costas by Greg Gutfeld that he was protected by armed security, Costas blanched. Costas responded, "In truth, Greg was accurate if you consider 180 degrees from the truth accurate. I have never had a personal bodyguard a single day in my life. There are security people at NFL games that the NFL employs, and there is always massive security at an Olympics, and there...is NBC security." But Gutfeld never said that Costas had hired a personal bodyguard. Just pointing out that Costas was benefiting from the gun culture he was simultaneously attacking. He doesn't have to be armed, because the companies he works for have the power and money to make other carry arms for him.

Then there is professional self-righteous loudmouth Rosie O'Donnell. Once, on her now-defunct television talk show, she went into a long rant about Second Amendment rights and directed an appeal to gun owners across America: "I don't care if you want to hunt. I don't care if you think it's your right. I say, 'Sorry.' It is 1999. We have had enough as a nation. You are not allowed to own a gun, and if you do own a gun I think you should go to prison." Not long after that, one of her bodyguards applied for a concealed-carry permit in Connecticut.

Perhaps the biggest kahuna of hypocrisy in Hollywood is action star Sylvster Stallone, which is unfortunate because I love his shoot-'em-up action movies. At least one website collected an anti-gun quote attributed to him via *Access Hollywood*:

> *"I know people get (upset) and go, "They're going to take away the assault weapon." Who...needs an assault weapon? Like really, unless you're carrying out an assault...You can't hunt with it...Who's going to attack your house, a (expletive) army?" (February 2013)*
>
> *"It [the Second Amendment] has to be stopped, and someone really has to go on the line, a certain dauntless political figure, and say, 'It's ending, it's over, all bets are off. It's not two hundred years ago, we don't need this anymore, and the rest of the world doesn't have it. Why should we?"* (Access Hollywood, *June 8, 1998)*

I have a one-word response to this, of course: Rambo. I guess now that's Stallone's safely banked away his multimillions glorifying gun violence, he's fine to get on his high horse and gallop all over everyone's else's constitutional rights.

And let's not forget the granddaddy of gun control himself. As the *Daily Caller* reported on December 31, 2013, "When New York City Mayor Michael Bloomberg leaves office today he will enter civilian life protected by firearms. The same man who has spent much of his career and personal fortune trying to render good, law-abiding men and women defenseless, will now surround himself with a team of armed bodyguards. Bloomberg's security detail will be comprised of former police officers that he purchased away from the NYPD with the promise of early retirement, six-figure salaries, and other perks that go along with protecting America's most notorious anti-gun zealot."

By focusing on only the violence and not the cases where self-defense saves lives (a statistic that greatly outweighs the illegal uses of firearms used in illegal acts) Bloomberg and his celebrity coterie are attempting to conflate peaceful, law-abiding exercise of the Second Amendment with tragedy. In 1995 a pre-DOJ Eric Holder appeared on C-SPAN2 to discuss the strategy of psychologically conditioning—brainwashing—people to turn on the Second Amendment. Said Holder: "What we need to do is change the way in which people think about guns, especially young people, and make it something that's not cool, that it's not acceptable, it's not hip to carry a gun anymore, in the way in which we changed our attitudes about cigarettes."

They're the Joe Camels of gun control.

THE PSYCHOLOGY OF GUN CONTROL MARKETING

Joe Camel was the debonair Camel cigarette icon always pictured in exotic locales and often with beautiful women, fast cars, or all three. And always with a Camel cigarette in his mouth. Marketing is just another form of psychology, and Joe Camel was a successful marketing ploy. Too successful, apparently. The American Medical Association Journal published a study in the early nineties showing that as many six-year-olds knew that Joe Camel represented cigarettes as well as they knew that Mickey Mouse represented Disney. The company was accused of targeting minors, typical American litigation ensued, and Joe Camel was no more. (The company still uses a camel, but it can't be fun looking.) Michael Bloomberg is looking for his Joe Camel effect. He hopes that celebrity coolness and popularity will translate to his anti–Second Amendment agenda. So far it hasn't worked as well as he'd like, but that hasn't stopped Bloomberg from trying. If ever there was a physical manifestation of Einstein's definition of insanity, it's Michael Bloomberg.

An alternative campaign cropped up on YouTube to challenge the credibility of the celebrities. A video titled "Demand A Plan? Demand Celebrities Go Fuck Themselves" re-created the video using the original footage, but simply spliced in the celebrities's gun-glorifying movie roles and performances after each read. "Demand A Plan" doesn't appear to be existent any longer, but Bloomberg and the anti-gun lobby remain undeterred.

It would be fabulous if anti-gun celebrities fought against shrouding children in ignorance of firearms and respect for life. It only seems more apparent that their belief is rooted in ignorance and emboldened by bigotry. When it was pointed out countless times to Carrey, Morgan, Moore, and others that the sorts of firearms they reference are not available to the general masses, that one cannot simply walk into a Super Walmart and throw one in the cart along with a box of tampons and an in-flatable lawn Santa, they ignored and name-called anyone who tried to reason with them. Grown men, they are, sticking their fingers in their ears and screaming "LALALALALA." Mean-while, other celebrities are simply uninformed on firearms and gun laws in general. They speak out against the Second Amend-ment because their "feels" (aka feelings) tell them so. In a speech for an event with Michael Bloomberg's Mayors Against Illegal Guns, crooner Tony Bennett stated:

I still haven't gotten over Connecticut. I'd like the assault weapons to go to war, not on our own country, and I'd like assault weapons eliminated.[4]

Bennett really believes that the same firearms used in Iraq and Afghanistan are the exact same firearms easily available to average Americans in the United States.

Bennett demonstrates his ignorance of existing gun laws by stating that he doesn't want citizens to be able to purchase select-fire capability (auto) firearms that they already are virtu-ally barred by law from purchasing. Bennett is for the exact laws we have now. YAY! Unless Bennett is claiming that handguns, which are the type of guns most used in crimes committed by blockheads with irresponsibly used firearms, are full auto, his statement makes no sense. I seriously doubt that Bloomberg or anyone else has explained this to him.

I discovered this during a conversation I had with Whoopi Goldberg backstage after I guest-co-hosted *The View*. Gold-berg, a gun owner herself, admitted that she's fine with owning firearms, but said that she didn't think people should be able to "go in and just buy AK-47s" with little or no checks or balances.

"But Whoopi," I remarked, "they can't. I can't."

It's true, it's impossible to wake up one day, decide that you want a fully automatic firearm, and up and purchase one. For one, it's cost-prohibitive. Additionally, law prohibits civilians from owning Class III (machine guns, etc.) firearms manufactured after 1986 due to the Firearm Owners Protection Act. Those made before are often referred to as "transferables." According to the Bureau of Alcohol, Tobacco, Firearms and Explosives (ATF), you must go through multiple steps, including getting your local sheriff to sign off on paperwork that basically states you can legally own the firearm (and have ownership transferred to you), obtain a full background check by the FBI, obtain a Class III license, and swim through even more red tape; additionally, you need to have about $20,000 lying around the house, because the 1986 law has driven up the price of full-auto firearms to astronomical levels (this doesn't include the near $2,000 you'll have to pay in various taxes alone before the purchase).

I explained the law to her, to which she remarked, exasperated, "Well why aren't people being told that?"

Whoopi and I disagreed on New York's SAFE Act, which, among many things, allows the state to determine whether or not your firearm storage is suitable. It also establishes a gun registry and broadens the definition of an "assault rifle" to be determined by two cosmetic features rather than just one. She said that she had nothing to hide, no problem, the state can come into her home and check to make sure her firearms are safely stored. I disagreed. We can't leave our civil liberties up to the state to determine. People against the death penalty routinely argue the state's incompetency in determining who lives and dies. Yet the same people now argue that the state is competent enough to determine how someone else protects her own life and even stores her firearms.

THE *VIEW* DRAMA

In February 2014, the announcement that I was asked to guest-co-host *The View* infuriated Michael Bloomberg's Moms Demand Action founder Shannon Watts, who spent literally every waking hour tweeting to the *View* staff, and organizing Facebook petitions and e-mail campaigns to have me kicked off of the show. Watts went full Hedra Carlson, and you never go full Hedra Carlson (from the movie *Single White Female*).

Why did I deserve such attention? Because I am pro–Second Amendment. Watts tweeted, "@theviewtv #DanaLoesch gets $$$ from gun lobby to promote gun propaganda that endangers women, children #momsdemand." She linked to a far-left website that feigned outrage when I made the point at a Colorado 2A rally that Dr. Martin Luther King Jr. was repeatedly denied a carry permit despite his life being threatened. She spent the entire week leading up to my appearance accusing me of being a "paid employee" of every outfit from Magpul and the NRA to the mythical gun lobby: "Gun lobby and #Magpul pay #DanaLoesch to promote lies about guns—not appropriate guest for @theviewtv."

I'm not even sure what the "gun lobby" is, exactly. I wear shoes, so I suppose that makes me a member of the "shoe lobby." I also like free speech, so I assume that makes me a member of the "speech lobby," as well? The NRA doesn't pay me, I pay *them* membership dues. What's the litmus test to decide employment here?

Watts and Bloomberg weren't finished, however. Two months later, the NRA held its annual convention in Indianapolis, home to one of the affiliates for my national show, and home to Bloomberg's Shannon Watts. I attended the event on behalf of Mercury One charities and to cover it for TheBlaze. A few times over the year Watts's expensive NYC- and D.C.-based PR firm sent me media requests for a number of their fascistic boycotts of businesses and other companies that didn't ban guns from their premises or other happenings. When I would respond affirmatively to the requests I was ignored. I decided to take them up on their offer in person. I figured since Watts basically cyber-stalked me online for the better part of a year (before I even ever responded), she would welcome the opportunity to discuss her claims against me, mother to mother. So I went.

I arrived at the airport with my television producer, George Szucs, and two camera men from TheBlaze. We drove to the public park just a couple of blocks from the convention center, readied the cameras, and turned on the mic. I walked through the middle of the crowd and spotted Watts, at which point I pleasantly introduced myself and shook her hand. As was seen on the tape, I had no sooner told her that it was nice to meet her when her demeanor turned curt and she snapped that she didn't want to speak to me because, as she said, "you have been insulting online." The woman who spent a year telling me that I had blood on my hands, endangered women's lives, and was a "paid shill" for Magpul/the NRA/the gun lobby accused me of being "insulting."

Sometime before, after one of Watts's endless Twitter rants directed at me, I finally remarked that she seemed like a lonely woman who sits in her driveway drinking boxed wine and ran out, and thus was left to aggravate law-abiding 2A moms. I facetiously called her Bloomberg group "Moms Demand Boxed Wine" and "Moms Demand Franzia." It's interesting to note that after the rally Watts and a few of the moms from the rally went to a bar and posted photo after photo in their Twitter timelines of themselves drinkin' it up (alcohol is a bigger killer than guns, but whatever), so apparently, my speculation wasn't far off. My intent wasn't to do to her what she does to me online, but rather have a genuine conversation. I wanted to know if she would retract the multiple statements she made where she accused me of being in the pocket of Magpul/the NRA/the gun lobby. I also wanted to know whether or not she believed that she represented all moms. While there were thousands and thousands of moms attending the NRA convention there were fewer than the 300 promised at well-to-do Bloomberg/moms rally, which was catered with mass-produced T-shirts and signs.

Watts interrupted my introduction and then turned her back on me. As if on cue, two burly dudes, one of whom was bald and in a black suit, marched over, took position at her sides, and escorted her away. I had spotted them before crossing the street and approaching the park; they noticed me quickly and moved early to flank her, so Bloomberg doesn't employ total blockheads, at least. I noticed that the jacket of the security guy in the black suit flared out at the side as jackets tend to do when covering holsters. (When asked, Everytown's communications director, Erika Soto Lamb, confirmed that they do indeed employ armed security.) I proceeded to follow and politely ask my questions. Because Watts had so aggressively targeted me on Twitter, Facebook, and apparently circulated an e-mail petition to get me booted from ABC, I wanted more than just a cowardly brush-off.

So I asked my question anyway, over and over, the physical manifestation of how she had treated me on Twitter, except that I was polite and honest. My producer and camera crew followed. Watts's armed security bumped into me, hip-checked me, ran me off the sidewalk, and rushed in front of me only to stop right in front of my toes, causing me to walk into them from behind and nearly lose my balance, all of which was visible on the video (which was released in its entirety replete with multiple angles from multiple videographers). Small, subtle movements, not unlike what they teach in krav maga, designed to create space and deter momentum. They weren't giving me their full force, but they were giving me physical force, make no mistake.

I asked Watts why she felt she deserved the armed security she's working so hard to deny other mothers. No answers. We stood around uncomfortably as Bloomberg's people called the car to expedite its arrival and Watts's armed security stared at me. I was undeterred. I continued politely asking questions. Finally, a black SUV with New York plates pulled up to the curb, and Watts's armed security tucked her inside before slamming the door and hitting the vehicle twice to signal "go."

After pursuing the NRA and protesting the convention, Watts and her merry band of surrogates claimed that I "stalked" her by attending a public event on public property and asking her why she spent the better part of a year attempting to discredit me. If we are to have a discussion of stalking and bullies, we can start with Troughton-Watts, who went at me for months online before I responded, to say nothing of her behavior over *The View*.

Watts has every right to disagree with the Second Amendment. I have every right as a victim of her bully tactics to call her to task on her remarks and her public attempts to discredit me, which I believe has led to threats against me and my family. I have scores of screenshots from Twitter remarks, Facebook comments, even e-mails from people who've wished me shot or wished for harm to come to my children, all Moms Demand Action supporters.

I don't have a rich city-mayor sugar daddy spending $50 million dollars on a PR campaign. I don't need to. As a truly empowered mother, I care too much about the safety of my family to play roulette with 911. I care too much to pay someone else to carry my gun for me.

Watts likes to say that the NRA's Wayne LaPierre is "paid millions" and that "my salary is zero dollars." So who pays that pricey PR firm Berlin Rosen? Who pays for the publicists that push her in front of MSNBC and CNN cameras? The flights around the country to aggravate peaceful gun owners? Who pays for the chauffeured SUV with tinted windows to drive her around? Who pays for pushy bald dudes in poorly tailored suits to carry her guns at public events? Am I to believe that all of these people provide these services to Watts for free out of the kindness of their hearts? Airlines are greedy bastards; it was announced just this year that Frontier is charging for use of the overhead bins, so am I to believe that they take one look at Watts and give her the kindness discount? Or maybe she pays these people with magic? Or, even more likely, does she simply annoy the will to live from these people like she tries to do to pro–Second Amendment moms online?

Bloomberg's Shannon Watts is a traitor to the very anti-gun platform she tries to push on all of us, for the simple fact that she had armed security guards present at her rally, as confirmed by the group's communications director. That she chose not to sully herself by carrying her own guns is irrelevant. Really, I'm glad that she doesn't carry. Her irrational behavior and obsession with women who support the Second Amendment defines the sort of person I would fear to see carrying a firearm. There are many other women, however, whose lives might well have been saved if they had a gun. Which is why it's so curious that so many leftists want to leave them disarmed and vulnerable.

Chapter 6

Gun Control, a Rapist's Best Friend

Lee: Did you know Kim carried a gun?

Abernathy: Yes. Now, do I approve? No. Do I know? Yes.

Kim: Look, I don't know what futuristic utopia you live in, but the world I live in, a bitch need a gun.

Abernathy: You can't get around the fact that people who carry guns, tend to get shot more than people who don't.

Kim: And you can't get around the fact that if I go down to the laundry room in my building at midnight enough times, I might get my ass raped.

Lee: Don't do your laundry at midnight.

Kim: Fuck that! I wanna do my laundry whenever the fuck I wanna do my laundry.

Abernathy: There are other things you can carry other than a gun. Pepper spray.

Kim: Uh, motherfucker, tryna rape me? I don't wanna give him a skin rash! I wanna shut that n—— down!

Abernathy: How about a knife at least?

Kim: Yeah, you know what happens to motherfuckers carry knives? They get shot! Look, if I ever become a famous actress, I won't carry a gun. I'll hire me a do-dirt n——gga, and he'll carry the gun. And when shit goes down, I'll sit back and laugh, but until that day, it's Wild West, motherfucker!

—FROM QUENTIN TARANTINO'S *DEATH PROOF*

In January 2013, a group of anti–Second Amendment advocates gathered in the Dayton, Ohio, snow to protest Bill Goodman's Gun and Knife show inside Hara Arena. One gun grabber, a man by the name of Jerome McCorry, was quoted on camera telling a reporter, "We know that guns are being sold on the floor inside Hara Arena illegally. No background checks, no identification of any kind."

The inclusion of this man-on-the-street interview in the local newscast raised the eyebrows of listeners of my radio show and readers online, who e-mailed me. McCorry, as it turns out, is a convicted rapist and a listed sex offender. He was identified on camera as the president of the Adam Project, whose headquarters is the same as McCorry's home address. He has been a repeated, trusted source for gun control for the *Dayton Daily News* and WHIO-TV, which have repeatedly featured him as the area voice of gun control for many of their stories. Not surprisingly, neither of these mainstream media outlets dared inform their readers or viewers that they were giving a convicted felon a platform to lecture law-abiding Americans on what guns they can own.

Don't you think McCorry's sex offender past is relevant?

A convicted rapist advocating for the disarming of law-abiding Americans?

Wouldn't a more appropriate caption for the interview with McCorry read, "Rapists agree: gun control is great!"?

It wasn't until I covered this story that WHIO-TV finally admitted McCorry's past on Facebook and Twitter.[1] (I published screenshots on DanaRadio.com). In their Facebook response, WHIO-TV stated: "We talked with supporters of gun rights, as well as protesters, including the Rev. Jerome McCorry. We understand his controversial past, and have reported on this. More recently he has been highly visible throughout the community championing a number of causes and has the endorsement of respected law enforcement leaders and community leaders. He is voicing his message of community harmony through peace and non-violence."

There was no word as to whether he also has the endorsement of his rape victim.

Perhaps the oddest part of WHIO-TV's response was its decision to classify rape as "controversial." Having a man violently and forcefully penetrate you against your will is considered "controversial."

RAPE SURVIVORS SPEAK OUT

One October night, Amanda Collins, a student at the University of Nevada, Reno, walked back to her car after class. Amanda, a concealed-carry holder and martial arts student, had just completed a midterm and had left her classroom with a group of classmates because, as she said, "you're always taught that there is safety in numbers."

The group walked to the parking garage. Collins was the only one parked on the ground floor, so she said good-bye to her classmates and headed toward her car, surveying her surroundings. Even though she was a permitted concealed-carry holder, Amanda was unarmed that evening, because the campus was designated as a "gun free zone" to "protect" students like her. School officials felt that the placement of signs around the premises provided an invisible defense shield against criminals illegally possessing firearms. It was a stern warning to murderers and rapists: Law-abiding students were disarmed, so murderers and rapists better not get any funny ideas. Because Collins abides by the law, she left her licensed firearm at home.

James Biela, a serial rapist, was also on campus that night, scoping out his next victim. His sights set on Collins, he confronted her and put a pistol to her temple. It was there, in the hushed darkness at the University of Nevada campus parking garage, that Biela brutally raped Collins. The university's campus police headquarters was less than a hundred feet away.

The gun-free zone did not save Amanda Collins. The "Gun Free Zone" sign did not create an invisible force field around the campus, and it did not magically disarm James Biela. As with all gun control, the only people who followed the rule were non-criminals. The campus police, one hundred feet away, did not save her.

The university's response was to install a couple more police call boxes, which seems futile considering that Collins was raped yards away from the largest call box—the actual campus police headquarters. Meanwhile, Biela was still free, and more rapes were reported. Collins understandably felt afraid and utterly helpless against future attack. She wondered if Biela continued to watch her.

Collins's father discovered a loophole in the university's bylaws that allowed the university's president to use his or her discretion and grant permission for a student to conceal-carry on campus. Collins and her parents wrote a letter to the school's president, Milton Glick, explaining the circumstances and asking for permission for Collins, a trained concealed-carry permit holder, to carry on campus.

Before considering the request, the university required Collins to undergo a series of interviews, including one with the campus chief of police—the same campus police that failed to protect Collins when she was brutally attacked outside of their campus station. Eventually, the university granted Collins permission to conceal-carry on campus, but with six caveats, the first of which was that she was not allowed to disclose to anyone that she was carrying a firearm or her permission would be revoked.

The condescension from the university angered Collins. It wasn't as though she skipped around the campus telling everyone that she was a concealed-carry permit holder anyway. As Collins put it, "They were granting me my Second Amendment right at the expense of my First."

Biela would later assault other women and murder nineteen-year-old Brianna Dennison, all of which weighs heavily on Collins's mind. "Everyone deserves a chance to defend themselves," Collins told the press. "I know, having been the first victim, that Brianna Dennison would still be alive had I been able to defend myself that night."

Meanwhile members of the Colorado State Legislature debated among themselves the right of college students to conceal-carry on campuses. But the largely Democratic body chose not to put a referendum regarding concealed-carry on Colorado campuses—and a number of other anti–Second Amendment laws—on the ballot. That's when Collins made the brave decision to step out from the blurred visage of anonymity that she had worked so hard to maintain throughout Beila's trial for the murder of Dennison and speak in favor of a woman's right to choose her self-defense.

"This is bigger than just me," Collins said in a video for the NRA. "It was a decision I made to prevent anyone else from being in the position that I'd found myself in. Women and men being unable to defend themselves needs to stop."

Colorado State Democrats weren't persuaded. Even though none of them were present the night that Collins was attacked, they all believed they knew what would have happened had Collins the right to protect herself.

"Statistics aren't on your side," said a smug Colorado state senator Evie Hudak, after Collins's powerful testimony at the hearing on Colorado's statewide college campus gun ban. In audio widely available on the Internet, Hudak says: "I just want to say, statistics are not on your side, even if you had had a gun. You said that you were a martial arts student, I mean person, experienced in tae kwon do, and yet because this individual was so large and was able to overcome you even with your skills, and chances are that if you had had a gun, then he would have been able to get that from you and possibly use it against you."

Hudak offered no statistics to back up her assertion, and she conflated martial arts with firearm defense, apparently without realizing that one of these tactics requires close contact with an attacker. She projected her own views regarding women's weakness onto Collins and surmised that no woman can stop a rapist.

Hudak's prejudiced characterization of women and firearms was reminiscent of another Colorado lawmaker. State Rep. Joe Salazar is a banner man for the war on women, particularly for the assault against a woman's right to self-defense. Salazar brazenly stood at the dais and flatly stated, in remarks available online, that women were simply too hysterical and too stupid to own firearms.

"It's why we have call boxes," said Salazar. "It's why we have safe zones. That's why we have the whistles. Because you just don't know who you're gonna be shooting at. And you don't know if you feel like you're gonna be raped, or if you feel like someone's been following you around or if you feel like you're in trouble when you may actually not be, that you pop out that gun and you pop…pop a round at somebody."

When I first saw this video I had to take a moment. Was he really saying what I thought he said? Could a man really be that patronizing and ignorant? According to Salazar's mansplaining, we women are just too stupid to carry firearms on a college campus because we don't know if we just feel like we're gonna be raped or if we're just feeling paranoid about the dude overpowering us and ripping off our pants in a dark parking lot. If only we could magically pause our situation and put our hypersensitive female freakouts on hold long enough for Super Representative Joe Salazar to teleport to our locale *I Dream of Jeannie* style and analyze the situation for us.

The most insanely amazing thing about this train wreck of chauvinism is that it didn't stop with Salazar. At no point during these hearings did any Democrat scratch his head and think, "Oh geebus, maybe we should turn off his mic." It was like each of them tried to outdo the other in a medieval joust of epic stupidity. After Salazar came his statehouse colleague Paul Rosenthal, whose remarks may also be viewed online:

Another point that was brought up is that a gun is the only method a person, a student has at self-defense. There are other methods: there's mace, what about a taser? The buddy system! Um, other methods at self defense, judo, or what have you. There are other methods. It's not just the only method out there known to man or woman today is a weapon. Uh, uh, of a firearm.

Let's see: Amanda Collins used the buddy system (until she got to the parking garage) and was trained in martial arts. Guess what? She was *still raped*. Yes, mace works if you are close enough and spray your attacker in the face. So make sure you're in position! You wouldn't want to hurt or kill a man who wants to rape you so badly that you may have difficulty walking to a safe place to call for 911.

Let me be clear: A woman has the right to make a mess for the medic out of any attacker. It's the occupational hazard of being a rapist: You may get shot by your victim. And rapists deserve it. A woman has the pro-choice right of self-defense.

Bizarrely, the act of women defending themselves from attackers is becoming taboo. During the 1994 Miss USA Pageant

Miss Nevada, Nia Sanchez, was asked about the epidemic of women sexually assaulted on college campuses. Miss Nevada, a fourth-degree black belt in tae kwan do, thoughtfully replied that women should be empowered to defend themselves. This outraged the fembot feminist army, who were melancholy from not having anything in the news for a week or so over which to be outraged. The alarm sounded at the Fembot Headquarters as angry women's studies acolytes manned the Twitter cannons and tweeted outrage after outrage. "That's victim shaming," tweeted one. "Way to support rape culture," remarked another. "How about teaching men not to rape?"

Jesus take the wheel, why did we never think of that? It's almost like sexual assault and rape aren't already illegal, except, oh…they are illegal. Whereas I view self-defense as empowering, these women view it as a sign of weakness. These same women will eschew self-defense as "rape culture" but won't identify sending dong pics, groping and assaulting female staff, or having a string of women accuse you of sexual assault (Weiner, Filner, Clinton, respectively) as "rape culture." The true intent is emerging: It isn't just firearms for self-defense to which gun control lobbyists object, it's really self-defense in any form. You don't have the right to not be controlled.

While in Colorado, I saw Rep. Rosenthal at the "Farewell To Arms" event organized by Free Colorado and other grassroots groups, with participation by Magpul. I made my way over. As can be seen from the online video of our encounter, Rosenthal was carrying a Magpul swag bag with a few standard-capacity magazines inside. The moment the camera was on him he got awkward, handed the bag to another attendee, and insulted one of the biggest companies (Magpul) in his state. He didn't much like me, and as he left I shouted to him that he should take a buddy for safety.

If you think it can't get more insane, it does! The University of Colorado at Colorado Springs published a handy-dandy guide about "What To Do If You Are Attacked." Hands to sky I am not making any of this up.

1. Be realistic about your ability to protect yourself.
2. Your instinct may be to scream, go ahead! It may startle your attacker and give you an opportunity to run away.
3. Kick off your shoes if you have time and can't run in them.
4. Don't take time to look back; just get away.
5. If your life is in danger, passive resistance may be your best defense.
6. Tell your attacker that you have a disease or are menstruating.
7. Vomiting or urinating may also convince the attacker to leave you alone.
8. Yelling, hitting or biting may give you a chance to escape, do it!
9. Understand that some actions on your part might lead to more harm.
10. Remember, every emergency situation is different. Only you can decide which action is most appropriate.

I have so many insults about the intellect of the people who wrote this list, there may not be enough pages in this book to contain it all. The epic genius who drafted this list and published it on the school's website believes women never envision how they'll get away from an attacker. According to him, they just shoot at things, randomly, like rabid dogs bite randomly.

Number 5 tells the victim to just lay back and take her rape.

Numbers 6 and 7 show that whoever wrote this list doesn't know what rape is. He thinks rape is about sexual attraction? Rape is about *power*. The act of rape is about control, control over a woman's intimacy and physical being. If a victim said she was especially vulnerable, this would only heighten his arousal.

Number 9 is straight-up victim shaming. The controversy was such that the university finally removed the guide and issued an apology for publishing their victim-shaming "advice," but not an actual act of repentance for believing that women can't be trusted like a men to carry a firearm.

Let me newsflash some facts to the authors of this barbaric list:

1. A rape occurs on an American college campus every twenty-one hours.[2]
2. One out of four collegiate women will be raped during her academic career.[3] So much for Salazar's "call boxes and safe zones" strategy.
3. During the year 2000 alone, 246,000 women survived a rape or sexual assault, which equates to twenty-eight women every hour.[4]
4. Eighty-four percent of rape survivors attempted to reason with their rapist.[5]
5. Nearly 70 percent of those who survived sexual assault reported that they employed self-protection tactics during their attack, that is, resisting or running from the attacker.[6]

Anti–Second Amendment advocates like the kind who clearly crafted this idiotic list want women to arm themselves with only their own vomit, urine, and fingernails. It's for the woman's own good. After all, as Salazar seemed to suggest, we wouldn't want to hurt the rapist. I never want to hear another Democrat, liberal talking head, or progressive blogger accuse conservatives of being soft on rape ever again.

Fortunately, there are still some places left in America that aren't as rape friendly as Colorado campuses. Let's take a look at a few of the women who have used guns to defeat rapists and save themselves from brutal assaults.

DONNA HARPER

Sixty-six-year-old Donna Harper was terrified when she was awakened early one morning in October 2011 by an intruder trying to break into her home. The man, thirty-seven-year-old Jesse Theis, continued to force entry even after Harper fired two warning shots through a window to scare him away. Theis continued, and Harper shot him in the abdomen, killing him. Shasta County Chief Deputy Josh Lowery told CBS Channel 12 that Theis meant Harper "lethal harm." Unarmed, Harper would have been another statistic, unless gun control advocates believe that an elderly woman could have fought off a thirty-seven-year-old man.

A COURAGEOUS TWELVE-YEAR-OLD

A twelve-year-old girl took charge of her own security in 2012 when a man invaded her home while her mother was at work. Debra St. Clair's young daughter called her at work and told her that a stranger kicked in the back door. While racing home, St. Clair told her daughter to go get the family gun, hide in a closet, and dial 911. The girl called 911, but the police didn't arrive in time. The man located the girl and tried to open the closet door. That was when the girl shot him through the door. Her panicked voice narrated the events to the 911 operator, who kept assuring her that police would arrive any moment. The intruder was wounded, arrested, and jailed. Had this responsible mother not educated her daughter about firearms, and had this girl not had the means with which to protect herself, this story would have ended tragically. The intruder would have opened that closet door—and then what?

DONNA JACKSON

Donna Jackson, fifty-seven years old and from rural Oklahoma, called 911 and pleaded for police help for over ten minutes as a man forced entry into her home. As the man, Billy Riley, busted in by throwing a patio table through a glass sliding door, the operator notified her of her rights of self-defense. Jackson retreated to a back room and barricaded herself behind the door. "I will shoot him," she told the operator. In the 911 call, available online, you can hear the man busting through the last door before Jackson fires. She's grieved at having to do so, but was not going to be defenseless. There isn't any doubt that Jackson would be dead today had she not had the choice of self-defense by firearm.

A MOTHER IN DETROIT

A mother on Detroit's west side protected her two young children from home invaders who broke down her front door. The woman fired defensive shots at the intruders, all of which was caught on the family's security cameras, which had been installed after repeated break-ins. What might have happened had this mother not been armed?

A MOTHER IN GEORGIA

A mother in Georgia fled to her attic with her small children after spotting a man breaking into her home with a crowbar. Hiding in the attic wasn't safe enough, as thirty-two-year-old Paul Slater eventually found the family. Slater clearly was interested in more than just material items, since he stalked the mother and her children all the way to their attic. But Slater got more than he bargained for when he finally found the hiding family. He didn't expect the mother's .38 revolver, which she fired six times, every time Slater refused to retreat, hitting him in the face and neck. (Yes, sometimes you need more than one shot. In this case, she needed to empty the entire chamber.) Slater finally ran, but due to his injuries police were able to arrest him. Imagine if this mother had been unarmed.

SARAH MCKINLEY

Sarah McKinley was eighteen years old when her husband succumbed to lung cancer on Christmas day. Six days later, on New Year's Eve, the newly widowed teen mom was home with her newborn son when two men, armed with knives and aware that there was medicine in the house, attempted to force their way into McKinley's house. In response, McKinley calmly collected her late husband's shotgun and handgun, put a bottle in her son's mouth, called 911, and informed the operator of her intent to shoot if the intruders did not retreat. The 911 dispatcher told McKinley to protect her baby. The intruders busted down her door and McKinley fired, killing twenty-four-year-old Justin Shane Martin. The second intruder, twenty-nine-year-old Dustin Louis Stewart, turned himself in to police. Could an unarmed eighteen-year-old new mother protect herself and her newborn against two violent men? No.

FIREARMS: THE ULTIMATE EQUALIZER FOR WOMEN

Even though there are enough stories of women relying upon firearms to defend themselves and their families to fill multiple books, these are the women people like Michael Bloomberg and other members of the anti–Second Amendment lobby want to disarm. Their favorite argument? A woman with a gun in the home is more likely to die by it than protect herself with it.

Statistics don't support this. It's true that if you abuse alcohol and drugs and don't abide by the law, your possession of a gun is a risk to yourself. But if you are a law-abiding, responsible gun owner, you're better off armed—as the stories in this chapter show. Only by conflating lawbreakers with law-abiders do Bloomberg and his allies manufacture misleading statistics to oppose gun ownership.

The simple fact is that firearms are attributed sixty times over to saving lives rather than taking them. In fact, Dr. Arthur Kellermann, the man behind the faulty *New England Journal of Medicine* study published in 1993 that gave rise to Bloomberg's claim, refused for years to share the data behind his much-debated conclusion due to the reason listed above and because other studies (Kleck/Gertz; CDC; researcher Don Kates, "Tennessee Law Review[7]) have noted that "home gun homicide victims [in the flawed study] were killed using guns not kept in the victim's home." Bloomberg promoted a faulty study for the sake of pushing a narrative wholly unsupported by science.

Criminologists Dr. Gary Kleck (a Democrat who began as a gun-control advocate until cold, hard statistics convinced him otherwise) and Marc Gertz revealed in their thesis "Armed Resistance to Crime: The Prevalence and Nature of Self-Defense with a Gun," published in 1995 in the Northwestern University School of Law's *Journal of Criminal Law and Criminology*, that firearms are used for self defense roughly between 2.1 and 2.5 million times a year. Of these, over 1.9 million cases involve a handgun. Half a million cases a year occur away from home, and of these, nearly 10 percent involve women defending themselves from sexual assault or another form of abuse. Do the math: Firearms are used sixty times more to protect, rather than to take, lives. John R. Lott Jr., a leading researcher on gun control who's done inimitable work with his newly launched Crime

Research Prevention Center, wrote in his book *More Guns Less Crime*:

> *The National Crime Victimization Survey data show that providing a woman with a gun has a much greater effect on her ability to defend herself against a crime than providing a gun to a man. Thus even if few women carry handguns, the change in the "cost" of attacking women could still be as great as the change in the "cost" of attacking men, despite the much higher number of men who are becoming armed. To phrase this differently, if one more woman carries a handgun, the extra protection for women in general is greater than the extra protection for men if one more man carries a handgun.*

It's a mystery why politicians and anti–Second Amendment advocates want to disarm women and make them potential victims of rapists and murderers.

I'm especially amazed that feminists will preach countless tales advocating for the empowerment of women in almost all ways except for the one that matters most—protection of their physical safety. Throw a firearm into the equation, and modern-day feminists adopt the patriarchal prejudice represented by Colorado Democrats: Women suddenly become stupid, weak little creatures, unfit to carry a firearm.

Fortunately, law-abiding American women—and men—are refusing to allow people irrationally afraid of guns—hoplophobics—and convicted rapists like Jerome McCorry to take away their pro-choice right of self defense. After the attempt by Colorado Democrats to restrict Coloradans' Second Amendment civil liberty, voters revolted in a landslide recall, tossing out Senate president John Morse and state legislator Angela Giron over their opposition to the Second Amendment. State lawmaker Evie Hudak, who famously told rape survivor Amanda Collins that "statistics aren't on your side" regarding concealed-carry, hastily resigned ahead of her energized recall. And the grassroots are nowhere near finished with the electoral retribution.

Meanwhile FBI background checks for gun purchases—the kind that Everytown communications director Erika Soto Lamb said on Twitter doesn't exist—eclipsed 2012's count by 20,000 before the year's end in 2013.[8] Indianapolis gun permits for women have soared by over 42 percent from 2012, 14.6 percent for men. Women comprised 25 percent of the seventy thousand attendees at the 2014 NRA convention in Indianapolis, and this number is steadily increasing year by year.[9]

Women are becoming a desirable demo in the firearms market, with manufacturers now tailoring everything from furniture (grips, trigger guards, buttstocks) to specific models to a female audience. I noticed the new carbon prototypes at the Magpul booth at the 2014 NRA Convention were slimmer for smaller, female hands, and furniture was more streamlined. Women aren't just attracted to firearms for personal safety and home security; more women every year are embracing hunting as a way to reconnect with nature, cultivate family time, and bypass the supermarket for organic, low-fat meat. Women are starting shooting clubs, firearm groups, and helping their fellow sisters obtain their concealed-carry permits. Two years ago former Chicago police officer and firearms enthusiast Karen Bartuch of Alpha Girls and clothing designer and retailer Marilyn Smolenski began hosting the annual Firearms and Fashion show to benefit the Chicago Police Memorial Foundation. The women showcased self-defense jewelry, conceal carry apparel, designer holsters, and accessories. The show had to turn attendees away, as the success meant they exceeded their audience capacity both years. *Chicago Sun-Times* columnist Carol Marin took exception to a female former cop helping women realize their options with concealed-carry clothing and accessories, and penned a downright ignorant piece blasting the women and essentially accusing them of facilitating the crime culture that has become signature Chicago. Marin wrote:[10]

> *In a city that can't shake its shooting reputation, here we have a firearms/fashion show billed as a way to "empower women." And it comes just days after a 14-year-old girl was shot and killed by another 14-year-old girl who will never grow up to be a woman.*

One of the arguments so often used to deny Americans their Second Amendment civil liberty is to falsely claim that gun owners lack adequate training. It really isn't a question of training; anti-gun extremists don't even want our troops to carry on base, which has resulted in several massacres over the past few years on our military bases, twice at Fort Hood. If it was an issue of training they wouldn't object. I hardly doubt that anyone would argue that our soldiers aren't well versed in firearms training, regardless of rank. Here, too, in the instance of the Chicago media criticizing the Firearms and Fashion show, Bartuch is a former police officer and trains other women in using firearms. This was ignored, and op-ed columnists publicly asked how the Chicago police chief, a man, could allow an event of this nature. Do these critics assume that Bartuch's sex invalidates her as a trained gun owner? It goes to show that the false concern over training is just that: false. If only the average anti-gun extremist possessed one-eighth of the firearms knowledge that the average gun owner possesses.

The effort of anti-gun extremists to ignore the growing number of female gun owners and concealed carriers underscores the sexist attitude inherent to gun control: Leave women without an equal means of force for defense and ignore those who want to preserve their right of choice concerning defense. Bloomberg wasn't there on the exhibitor floor at the 2014 NRA convention. I was. So were literally thousands of women, women who didn't simply go to indulge their husbands for the day, women who were just as interested as their male counterparts in checking out the latest from Browning or fawning over the slimmer Glock varieties.

These women are the face of the empowered American female. Michael Bloomberg better get used to females keeping and bearing arms. We had the divine right to bear arms before men decided we could vote. In fact, guns have been used many times over the years to protect women and minorities from the plans of certain anti-liberty white men.

Chapter 7

The Left-Wing Lynching

...a good revolver, a steady hand, and a de-
termination to shoot...
—FREDERICK DOUGLASS, ON THE BEST
RESPONSE TO THE FUGITIVE SLAVE ACT

Martin Luther King Jr. was denied a gun permit as a result of gun control laws put into effect by white male Democrats. Out of all the law-abiding, peace-loving people, this man was denied the means to protect himself while those who wished to do him harm for believing in equality were allowed to carry. Dr. King was disarmed by Democrat laws. That is just one in a series of examples of the explicit racism behind left-wing gun grabs. It should be taught in schools, how the origination of modern-day gun control laws were designed to prevent racial equality. The examples of this, which I detail in this very chapter, are ignored by the left, who become infuriated whenever the topic is broached. What can I tell you? The truth hurts.

Here's the dirty little secret about gun control: Everyone knows who white elitists like Dianne Feinstein, Elizabeth Warren, Rahm Emanuel, and Michael Bloomberg envision when they preach to Americans about keeping guns out of the hands of "criminals." Hint: They aren't thinking about fresh-faced teenage girls in Omaha. No, they are thinking about "the scary black man" that they've seen on television during riots in Detroit or LA. It's not a white man carrying a gun on a farm in Montana that scares them. Instead they talk about gun violence in "urban areas." And guess who lives there? Their racism is deep-seated, even if it goes unnoticed by the mainstream press, even if they frequently tut-tut to conservatives about their intolerance and supposed racial insensitivity on just about every other issue.

There is a cruel irony at the heart of all of this. As a result of such inherent and instinctive racism, the predominately white, patriarchal masters in Washington are actually making African-American kids less safe and more vulnerable to violence. The Wise White Men (and some Women) of Washington, D.C., are aiding and abetting race wars instead of stopping them. And they are doing so with tactics borrowed from the Ku Klux Klan—which wanted nothing more than to take guns away from black Americans.

Find that hard to believe? Well, consider the case of five-year-old Ossian Sweet. This little boy was out alone on a spring night in 1901 when he saw a black teenager being burned at the stake by a white mob. Sweet hid in the bushes while the mob's screaming victim was swallowed up in flames. For the rest of his life, Sweet would remember that night in central Florida—the smell of kerosene, the crowd taking off pieces of charred flesh as souvenirs, and the howls of agony by the burning teenaged boy.

The son of a former slave, Ossian Sweet did not let the trauma of the lynching stop him from one day working his way through one of the nation's few black colleges. He graduated from Ohio's Wilberforce University—named after the English statesman responsible for England's abolition of the slave trade—and went from there to Howard University, where he became a medical doctor.

Even when Sweet was studying medicine, nearly twenty years after he watched in horror from the bushes as a teenager was lynched, he couldn't escape racial violence. During a five-day race riot in Washington, D.C., in 1919, Sweet saw a white gang stop a streetcar, drag a black passenger to the sidewalk, and beat the innocent man without a hint of mercy.

Ossian Sweet knew what a racist mob was capable of when, in 1925, he found himself on the receiving end of one. Sweet had bought a house in an all-white neighborhood of Detroit, and when a mob arrived threatening his home and his family, Sweet and several friends fired into the mob and killed one of the attackers. The guns in their hands saved Sweet's home and likely his life. If Dianne Feinstein, the KKK, and Rahm Emanuel had had their way back then, Ossian Sweet would have been dead.

You might think the lesson of Ossian Sweet's story is that angry racist lynch mobs were a terrible problem a hundred years ago. Well, they were, but that's not the lesson Michigan's anti–Second Amendment advocates took away from it in 1925. Like their successors in today's Democratic Party, they didn't want African-Americans like Ossian Sweet to possess the ability to protect themselves. They liked their "scary" black neighbors unarmed and defenseless. So Michigan started seizing guns from African-Americans, requiring and denying gun permits, and generally infringing on their Second Amendment rights.

The Michigan gun grab was far from unique. The long, ugly history of gun grabs or—excuse me, "common sense, prudent gun control measures"—is steeped in racism. It's about rich white folks thinking that they're going to be robbed and killed by one of the "skid row" characters once played by Eddie Murphy on *Saturday Night Live*. For most of American history, many gun grabbers cared less about limits on guns than they cared about limits on people they perceived to be "uppity blacks." The social order they knew depended on defenseless African-Americans, so black gun owners were a threat that couldn't be tolerated.

This sad, transparent, and pathetic state of affairs began as early as 1640, when Virginia's House of Burgess passed a law denying free blacks the right to bear arms. Colonial South Carolina restricted free African-Americans's gun rights in a 1712 statute called "An act for the better ordering and governing of Negroes and Slaves." (Even back then, gun grabbers were using words like "ordering" when the effect was more sinister and oppressive. How little things have changed with the passage of time.)

English colonies weren't the only ones in North America determined to use gun control to keep blacks subservient. In certain circumstances, the French Black Code in colonial Louisiana not only allowed, but required, white Louisianans to beat armed blacks. According to the code, whites had a duty to disarm blacks, and if force was required to do so, whites had to beat "any black carrying any potential weapon, such as a cane."

After American independence in 1776, free blacks hoping to protect themselves still couldn't catch a break. Many whites loved their guns, but they hated the idea of black people with guns. They knew that you've always got to disarm a group of people before you can oppress them.

That's why the Kentucky Comprehensive Act of 1798 required African-Americans—unlike whites—to obtain a license if they wanted to protect themselves on the frontier with a gun. And in other states, "weapons" were defined more broadly, and some laws included dogs. Maryland required blacks to get a license before they could protect themselves and their families with a dog, and Mississippi flat-out banned blacks from owning a dog.

If white gun grabbers were worried about guns in the hands of black Americans before 1831, they became downright terrified of it that summer, when Nat Turner led the bloodiest slave rebellion in American history. For two days, Turner and more than seventy slaves and free African-Americans waged war against the white population of southeast Virginia's Southampton County. Turner's goal was to free his fellow slaves, and they had fortune on their side as they vastly outnumbered the white population of the county.

What Turner didn't have on his side were guns. Frederick Douglass would one day call "a good revolver" the "best response to the slave catcher," but Turner and his rebels had trouble getting guns. After over 150 deaths, an armed white militia with three companies of artillery defeated Nat Turner's rebellion.

Remember: The colonists beat the British because they had the same guns. Fifty years later, Nat Turner lost because he didn't.

After two days, the fighting was over, but its effects weren't. From plantation to plantation across Virginia and the rest of the South, slaveholders were asking one question: What if Turner's men had been better armed? It was a rhetorical question; slave holders in Virginia doubled down on gun control. They passed a law that said free blacks couldn't "keep or carry any firelock of any kind, any military weapon, or any powder or lead." Leaving no stone unturned, they also repealed laws that had once allowed the rare African-American to get a license for a gun. Similarly, North Carolina barred "any free negro, mulatto, or free person of color" from carrying or keeping in his home any unlicensed "shot gun, musket, rifle, pistol, sword, dagger or bowie-knife."

Tennessee's anti–Second Amendment advocates responded to Nat Turner's rebellion by going even further. They actually changed the words of the Tennessee Constitution. Previously, it's eleventh article had said that "freemen of this State have a right to keep and to bear arms for the common defence." After Nat Turner scared slaveholders with his reach for equality, Tennessee's amended constitution stated "free white men of this State have a right to keep and to bear arms for their common defence."

It wasn't long before racist judges realized that if these gun-grabbing laws were going to survive constitutional scrutiny, the judges needed to find a way around the Second Amendment and similar provisions in state constitutions. Those constitutions protected the gun rights of Americans. Weren't free blacks Americans? Racist judges answered no.

To get to that conclusion, the judges had to use some pretty twisted logic. It went like this: Belief #1: Americans have gun rights. Belief #2: Free blacks shouldn't have gun rights. Conclusion: Free blacks aren't Americans. North Carolina's Supreme Court led the way with this kind of muddled thinking. In 1844, it held constitutional a law that imposed "upon free men of color, a restriction in the carrying of fire arms, from which the white men of the country are exempt." It admitted that the state's constitution protected citizens' gun rights, but it argued that "free people of color cannot be considered as citizens." Georgia's Supreme Court did the same thing. It took one look at a similar anti–Second Amendment law and claimed that "free persons of color have never been recognized here as citizens; they are not entitled to bear arms."

It didn't take long before the United States Supreme Court came on board. Most people have heard of the Dred Scott case, which determined blacks weren't citizens and that the federal government had no business regulating slavery. My hometown of St. Louis was the judicial stage for Scott's trial. Many may even know that the controversial decision played a large part in the lead-up to the Civil War. But hardly anyone bothers to look at the Supreme Court's motivation in making that decision. What rationale did the Justices use to declare that black Americans can't be citizens? Citizens can own guns.

Writing for the court in *Dred Scott v. Sandford*, Chief Justice Roger Taney—a proud Southerner who destroyed an otherwise distinguished legal career with this shameful catastrophe— explained that if free blacks were "entitled to the privileges and immunities of citizens, it would exempt them from the operations of the special laws and from the police regulations which [the states] considered to be necessary for their own safety." And what was one of the most important of those "special laws"? Racist gun control laws. Allowing free blacks to be citizens "would give them the full liberty…to keep and carry arms wherever they went," said Taney. They can't be considered citizens, because citizens can own guns, was Taney's logic.

Heaven forbid free black men have the equality under the Second Amendment that white men enjoy. He cared so much about gun control that he distorted the meaning of *citizen* and helped ignite a Civil War that killed over six hundred thousand Americans. If you guessed Roger Taney was a Democrat, you'd be right. Little has changed with the ideology of the anti–Second Amendment left. The new Republican Party was founded in 1854 to stop the spread of slavery and abolish it entirely. A key way to go about this goal was to ensure that black Americans were citizens and could bear arms.

After the Civil War, black Southerners enjoyed a brief window in which they were able to own guns. Many of them had served in the Union Army and still had their rifles when the war ended. Others could afford cheap handguns called "Suicide Specials" that were sold for as little as fifty or sixty cents.

These guns threatened to change everything, as a group of white racists in Greensboro, Alabama, learned in 1867. They didn't like the idea of a black voting registrar, so they murdered him. They probably thought nothing of it. After all, who was going to stop them? The police? A judge? They were protected by law, after all. But before they knew it, an emancipated African-American in town was organizing other freedmen into a permanent, armed militia, the kind of which is explicitly detailed in the Second Amendment. What's more, his wasn't the only one. "Union League" militias started popping up all over Alabama to protect African-Americans and white Republicans.

If those militias and private citizens had been allowed to keep their guns, the whole history of the postwar South would have looked a lot different. The story of Dr. Martin Luther King might have read differently with the absence of a Jim Crow system against which to protest. Maybe Dr. King would not have been repeatedly denied a gun permit of his own by segregators.

For the brief window when black Southerners were armed, they were able to vote and protect their civil rights. In at least one Southern state, South Carolina, blacks even outnumbered whites. If they could use guns to protect their right to vote, they could gain a majority in the state legislature, pass civil rights laws, and use their guns to enforce those rights.

Unfortunately, the anti–Second Amendment advocates struck again. In 1867, a former Confederate cavalry commander in Pulaski, Tennessee, founded the most effective gun control organization in American history—even more effective than the Democratic Party. It was called the Ku Klux Klan. As UCLA law professor Adam Winkler writes, "Whites believed that they had to confiscate black people's guns in order to reestablish white supremacy and prevent blacks from fighting back. Blacks who refused to turn over their only means of self-defense were lynched." In other words, the forerunner to Mike Bloomberg, Michael Moore, Jim Brady, and other white males trying to take away our guns was Nathan Bedford Forrest.

The KKK's model was imitated throughout the South. In Alabama, the night riders named themselves the "Men of Justice." In Louisiana, they called their group the "Knights of the White Camellia." In South Carolina, it was the "Sweetwater Sabre Club." In Texas, they were the "Knights of the Rising Sun." If there was one thing these terrorist organizations seemed to love, it was fancy-sounding, ridiculous names. If there was one thing they hated, it was gun ownership by black Americans.

Gun control groups like the KKK were brutally effective. As a Northern lawyer and civil rights worker of the era wrote,

"Almost universally the first thing done [by the KKK] was to disarm the negroes and leave them defenseless." Massachusetts senator Henry Wilson complained that in Mississippi, "men who were in the rebel armies are traversing the State, visiting the freedmen, disarming them, perpetrating murders and outrages upon them." Massachusetts congressman Benjamin Butler agreed. "Armed confederates," he said, "have preceded their outrages upon [the black Southerner] by disarming him, in violation of his right as a citizen to 'keep and bear arms' which the Constitution expressly says shall never be infringed."

Butler helped introduce in Congress an anti-KKK bill in 1871 called "an act to protect loyal and peaceful citizens of the South." As originally drafted, it made it a crime to "deprive any citizen of the United States"—by 1871, the Fourteenth Amendment had made African-Americans citizens—"of any arms or weapons he may have in his house or possession for the defense of his person, family, or property." Butler explained that it was "intended to enforce the well-known constitutional provision guaranteeing the right of the citizen to 'keep and bear arms.'" He said it was "necessary" because when "these midnight marauders made attacks upon peaceful citizens, there were very many instances in the South where the sheriff of the county had preceded them and taken away the arms of their victims." In one county, "all the Negro population were disarmed by the sheriff…and then, the sheriff having disarmed the citizens, the five hundred masked men rode at night and murdered and otherwise maltreated the ten persons who were there in jail in that county."

The anti-KKK bill was only one of several attempts by Congress in the Reconstruction Era to protect the gun rights of black Southerners. The Freedman's Bureau Act provided that freedmen were entitled to the "full and equal benefit of all laws...concerning personal security...including the constitutional right to bear arms." Senate Bill No. 9 said state laws like gun control laws that denied rights based on race were void. The Civil Rights Act's supporters explained that "in most of the southern States, there has existed a law of the State based upon and founded in its police power, which declares that free Negroes shall not have the possession of firearms or ammunition. This bill proposes to take away from the States this police power."

Unfortunately, these measures didn't work. Nice laws are all official, well, and good, but if the local police are unwilling to enforce those laws—and if the citizens who depend on the laws don't have the guns to enforce the laws themselves—laws are meaningless. A law's strength is steeped in its justification, its enforcement, and its observance. Opposite of that is an erosion of law for the sake of a racist agenda.

By the end of Reconstruction, black Southerners had been disarmed by groups like the KKK and white supremacist sheriffs. Racists with guns terrorized unarmed blacks to keep them from voting, and once the racists got control of state legislatures, they started codifying the gun grabs of the Klan and its allies.

Because of the Fourteenth Amendment, which made black Americans citizens and required "equal protection of the laws," Southern legislatures couldn't reenact the old prewar laws that put gun restrictions only on African-Americans, but just like their anti–Second Amendment advocates of today, they looked for ways around inconvenient constitutional provisions.

The racist gun grabbers settled on two loopholes, and unlike today's so-called faux gun show loophole, these loopholes were real. The first was a set of laws that made guns too expensive for black Southerners to afford. Tennessee banned all handguns other than "army or navy" model revolvers. These high-quality revolvers were expensive, and many whites already owned them. Blacks didn't, and couldn't afford them. Arkansas took note, liked what it saw, and did the same thing.

Alabama, Texas, and Virginia also made guns too expensive for African-Americans to afford. Instead of banning cheap guns, they made them expensive, and placed heavy taxes on handguns. The goal, according to its racist supporters, was to disarm "the son of Ham." And in South Carolina, a statute allowed pistol sales to only sheriffs and special deputies—which meant pistols would be sold only to whites. You don't have to have seen *Blazing Saddles* to know that black sheriffs weren't too common.

The second strategy—the second gun control loophole—was to require handgun registration and permits. Local law enforcement officials—always white—would have the discretion to decide whether to grant the permit or not. Shockingly in the South of a hundred years ago, African-Americans didn't get permits very often. Mississippi, Georgia, North Carolina, Missouri, Arkansas, and Florida all went this route.

There was no doubt in anyone's mind about what was going on with gun control laws that were race neutral on their face. As a concurring justice on the Florida Supreme Court made clear, Florida's permit law "was passed for the purpose of disarming the negro laborers...and to give the white citizens in sparsely settled areas a better feeling of security. The statute was never intended to be applied to the white population and in practice has never been applied." In fact, often a sheriff would grant a gun permit within seconds of meeting an applicant—just long enough to make sure the applicant wasn't black.

Gun permit requirements were ideally suited to abuse by white prosecutors. According to professor of sociology William Tonso, "since the illegal possession of a handgun (or of any gun) is a crime that doesn't produce a victim and is unlikely to be reported to the police, handgun permit requirements or out-right handgun prohibitions aren't easily enforced." He adds that "when laws are difficult to enforce, 'enforcement becomes progressively more haphazard until at last the laws are used only against those who are unpopular with the police.'" It would be an understatement to say that black Southerners a hundred years ago were "unpopular with the police." If Al Sharpton had lived then, he wouldn't have had to invent his stories about police brutality and inequality.

ONE OF THE FIRST FEDERAL GUN GRABS

Of course, black Americans are not the only people who have had to endure bigotry in American history, and they aren't the only ones who've been the target of bigoted gun grabs.

Five days after Christmas 1890, the Seventh Cavalry arrived on the Pine Ridge Indian Reservation to confiscate the arms of the Miniconjou people, part of the Lakota, "for their own safety and protection." A misunderstanding occurred when a deaf tribesman named Black Coyote refused to part with his gun. He said he paid too much for it. Unable to hear the soldiers's orders, a struggle ensued, his gun discharged, and the cavalry opened fire, killing nearly three hundred innocent Lakota men, women, and children. The bloody massacre was among the first federally sanctioned gun grabs. It happened at a place known to history as Wounded Knee.

In addition to African-Americans and American Indians, eastern and southern European immigrants faced prejudice a hundred years ago, especially in the North. Bigotry wasn't unique to the South, and xenophobic Northerners were almost as scared of armed immigrants as Southern white supremacists were scared of armed African-Americans. Northern nativists blamed immigrants for crime and the anarchist movement that assassinated the leaders of Russia, France, Spain, Italy, Portugal, Greece, and—when a bullet brought down William McKinley—the United States.

In 1911, New York passed the notorious Sullivan Law. It required a permit for a handgun and gave local law enforcement enormous discretion over whether to grant the permit. Police departments like New York City's could be as arbitrary as they wanted in choosing whether to let someone own a handgun. The rich and powerful could have one. Legal immigrants couldn't. They were considered racially inferior. They couldn't be trusted with guns.

So who could be trusted with a firearm? Ironically, the police trusted enemies of the Second Amendment. The *New York Times* never gets tired of editorializing in favor of gun control—on and outside of the editorial page—but its publisher for most of the twentieth century, Arthur Sulzberger, was one of the few New Yorkers allowed to have a handgun permit. Other enemies of the Second Amendment in New York, like Nelson Rockefeller and John Lindsey, also had permits. And, considering the history behind the Sullivan Law, why should anyone be surprised? Like other racist gun control laws, the Sullivan Law was never meant to apply to them.

Laws like it were, of course, meant to apply to people like Martin Luther King, and in the 1950s he became a victim of gun control.

King is famous for nonviolent resistance, but he believed that "violence exercised merely in self-defense" was "moral and legal." He explained that "the principle of self-defense, even involving weapons and bloodshed, has never been condemned, even by Gandhi." According to King, "when the Negro uses force in self-defense, he does not forfeit support. He may even win it, by the courage and self-respect it reflects."

Because King was a constant target of assassination threats, self-defense wasn't theoretical for him. It was the day-to-day reality for his young family. His house was like "an arsenal," according to one advisor. There were so many guns lying around that a visitor "almost sat on a loaded gun" one time. Dr. King even applied for a permit to carry a handgun after his home was bombed in the 1950s. But, since Alabama's white supremacist law enforcement authorities had arbitrary power to deny King's application for a handgun—indeed, keeping guns from people with King's skin color was the whole point of the permit law—Alabama refused his request.

About a decade after King was denied a gun permit, Congress got in on the race-inspired gun grabbing. There were terrible race riots in Newark and Detroit in 1967, and Congress responded by passing the Gun Control Act of 1968. It prohibited mail-order sales of guns, imported military surplus guns, and so-called Saturday Night Specials. Like the Suicide Specials of the Reconstruction-era South, Saturday Night Specials were very cheap and easily available. They weren't used more often in crime than more costly guns, but when crime was committed by young African-Americans, cheap handguns were often used. By targeting those guns, Congress could target the people it wanted to target, without bothering too many others. As even the gun control advocate and reporter Robert Sherrill conceded, the law in 1968 was "passed not to control guns but to control Blacks."

That was then, what about today? Does race still play a role in gun control? It's an issue worthy of examination. The California state legislature's research department found that almost all of the state's concealed-carry permits go to whites. In the past several decades, the housing authorities in Richmond and Chicago have targeted gun control at public housing projects—whose residents tend to be minorities. An ACLU study in St. Louis in the 1970s found that the police conducted over twenty-five thousand illegal searches "on the theory that any black, driving a late model car has an illegal gun"—even though the searches found only 117 guns.[1]

Consider also the security threats in many inner-city, predominately black neighborhoods. Their residents can't afford to outsource their security. They can't afford gates on their communities. They can't afford private security patrols. They can't afford electronic alarm systems. Instead, they live in areas with too few police, where 911 responses are slower than elsewhere, and where threats to their homes and families are high. Innocent men and women in these neighborhoods need guns for protection even more than most other Americans, but white liberal elites—safe behind their gated communities and inside their condo buildings with a security guard in every lobby—

refuse to allow them their Second Amendment rights. Instead, they'll grab their guns.

The author of *The Racist Roots of Gun Control*, Clayton Cramer, says it bluntly: "In the last century, the official rhetoric in support of such laws was that 'they were too violent, too untrustworthy, to be allowed weapons.' Today, the same elitist rhetoric regards law-abiding Americans in the same way, as child-like creatures in need of guidance from the government."

Even today, leaders in Congress are shamelessly pimping an obvious racial fear and animus. They have made African-Americans less safe while making sure that they themselves are protected, like true 1 percenters. Despite their endless quoting of the Second Amendment and faux reverence, they have totally distorted the views of America's founders.

Progressives love to run around and brand conservatives who disagree with them on anything as racists. Well, now conservatives have a response. Let's see how they enjoy being reminded that their gun control views are wholly in line with those of the Ku Klux Klan. That ought to make Thanksgiving dinners with "coo-coo for Cocoa Puffs" left-wing relatives pretty interesting this year. In fact, there's even more to the often ignored or overlooked history of gun rights that will stoke liberal fury.

Chapter 8

Founding Firearms

A strong body makes the mind strong. As to the species of exercises, I advise the gun. While this gives moderate exercise to the body, it gives boldness, enterprise and independence to the mind...Let the gun therefore be the constant companion of your walks.

—BITTER GUN CLINGER THOMAS JEFFERSON

Rarely in history have so many people quoted the United States Constitution and yet seemed deliberately obtuse to its meaning than have the members of the United States Congress. Why that still comes as a surprise probably says more about me than it does about them. Let's face it. Liberals always have had a love-hate relationship with the Constitution—they love it when they can use it to abort babies or let gay people get married. They hate it when its language gets in the way of their big-government schemes, like censoring conservative media outlets or investigating troublesome, truth-telling journalists. They especially hate the fact that the Constitution explicitly—

yes, explicitly—protects gun owners. To get around that inconvenient truth, the left does what it does best: It denies that things say what they actually say, or mean what they actually mean. Or as everyone's favorite sexual harasser once famously put it, "It depends on what the meaning of *is* is."

The gun grabbers' useful idiot, Sen. Chuck Schumer, once claimed that his fellow Democrats needed to admit that there was such as thing as a Second Amendment that gave people "a constitutional right to bear arms." But before we think Senator Schumer was actually on our side, he went on in the same breath to call for a "compromise" that allowed the left to ban a whole bunch of different guns and thus infringe on that aforementioned constitutional right to bear arms.

Things got a little testy in the Senate in 2013 when Ted Cruz tried to explain to Dianne Feinstein that the Second Amendment protected gun owners. "I'm not a sixth grader," she snapped, as she continued to argue that the Second Amendment was irrelevant to her latest gun-grab legislation. (Respectfully, I would argue that most sixth graders understand the Second Amendment, and civics, better than Senator Feinstein.) Liberal academics, given a megaphone by various media outlets, have told us again and again that the Second Amendment doesn't mean what we think it means or it doesn't mean what it says. Always good for a laugh, the *Huffington Post* once went even further with the #WTFbananas headline: "The Second Amendment Demands Gun Control."

It's long past time for a basic tutorial on the Constitution. Our Founders meant for it to be read, not trampled underfoot. We should present it in a way that even someone with the reading comprehension of a dolphin could understand it. Or a member of Congress.

THE MERRY MONARCH

The king of England, Charles II, was known as the "Merry Monarch," in part because anyone in the mid- to late 1600s would have seemed relatively "merry" after the reign of the brutal Oliver Cromwell, and in part because Charles II was fond of wine and women. He was not, however, all that fond of Protestants, who unfortunately for him, made up 98 percent of his country.

Believe it or not, the story of America's Second Amendment begins with that Merry Monarch. In 1671, Charles II ordered that any regions home to his political enemies—and, to be sure, he had a lot of them—should be disarmed while other lands were otherwise untouched. His son, James II, later continued his policies of enforcing autocracy and suppressing dissent by disarming anyone who disagreed with him.

The English didn't take kindly to monarchs who took away rights they believed were given to them by God, and having once beheaded James II's grandfather for infringing on their rights, this band of bitter clingers deposed James II at the first opportunity. They called this the "Glorious Revolution," because it involved less bloodshed than most rebellions, and with a swift stroke, the English said good-bye to James II and hello to his successors, William and Mary.

The English who defeated James II weren't about to replace one despot with another, though. They had learned what a king was capable of when he combined a strong army with a policy of disarming his political opposition, and so they required William and Mary to agree to a Declaration of Rights that guaranteed to their subjects the right to bear arms. That Declaration was soon codified in 1689 as the English "Bill of Rights."

In the near century that followed before American independence, English courts applied the Bill of Rights to protect the right of Englishmen to keep and bear their arms. In the case *King v. Gardner*, the King's Bench agreed in 1739 with a defendant who argued that he could not be convicted for owning a gun "necessary for defence of a house, or for a farmer to shoot crows." In 1744, the Court of Common Pleas in *Mallock v. Eastly* held it was well-settled that "a man may keep a gun for the defence of his house and family." Later, in 1752, the King's Bench again explained in *Wingfield v. Stratford* that "a gun may be kept for the defence of a man's house, and for divers other lawful purposes."

As the United States Supreme Court would later state, "by the time of the founding, the right to have arms had become fundamental for English subjects," and the founders saw gun ownership as an important part of being a person free and independent from an autocratic government. When Thomas Jefferson drafted the Virginia Constitution, he inserted the right to bear arms in three separate drafts, though the wording in each varied slightly. In the first draft, he wrote, for example, that "No freeman shall ever be debarred the use of arms." Besides bitter clinger Thomas Jefferson, James Madison wrote that oligarchies were only safe with a "standing army, an enslaved press, and a disarmed populace." The Founding-era poet, diplomat, and statesman Joel Barlow believed a "people [who] will be universally armed" flowed from "the original, unalterable truth, that all men are equal in their rights." It's funny how much liberals love to quote our Founding Fathers, especially on the Fourth of July, but then ignore many of their actual points of view. Inconvenient truths, indeed.

It was against this backdrop that British troops arrived in Boston in 1768 to enforce a collection of unpopular taxes. Many in Boston saw the taxes as tyranny, and as English subjects born and bred to believe in a right to bear arms in defense of their liberties, Bostonians saw nothing illegal about, in Samuel Adams's words, "calling upon one another to be provided with" arms to defend themselves against tyranny. Adams explained that "the privilege of possessing arms is expressly recognized by the Bill of Rights" of 1689, and he cited Blackstone's treatise holding that Englishmen are born with the "right of having and using arms for self-preservation and defence." His brother John Adams similarly stated in his closing argument in a case involving the Boston Massacre, "Here every private person is authorized to arm himself."

The *New York Journal*—in its day called the "Journal of the Times"—agreed with both Adams brothers, declaring "it is a natural right which the people have reserved to themselves, confirmed by the [English] Bill of Rights, to keep arms for their own defence; and as Mr. Blackstone observes, it is to be made use of when the sanctions of society and law are found insufficient to restrain the violence of oppression."

Despite the colonists's belief in the natural right to armed self-defense—or perhaps because of it—British authorities attempted to disarm colonists in Boston and elsewhere. The colonists complained that England had "a design of disarming the people of America, in order the more speedily to dragoon and enslave them." The Revolutionary War began on April 19, 1775, when British troops attempted to seize arms from private property in a little Massachusetts town called Concord. That the American colonists went on to win that war was possible only because those patriots were armed. With guns. And rifles. And bullets. You know, all the things progressives today want to ban. All the things progressives today think the Founders wanted the Constitution to ban. It's a cruel irony the way they mock they very democracy they claim to represent. The British general Cornwallis, after all, surrendered to an American army, not an American diplomat. He surrendered to force of arms, not the force of words. If people like Chuck Schumer and Al Franken and Rahm Emanuel were in charge during colonial times, George Washington would have been captured, Adams and Jefferson hung, and today we'd all still be making out our annual taxes to the Chancellor of the Exchequer and exchanging currency on which the profiles of monarchs are minted.

In particular, the patriots were armed from the start of the war with the British Brown Bess, which was the firearm of choice for the British Army. In addition, the founders were familiar with weapons's evolution and technological advancement. In the time prior to the Revolution and during it, match-lit muskets progressed into matchlock muskets, which progressed into flintlocks. In fact, muskets were slowly being replaced by long rifles during and after the Revolution. Rifling gave shots increased accuracy over greater distances.

In 1718 the Puckle gun, the first machine gun, appeared, and by the time of the revolution, the "assault rifle," was an available technology. It was called the Belton gun, and it modified flintlock muskets so that the shooter could engage in rapid firing with a single loading. The technology was demonstrated before well-known scientist David Rittenhouse and Gen. Horatio Gates, and the Continental Congress had hopes of purchasing Belton guns. It was only Belton's insistence on a price Congress believed to be excessive that stopped the cash-strapped Congress from buying what today would be called an assault rifle.

After Americans used their guns to defeat tyranny and win their independence, they were governed for more than a decade under the Articles of Confederation. Because the kings Charles II, James II, and George III had used large armies to oppress political opponents, Americans were skeptical of standing armies, and the Articles of Confederation banned them. Its sixth article provided, "No vessel of war shall be kept up in time of peace by any State...nor shall any body of forced be kept up by any State in time of peace." Although there were exceptions to Article Six's ban, what had no exceptions was the Articles of Confederation's refusal to create an executive branch. There would be no standing army for the executive to command, because there would be no executive.

That changed with the Constitution. Written in 1787, the Constitution addressed inadequacies in the Articles of Confederation, but it struck fear into the hearts of many Americans when it created a president and made him the commander in chief of a federal army. Opponents of the Constitution warned that a standing army would be an "engine of arbitrary power." They believed, in the words of New Hampshire's 1784 Constitution, that "nonresistance against arbitrary power, and oppression, is absurd, slavish, and destructive of the good and happiness of mankind," and they were afraid a standing army would crush any such resistance.

Those who shared that fear had the power to sink the Constitution. Unless nine of the thirteen states ratified the Constitution in state conventions, it would be a dead letter. And unless the fear of a standing army was mollified, there was no way nine states would vote to ratify the Constitution. These folks had just fought a war for their freedom. They weren't about to risk replacing a British tyrant with an American one. Washington shared this fear and was sensitive to it when the delegates assembled for the drafting of the Constitution. So sensitive was he that as president he made the careful effort to include Congress in every decision made in battle strategy, respective of the people.

The Constitution's supporters replied that a standing army shouldn't be feared because the American people would be armed. With their guns, they could protect themselves against any future tyranny threatened by a standing army. As Noah Webster argued in the first pamphlet by a federalist (the name the Constitution's supporters gave themselves), "Before a standing army can rule, the people must be disarmed; as they are in almost every kingdom of Europe." In contrast, the national government "in America cannot enforce unjust laws by the sword; because the whole body of the people are armed, and constitute a force superior to any bands of regular troops that can be, on any pretence, raised in the United States."

In state ratifying conventions, federalists made the same point. At the convention in Massachusetts, one federalist asked rhetorically how a standing army "could subdue a nation of freemen, who know how to prize liberty, and have arms in their hands?"

Alexander Hamilton and James Madison made a similar argument in *The Federalist Papers*, a collection of editorials published in New York newspapers in an attempt to persuade on-the-fence Empire Staters to support the Constitution. In *Federalist* 29, Hamilton argued that "if circumstances should at any time oblige the government to form an army of any magnitude, that army can never be formidable to the liberties of the people while there is a large body of citizens, little, if at all, inferior to them in discipline and the use of arms, who stand ready to defend their own rights and those of their fellow-citizens."

Similarly, Madison argued in *Federalist* 46 that "besides the advantage of being armed, which the Americans possess over the people of almost every other nation, the existence of subordinate governments, to which the people are attached, and by which the militia officers are appointed, forms a barrier against the enterprises of ambition, more insurmountable than any which a simple government of any form can admit of."

Madison explained that America would not be like the European mainland, where standing armies could oppress citizens because the citizens were not armed. "In the several kingdoms of Europe," he wrote, "the governments are afraid to trust the people with arms." But if Europeans had firearms, as well as local governments and local militias, "it may be affirmed with the greatest assurance, that the throne of every tyranny in Europe would be speedily overturned in spite of the legions which surround it."

The opponents of the Constitution were not, however, easily persuaded. They had a simple reply to Hamilton, Madison, and the other federalists: Nothing in the Constitution prevented the government from disarming the people. Patrick Henry bellowed at the Virginia ratifying convention about a future in which "your arms, wherewith you could defend yourselves, are gone." If the people were disarmed, Henry and his allies argued, then the standing army could be used to oppress them. After all, anti-federalist George Mason reminded Virginia delegates that King George III had planned "to disarm the people," because it "was the most effectual way to enslave them." According to an anti-federalist at the Pennsylvania ratifying convention, "the people in general may be disarmed" under the scheme established by the Constitution.

In early 1788, it looked as if that argument by the Constitution's opponents would carry the day. Although five states had ratified the Constitution by February 1788, anti-federalists appeared to outnumber federalists in most of the remaining states, and they made clear that their support for the Constitution depended on the federalists finding a way to alleviate their fears of an oppressive federal government.

The clearest way to alleviate those fears was to amend the Constitution to address them, and so, with their leverage, the anti-federalists began to demand certain amendments. Foremost among them was an amendment to ensure that Americans would never be disarmed.

In Pennsylvania, delegates skeptical of the Constitution called for an amendment providing "that the people have a right to bear arms for the defense of themselves and their own State, or of the United States, or for the purpose of killing game; and no law shall be passed for disarming the people or any of them, unless for crimes committed, or real danger of public injury from individuals." In Massachusetts, Samuel Adams demanded a guarantee "that the said Constitution be never construed to authorize Congress to...prevent the people of the United States, who are peaceable citizens, from keeping their own arms."

Pennsylvania and Massachusetts were not alone. New Hampshire demanded a guarantee that "Congress shall never disarm any Citizen except such as are or have been in Actual Rebellion." Virginia called for an amendment providing "that the people have a right to keep and bear arms; that a well-regulated militia, composed of the body of the people trained to arms, is the proper, natural, and safe defense of a free state; that standing armies, in time of peace, are dangerous to liberty." And in almost identical language, New York insisted on a guarantee that "the people have a right to keep and bear arms; that a well-regulated militia, composed of the body of the people capable of bearing arms, is the proper, natural, and safe defense of a free state."

Calls for amendments to protect other rights were also made in state ratifying conventions, but none received more attention than the right to bear arms. While there were three demands for an amendment to protect freedom of speech and one for a protection against double jeopardy, five separate state conventions made calls for what would become the Second Amendment of the Bill of Rights.

There's little appreciation today for how close opponents of the Constitution came to defeating it. The vote at the Massachusetts convention in February 1788 was 187 to 168. In subsequent months, a switch of just six votes would have defeated ratification in Virginia and New Hampshire, and a change of a mere two votes would have defeated it in New York.

There's also little appreciation today for the certainty that the Constitution would have been defeated during the ratification debates if its supporters had not agreed to meet skeptics's demands for a Bill of Rights that included protection of the right to possess firearms. In other words, not only does the amended Constitution protect Americans' right to own guns; there wouldn't be a Constitution if that right had not been protected in the Second Amendment.

Fortunately, the Constitution's ratification was saved by its supporters' willingness to promise skeptics a Bill of Rights that included what became the Second Amendment.

Most of those supporters believed a Bill of Rights was unnecessary, because rights like freedom of religion, freedom of speech, and the freedom to own firearms were natural rights. They were God-given. They didn't need to be created by amendments to the Constitution, because they couldn't legally be taken away by any lawful government. As the Supreme Court said in 1897, the Second Amendment was "not intended to lay down any novel principles of government, but simply to embody certain guarantees and immunities which we had inherited from our English ancestors."

As a result, when James Madison drafted the Second Amendment, he wrote it as if "the right of the people to keep and bear arms" already existed. The Second Amendment that he wrote and that the First Congress passed said that this pre-existing "right of the people...shall not be infringed." In its final form, it says—and, contrary to the wishes of gun grabbers everywhere, continues to say—"A well regulated militia being necessary to the security of a free state, the right of the people to keep and bear arms shall not be infringed."

The amendment was passed by Congress in 1789 and adopted by the states in 1791. The next year, Congress demonstrated the importance the founders placed on gun ownership when they passed a law requiring gun ownership. It provided that "each and every free able-bodied white male citizen of the respective States, resident therein, who is or shall be of age of eighteen years, and under the age of forty-five years…shall, within six months thereafter, provide himself with a good musket or firelock, a sufficient bayonet and belt, two spare flints, and a knapsack, a pouch with a box therein to contain not less than twenty-four cartridges…and shall appear, so armed, accoutered and provided, when called out to exercise, or into service" for the militia.

In other words, the country's first "individual mandate" was a mandate to get a gun. And, unlike today's individual mandate to buy health insurance, the mandate to own a gun was constitutional.

IN THEIR OWN WORDS

Just to make sure everyone reading this book is well armed—pun intended—with the facts about the Founders and their intentions, the Buckeye Firearms Association compiled a list of quotes attributed to various Founders that demonstrated beyond any shadow of a doubt what our Constitution's drafters intended when they drafted and approved the Second Amendment. Do the new-century equivalent of sticking them onto your fridge: Post them to Facebook or Twitter. Among the quotes they listed:

"A free people ought to be armed."

—GEORGE WASHINGTON

"Those who would give up essential liberty to purchase a little temporary safety, deserve neither liberty nor safety."

—BENJAMIN FRANKLIN

"The laws that forbid the carrying of arms are laws of such a nature. They disarm only those who are neither inclined nor determined to commit crimes...Such laws make things worse for the assaulted and better for the assailants; they serve rather to encourage than to prevent homicides, for an unarmed man may be attacked with greater confidence than an armed man."

—THOMAS JEFFERSON (QUOTING EIGHTEENTH-CENTURY CRIMINOLOGIST CESARE BECCARIA)

"A strong body makes the mind strong. As to the species of exercises, I advise the gun. While this gives moderate exercise to the body, it gives boldness, enterprise and independence to the mind. Games played with the ball, and others of that nature, are too violent for the body and stamp no character on the mind. Let your gun therefore be your constant companion of your walks."

—THOMAS JEFFERSON

"The Constitution of most of our states (and of the United States) assert that all power is inherent in the people; that they may exercise it by themselves; that it is their right and duty to be at all times armed."

—THOMAS JEFFERSON

"On every occasion [of Constitutional interpretation] let us carry ourselves back to the time when the Constitution was adopted, recollect the spirit manifested in the debates, and instead of trying [to force] what meaning may be squeezed out of the text, or invented against it, [instead let us] conform to the probable one in which it was passed."

—THOMAS JEFFERSON

"I enclose you a list of the killed, wounded, and captives of the enemy from the commencement of hostilities at Lexington in April, 1775, until November, 1777, since which there has been no event of any consequence…I think that upon the whole it has been about one half the number lost by them, in some instances more, but in others less. This difference is ascribed to our superiority in taking aim when we fire; every soldier in our army having been intimate with his gun from his infancy."

—THOMAS JEFFERSON, IN A LETTER TO GIOVANNI FABBRONI, JUNE 8, 1778

"Arms in the hands of citizens may be used at individual discretion in private self defense."

—JOHN ADAMS

"To disarm the people is the most effectual way to enslave them."
—GEORGE MASON

"I ask sir, what is the militia? It is the whole people except for a few politicians."

—GEORGE MASON (FATHER OF THE BILL OF RIGHTS AND THE VIRGINIA DECLARATION OF RIGHTS)

177

"*Before a standing army can rule, the people must be disarmed, as they are in almost every country in Europe.*"

—Noah Webster

"*The supreme power in America cannot enforce unjust laws by the sword; because the whole body of the people are armed, and constitute a force superior to any band of regular troops.*"

—Noah Webster

"*A government resting on the minority is an aristocracy, not a Republic, and could not be safe with a numerical and physical force against it, without a standing army, an enslaved press and a disarmed populace.*"

—James Madison

"*Americans have the right and advantage of being armed, unlike the people of other countries, whose leaders are afraid to trust them with arms.*"

—James Madison

"*The right of the people to keep and bear arms shall not be infringed. A well regulated militia, composed of the body of the people, trained to arms, is the best and most natural defense of a free country.*"

—James Madison

"*To preserve liberty, it is essential that the whole body of the people always possess arms, and be taught alike, especially when young, how to use them.*"

—Richard Henry Lee

"A militia, when properly formed, are in fact the people themselves...and include all men capable of bearing arms."

—RICHARD HENRY LEE

"Guard with jealous attention the public liberty. Suspect everyone who approaches that jewel. Unfortunately, nothing will preserve it but downright force. Whenever you give up that force, you are ruined...The great object is that every man be armed. Everyone who is able might have a gun."

—PATRICK HENRY

"This may be considered as the true palladium of liberty...The right of self defense is the first law of nature: in most governments it has been the study of rulers to confine this right within the narrowest limits possible. Wherever standing armies are kept up, and the right of the people to keep and bear arms is, under any color or pretext whatsoever, prohibited, liberty, if not already annihilated, is on the brink of destruction."

—ST. GEORGE TUCKER

"Arms...discourage and keep the invader and plunderer in awe, and preserve order in the world as well as property... Horrid mischief would ensue were [the law-abiding] deprived the use of them."

—THOMAS PAINE

"*The Constitution shall never be construed to prevent the people of the United States who are peaceable citizens from keeping their own arms.*"

—SAMUEL ADAMS

"*The right of the citizens to keep and bear arms has justly been considered, as the palladium of the liberties of a republic; since it offers a strong moral check against the usurpation and arbitrary power of rulers; and will generally, even if these are successful in the first instance, enable the people to resist and triumph over them.*"

—JOSEPH STORY

"*What, Sir, is the use of a militia? It is to prevent the establishment of a standing army, the bane of liberty... Whenever Governments mean to invade the rights and liberties of the people, they always attempt to destroy the militia, in order to raise an army upon their ruins.*"

—REP. ELBRIDGE GERRY OF MASSACHUSETTS

"*For it is a truth, which the experience of all ages has attested, that the people are commonly most in danger when the means of insuring their rights are in the possession of those of whom they entertain the least suspicion.*"

—ALEXANDER HAMILTON

The Founders understood that a free and independent citizenry starts with a well-armed populace. This sentence does not appear in the Virginia Constitution as adopted. The only way progressives can change that is if they make enough people believe that things don't mean what they say they mean. The passing of time does not make our liberties anachronistic. You don't lose speech because there exists new ways to engage, nor do we lose our right to bear arms simply because of the advances in firearm technology. Time doesn't pervert the purpose, nor does technology. The Founders were clear. Agree with them or don't.

Chapter 9

Violent Europeans

It's been quite a while since Michael Moore made a movie anybody bothered to watch. But about ten years ago, he was to the radical left-wing as Justin Bieber is to prepubescent girls. When he made a mockumentary about gun control called *Bowling for Columbine*, the mainstream media treated it like it was a stone tablet being brought down from the mountain by Moses. It was "absolutely required viewing," gushed the *Miami Herald*. The *Washington Post* called it "a refreshingly nuanced view of the issue." The *Denver Post* was even more effusive: "At its best, which occurs often, Michael Moore's *Bowling for Columbine* rekindles the muckraking, soul-searching spirit of the 'Are we a sick society?' journalism of the 1960s." According to the *San Francisco Chronicle*, Michael Moore's movie "explains the very fabric of American society."

Well, well—it's not every day you can see the "very fabric of American society" explained in a little under two hours. What, you might ask, explains American society? Moore's answer (and the *San Francisco Chronicle*'s) is simple: guns. Moore's "logic" is simple: Guns lead to violence, and violence defines America.

The problem with this thinking is, well, just about everything about it.

Take, for example, the premise that America is unusually violent. "In Europe and Australia, most other free-world countries, they don't have this," we learn from Moore's movie. "They don't have people who snap and go on murderous rampages."

You hear this sentiment on cable news and see it on the editorial pages of major newspapers all the time. Back before Piers Morgan was fired from CNN, he said, "You have by far the worst rate of gun murder and gun crime of any of the civilized countries of this world."[1] According to the *New York Times*'s editorial page, "the American murder rate is roughly 15 times that of other wealthy countries, which have much tougher laws controlling private ownership of guns."[2]

It's long past time to call this kind of assertion by its name: a lie.

Let's take a quick look at the statistics before we take a hard, and sometimes painful, look at the "murderous rampages" that progressives believe other countries don't have.

The combined murder and suicide rate in the United States is lower than in Belgium, Switzerland, France, Bulgaria, Austria, Croatia, Denmark, Finland, Slovenia, Ukraine, Hungary, Belarus, Lithuania, Latvia, Estonia, and Russia. In many of those cases, our rate is far, far smaller than the rate in European countries. For example, our suicide rate is 43 percent of Finland's, and our murder rate is 25 percent of Russia's.[3]

Other continents have even worse crime. The murder rate in the United States is lower than the murder rate in "most of Southeast Asia, the Caribbean, Africa, all but one South American nation, and all of Central America and Mexico."[4] Additionally, among the world's nations, there's no correlation between fewer guns and less crime. To the contrary, among developed countries, the countries that have the fewest guns (like Turkey, Chile, and Estonia) often have the most crime.[5] On the other hand, Switzerland, which has more guns per capita than all but two other countries in the world, has a far lower murder rate than countries that heavily restrict guns, like Canada, Great Britain, and Australia. Even the *Washington Post*—in a rare moment of lucidity—has had to admit that "countries with the most guns don't necessarily have the most gun-related homicides."[6]

Honduras is a good example of the difference between gun control and crime control. The small Central American nation has a national registry of guns. It prohibits people from carrying guns openly in public. It puts limits on the number of guns an individual can own. And yet, Honduras has the most gun violence in the world. Even though there are only 6.2 guns per 100 Hondurans (compared to 88 guns per 100 Americans), there are 68.43 gun murders per 100,000 Hondurans (compared to 3.2 gun murders per 100,000 Americans). In other words, on a per capita basis, Honduras has 21 times more gun murders than America, even though it has 14 times fewer guns.[7]

Of course, progressives don't just want you to believe there is an unusually large amount of murders in America. They want you to dwell on tragic mass shootings like those at Columbine and Newtown. These mass shootings, they tell us over and over again, are a uniquely American problem, a symptom of our "gun culture."

Wrong again.

An average of 10.56 people die each year in the United States in shootings where at least four people are killed. We can all agree that that's 10.56 people too many. But it happens to be less than the 11.8 people who are killed in mass shootings in an average year in Western Europe.[8]

Even more revealing for purposes of the gun rights debate is that time and again, Europe's mass shootings happen in places where civilians are prohibited from carrying guns. Let's take a look.

In Finland, the Firearms Act of 1998 requires anyone who wants a gun to request a license from the government. Almost no one can carry a loaded gun in public. That didn't stop Pekka-Eric Auvinen's shooting rampage in November 2007. The eighteen-year-old student walked into a school and murdered eight people. The scene at the school was eerily familiar to anyone who has seen coverage of American school shootings: students and teachers barricaded inside classrooms; innocent educators murdered execution style in front of the students they had, only minutes earlier, been teaching; the execution of people like the school nurse who dared to try to help innocent children. A year later, a gunman walked onto a Finnish college campus and murdered ten people. Both schools were utopian, gun-free zones. Auvinen's victims were unarmed.

In France, the government has banned semiautomatic rifles and basic-capacity magazines. It even limits the number of bullets you can buy in a year. But none of that stopped Richard Durn's shooting rampage in March 2002. He went to a town council meeting and killed eight town councillors in cold blood. The meeting was in a gun-free zone. Durn's victims were unarmed.

In Germany, those who wish to own a firearm are subject to

some of the toughest gun laws in the world. Those who want a gun "merely" for self-defense are not allowed to own a gun. Of the few who are allowed to own a gun, the vast majority of them are prohibited from carrying a gun. None of that stopped Tim Kretschmer's shooting rampage in March 2009. The seventeen-year-old started by murdering five students in a high school classroom. Each was shot in the head. He then murdered four students in another classroom and killed a teacher in a chemistry lab. To escape Kretchmer, students jumped from school windows. Before Kretschmer was finally cornered near a Volkswagen showroom, he killed two more teachers, a gardener, and a salesperson and customer at the showroom—for a tragic total of fifteen slain victims, as well as nine other innocent people shot and injured. When asked his motive, Kretschmer said, "For fun, because it is fun." The school was another utopian gun-free zone. Kretschmer's victims were unarmed.

In Britain, handguns are in effect illegal, and other guns are heavily regulated. Its gun control laws are even stricter than Germany's, but they didn't stop Derrick Bird's shooting spree in June 2010. The fifty-two-year-old cab driver murdered twelve people in less than four hours and injured another eleven. Among them was a woman walking home from a shopping trip, a mole catcher talking with a farmer in a field, and a retiree on his bicycle. Bird's attacks covered five different cities in the region of Cumbria, which is supposed to be a gun-free area. Bird's victims were unarmed.

In none of these tragedies did the killer use a semiautomatic rifle—the kind of gun that American liberals blame for mass killings in the United States. And in none of these tragedies were civilians legally permitted to carry guns. The gunmen's victims were defenseless—as were the fifteen members of a local parliament killed on September 27, 2001, in Zug, Switzerland; the four people killed by a railway worker on October 29, 2001, in Tours, France; the eighteen people killed at a high school on April 26, 2002, in Erfurt, Germany; the three people killed by a single person on February 19, 2002, in Freising, Germany; the seven people killed on a hillside on October 15, 2002, in Turin, Italy; the two people killed by a fired coworker on October 1, 2006, in Madrid, Spain; the eleven people killed by a former student on November 20, 2006, in Emsdetten, Germany; the seven people killed at a town meeting on September 18, 2008, in Naples, Italy; the ten people killed at a college on September 23, 2008, in Kauhajoki, Finland; the ten people injured by gunfire at a nursery school on March 19, 2009, in Lyon, France; the three people killed at a vocational college on April 10, 2009, in Athens, Greece; the three people killed at a café on April 11, 2009, in Rotterdam, Netherlands; the one person killed and sixteen injured at a Sikh temple on May 24, 2009, in Vienna, Austria; and the four people killed at a shopping mall on New Year's Eve, 2009, in Espoo, Finland.[9] Shall I continue, or have I made my point?

How can liberals like Michael Moore say with a straight face: "In Europe and Australia, most other free-world countries, they don't have . . . people who snap and go on murderous rampages?" It's a mind-numbingly ignorant remark offensive to the victims of evil mass murderers in other countries, because it means those victims are being forgotten—as if liberals think European lives don't mean as much as American lives.

Mass killings in Europe became harder for liberals to ignore after July 22, 2011. In one of the cruelest and most horrific series of killings the world has ever seen, Anders Behring Breivik, a lone-wolf political extremist, killed eight people with a car bomb and then opened fire on a summer camp for children in Norway. Armed with a rifle and a pistol, he killed sixty-nine innocent people at the camp for teenagers. Campers ran, swam, hid in caves, and begged for their lives. Local fishermen rescued fleeing swimmers from the freezing fjord. The executions lasted for an hour and a half and played out live throughout news media.

The shootings in Norway were deadlier than the Columbine, Aurora, and Newtown shootings combined.

Of course, every single innocent death is a tragedy of unimaginable proportions to everyone who loved and depended on the victim. Every single murder is an act of incredible evil, whether it is isolated or one of dozens. My point in describing Europe's horrors is not to minimize those of America's. Rather, my point is that mass killings are simply not a uniquely American problem. They don't "explain the very fabric of American society," and they do not reflect a "sick society." To the extent there is a sickness in our society, it is a sickness in every society, and its cause is not the Second Amendment. It is a moral deficiency. Evil is as old as Cain, and to the extent it can be combatted, the prescription must include something more profound than even the most well-meaning of legislation.

ANYTHING CAN BE MADE A WEAPON

Mass killings don't even require guns. In 2009, a man in Belgium used a knife and a hatchet at a day care to kill an adult and

188

two babies. The babies were nine months old. He also stabbed but fortunately failed to kill another adult and eleven babies. Similarly, in 2008, a Japanese man used a kitchen knife at an elementary school to kill eight children. And in China, between 2010 and 2012, there were at least ten instances of individuals attempting to use weapons other than guns to kill large numbers of children at schools and day cares. China has censored many of the details, often including the number of fatalities, but it's likely that more than 134 people—mainly children—were stabbed, slashed, and bludgeoned. In one instance, the attacker used a hammer. In another instance, he murdered seven kids and two adults with a cleaver. In still another attack, the killer murdered four adults and two children with an ax. One child was four years old. The other was only one.[10]

Not only is America far from unique in terms of having to endure tragic mass killings, we are also not unique in the way liberals respond to such massacres. Consider what happened in Britain after sixteen people were killed in a small town called Hungerford by a deranged gunman in 1987: Britain already had fairly strict limits on handguns. After the shootings in 1987, Britain extended its tight limits to shotguns, while banning semiautomatic rifles. It also banned magazines that held more than three bullets.

Did this gun control work? No. In 1996, a deranged gunman killed sixteen children and a teacher in a Scottish elementary school. So what did the British do? Did they realize that you can't eliminate evil by banning guns? No. Instead, they passed even more gun control. They virtually banned and confiscated handguns.

Did this gun-control-on-steroids work? Of course not. As

described above, a cab driver in Cumbria went on a shooting rampage in 2010. Moreover, crime with handguns doubled. The murder rate increased 64 percent—at a time when the murder rate in the United States was falling by 23 percent.

When you focus on just England and Wales, the numbers are even more staggering. According to Dr. John Lott, an economist and researcher who has worked at the University of Chicago, Yale University, the Wharton School, and the University of Maryland, "the number of deaths and injuries from gun crime in England and Wales increased an incredible 340 percent in the seven years from 1998 to 2005. The rates of serious violent crime, armed robberies, rapes, and homicides have soared."[11]

Unlike before the latest round of gun control, British police are now carrying guns, because they have to defend themselves against armed gangs in the streets. Gun crime skyrocketed because the criminals realized that they could rob and rape and kill anyone they wanted without concern that their victims would be equally able to defend themselves. The only people gun control "controlled" were law-abiding citizens, and it controlled them by disarming them and making it twice as likely they'd be assaulted.[12]

Is this what Piers Morgan means when he says that "gun control has worked very successfully in Britain"?[13] Sure, Britain has a relatively low murder rate. But it had that rate even before it passed its first gun law in 1920. Way back in 1904, London reported only two gun murders, even though it was a city of seven million people.[14]

Australia had a similar experience. In 1996, Martin Byrant murdered thirty-five people at a tourist site in Tasmania. Australia already had some of the most restrictive gun laws in the world—even tougher than Great Britain's. Nevertheless, Australia's government decided the solution was even more gun control: the 1996 National Firearms Agreement (NFA). It banned semiautomatic rifles and prohibited semiautomatic and pump-action shotguns. It made its strict licensing system for other guns even stricter. It even required Australians to sell thousands of guns to the government. In a single year, the Australian government spent $500 million buying 631,000 guns from civilians.[15]

Care to guess whether the amped-up gun control resulted in a major reduction in gun crime in Australia? It didn't. Assaults increased by 40 percent. Sexual assaults increased by 20 percent.

The best that can be said for Australia's murder rate is that it didn't go up. The Melbourne Institute of Applied Economic and Social Research at the University of Melbourne found that the gun buyback "did not have any large effects on reducing firearm homicide or suicide rates." A report published in the *British Journal of Criminology* concluded, "Homicide patterns (firearm and non-firearm) were not influenced by the NFA, the conclusion being that the gun buy-back and restrictive legislative changes had no influence on firearm homicide in Australia." The left-leaning Brookings Institution studied the crime in the country and found that a "modest decline" in murders began before the gun buyback and merely continued after it.[16] Other observers have seen a slight increase in murders, from about 240 per year in the period before the buyback to about 255 per year in the five years after the buyback.[17]

"According to [the Brookings] study," says Joyce Lee Malcolm, a law professor at George Mason University Law School, "the use of handguns rather than long guns (rifles and shotguns) went up sharply, but only one out of 117 gun homicides in the two years following the 1996 National Firearms Agreement used a registered gun. Suicides with firearms went down but suicides by other means went up. They reported 'a modest reduction in the severity' of massacres (four or more indiscriminate homicides) in the five years since the government weapons buyback. These involved knives, gas and arson rather than firearms."[18]

Britain and Australia aren't alone in failing to control crime by controlling guns. After Ireland imposed a handgun ban in the early 1970s, its murder rate more than tripled. And since Jamaica imposed a handgun ban around the same time, its murder rate has increased by nearly 600 percent. Its rate is now one of the world's worst, and it's twice as high as those of other Caribbean nations.[19]

Other countries have made different, wiser choices. Around the same time that Ireland and Jamaica were banning guns and seeing their murder rates begin to soar, Israel decided to let its citizens carry concealed handguns. "Up until the early 1970s," writes Dr. John Lott, "the Jewish state had to deal with the cold reality of terrorists who would take machine guns into shopping malls, schools, and synagogues and open fire. That type of attack doesn't occur anymore. Why? Israelis realized that armed citizens could stop such attackers before the attackers could shoot many people."

Here's what happened. "Prior to letting citizens carry concealed handguns, terrorist attacks in Israel were committed almost entirely with machine guns. Afterward, bombs were almost always used. The reason for the change was simple. Armed citizens can quickly immobilize a gun-wielding attacker, but no one can respond to a bomber once the bomb explodes. Nevertheless, armed citizens do still stop some bombings before they bombs go off." Today, 10 percent of Jewish Israeli adults have a license to carry a weapon.

Of course, you don't need to go all the way to Israel to see the protection that comes from arming law-abiding citizens. Would-be mass killers have been stopped by armed civilians before they could inflict further carnage at a Shoney's restaurant in Alabama in 1991; at Pearl High School in Mississippi in 1997; at a banquet hall in Pennsylvania in 1998; at the New Life megachurch in Colorado in 2007; at a bar in Nevada in 2008; and in a mall in Oregon in 2012. In each of those instances, a gunman appeared prepared to inflict upon his community another Columbine or Aurora or Newtown. But in each of those instances, an armed civilian stepped in sooner than the police could and saved countless lives.[20]

Some anti–Second Amendment advocates try to scare people by claiming that gun-carrying citizens who stop mass killers during a shooting spree are likely to accidentally shoot innocent bystanders. But Lott shows that "the evidence clearly demonstrates that in practice this is not a problem. Out of all the multiple-victim public shootings that have been stopped by permit holders, no one has identified a single such incident." Before the 1995 Safe School Zone Act prohibited concealed handguns, Lott could not find "a single instance when a permitted concealed handgun was improperly used at a school."[21]

In the past four decades, crime in the United States has been plummeting. At a time when we have more guns than ever, we have the lowest murder rate we've seen since the Kennedy administration. Pretty soon, countries in Western Europe that are seeing their crime rates rise will be looking to the United States and asking us what we're doing right.

When they do, we should tell them that there's no silver bullet to crime control. Tough sentencing laws help. More cops on the street help. But there's something else that is invaluable: the Second Amendment of the United States Constitution—because an armed society is a safer society.

Chapter 10

Reclaiming the Language

Every battle is won before it is fought.

—Sun Tzu

We can't have a real conversation on guns until people know what they're talking about. A clip isn't a magazine and there is no such thing as an "assault pistol" (I'm looking at you, Charles Blow from the *New York Times*). This chapter examines the most misused firearms terminology and answers the questions "What is an assault rifle?" and "Where did this term come from?"

One evening in the days following the Sandy Hook massacre I watched as one well-intentioned conservative went on Piers Morgan to defend gun owners who were zealously blamed for every massacre in American history, as is customary. Morgan was arguing with the conservative over "assault weapons." After Morgan used "assault weapon" a frillion times in the discussion the conservative relented to move the discussion along and adopted it, too, when answering in the affirmative that Adam Lanza used an "assault rifle." The debate was lost.

I'm not even sure the conservative in the debate could have

accurately or adequately explained what makes an "assault rifle" more assault-y than a regular rifle, in which case the conservative should either have excused himself from the debate or educated himself before forfeiting the debate.

The reason this conservative lost this particular gun debate—and the reason why the insipid "assault rifle/weapon" jargon continues to be the go-to phrase for clueless blowhards who know precisely nubbin about guns—is because they used their language.

The reason why other conservatives trip up is because they cede even the smallest definition, the smallest word or phrase, and give the left that bit of ground. To those not analyzing the semantics it may seem like nothing. To those who debate this issue day in and out, that's ground that we have to now recover. Determining the ground on which a battle takes place is the first step toward either victory or defeat.

The weeks following the Sandy Hook massacre offered a televised smorgasbord of noise featuring pundits, strategists, activists, all herded onto the media's terrain. I absolutely refused to be herded, as did others. When I appeared on CNN with Morgan we spent nearly five minutes—years in TV time—arguing over the term "assault rifle." There was no way in hell that I was going to lie about the characteristics of an inanimate object or redefine a term for the sake of getting along on national television. For three appearances after that we continued to argue about "assault rifles." During one such hit I even brought on camera with me a tiny AR-15 lighter (I thought Morgan would wince if I brought the real thing, even thousands of miles away in his Los Angeles studio and me in my St. Louis hot box). I demonstrated how select fire works. He finally, after weeks, reluctantly somewhat agreed that he was completely full of crap on the term. A few conservatives were annoyed with me. *Move on, already,* they sighed. *What's the big deal?* others asked.

The big deal is that we as conservatives don't get along to move along if that means compromising truth. If we're going to talk guns we'll do it on the terrain of truth, not the Dilly Bar raindrop land where so many talking head cases reside. I'm not going to accept a viewpoint based on perception and fueled by emotion as a fact, especially if it seeks to make me more vulnerable by removing from me my ability to choose my means of self-defense.

If you think Creed is a fabulous band and take no issue with Scott Stapp's grunting constipation vocals, it doesn't physically hurt me (much) to allow that viewpoint to stand uncontested. You loving Creed doesn't seek to remove from me a civil liberty in a world where civil liberties are becoming few and far between. You owning all of Creed's albums on both CD and MP3 isn't infringing upon my rights.

But you believing that a criminal may illegally and irresponsibly use a firearm against an innocent isn't a good enough argument to render the innocent without a firearm as a means of defense. You believing that I and others should be disarmed, and you actively pushing for your opinion to become policy and trump a civil liberty, ceases to be a case of "agreeing to disagree." It is a threat. The first step in battling anti–Second Amendment rhetoric is to not cede the language or accept an illegitimate turn of phrase.

IT'S NOT GUN CONTROL, IT'S ANTI–SECOND AMENDMENT ADVOCACY

I prefer not to call anti-Second Amendment advocates "gun grabbers" or "gun control advocates." Anti–Second Amendment advocates hate this about me and try to argue the point without success. Why do I prefer this term over the terms "gun grabbers," "gun control advocates," and the like?

Because those terms are misnomers. It betrays the true nature of the advocates' desire, which is an abridgment of the Second Amendment. If you are abridging a right, then you are curtailing that right, editing that right. If you abridge the Second Amendment you are doing two things:

Either way, an abridgment of a liberty means that a liberty no longer exists. People who advocate for gun control do not support the Second Amendment. The Second Amendment does not tell you to give the make and location of your firearm to a national registry. The Second Amendment does not force you to apply for permission from the state to carry your firearm. (Irony: One must go through more to obtain a CCW and protect life than to obtain an abortion and obliterate it.)

If you do not support the Second Amendment as it is written—it is, after all the law, as so many of our Democrat brethren like to say of the Affordable Care Act—then you do not support the Second Amendment. There is no gray area— this doesn't apply to criminals who choose to violate law and harm others thus endangering their own rights. I will not cede the recognition of my liberty for the courtesy of sugarcoating the stance of one who seeks to deprive me of that liberty. I will

not allow another party to begin a debate by using deceptive terminology.

Make them own it from the beginning. They clearly have a
problem with the Second Amendment, so don't hide it by using
superfluous language like "gun grabber." They don't want to grab
your guns; that term is too cutesy. They want to disarm you and
make you play Russian roulette with your safety and the safety
of your family. They want to make your limbs your only defense
against a gun-wielding rapist as you walk to you car at night. Be
concrete about who these people are and what they want.

WHISKEY TANGO FOXTROT IS AN "ASSAULT WEAPON"?

Once, while battling gun-genius-because-his-brother-served-
in-the-military Piers Morgan (the same man sacked by the
Daily Mirror for publishing Photoshopped photos of British soldiers abusing an Iraqi prisoner, thereby endangering their lives),
I made the remark that anything could be an "assault weapon,
even a spoon." The left howled with delight. An assault spoon!
How utterly ridiculous! Except that it has happened: Thirty-
four-year-old Travis Tulley was charged over allegedly stabbing
his father with a spoon in Salt Lake City. In 2011 a fellow was
charged with stabbing his grandmother with a spoon in Australia.

These cases do exist, but it's all irrelevant. Anything can be
used as a tool with which to assault someone. The lack of lis-
tening comprehension by some anti–Second Amendment advocates classifies as an "assault weapon" all by itself. It doesn't
matter the instrument, it does matter the intent. Anti–Second

Amendment advocates like to use make-believe terms to describe guns that are black and look scary. If a rifle doesn't look like the one Elmer Fudd carries, if it's black and has complicated-looking stuff stuck on it, it's probably "shootier," according to anti-2A reasoning, so it must be banned.

According to the FBI's Uniform Crime Reports, more violence is perpetuated with illegally obtained and illegally used handguns than rifles, but because rifles can look scarier, anti-2A advocates focus specifically on those. They say "assault weapon," because they can't identify what type of rifle it is or what it shoots. "Assault weapon" is a blanket term for "gun."

Bottom line: I don't use firearm illiterate, cutesy terms like "assault weapon" when describing my .22 or any other rifle I own. Challenge the anti-2A advocates to grow up and learn about the items they want to ban.

CIVIL LIBERTIES, NOT CIVIL RIGHTS

The freedom to keep and bear arms isn't a a right granted by the government. It is a reminder and a warning that the people have freedom from government intrusion. People, by way of being law-abiding citizens, have the inalienable right to use the same means to defend themselves as allowed by the security forces which they fund for their protection. What separates the citizen from the police? From the military? If you answer "training," your argument presupposes that law-abiding citizens who purchase firearms receive no training and desire no greater skill. This couldn't be further from the truth. Yours truly participates in tactical courses and hones her marksmanship regularly. One of my favorite exercises is to clear out a house where my objective is to protect my principal while eliminating threats room by room. It's a timed exercise, and if I fail to complete it in time or miss my mark, my principal is compromised. During such an exercise I'm not worried about my grouping. The purpose is, in the words of my friend and Green Beret Grady Powell, star of National Geographic's *Ultimate Survival Alaska* (and instructor at Asymmetric Solutions in Farmington, Missouri), to "make a mess for the medic and make it interesting for the morgue."

When I practice my marksmanship and learn to handle a new firearm I'll head to the range—Top Gun, if I'm in St. Louis. Not long ago we took a group of thirty or so friends, all of whom were new gun owners or looking to obtain their concealed-carry. Law-abiding gun owners are eager to learn. They want to know how to best improve their aim, not fronting like a doucher throwing bullets from a gun as so often depicted on TV. After you learn the basics, it's easy to tell who's legit and who's a poseur when it comes to handling firearms.

No one wants to be a poseur. Sadly, those who seek to abridge our Second Amendment liberty are incapable of such shame. They are the most uneducated and blatantly ignorant people on the subject yet pretend to know the most because they looked online for a couple of stats pulled from *Daily Kos* while pausing their reality TV show on housewives. Do not allow this basic level of cerebral silicone defeat you in an argument because you allowed them to redefine terms and frame the debate with false arguments and equivalences.

PEOPLE WHO SEEK TO DEPRIVE YOU OF A RIGHT DO NOT MERIT COURTESY

I can disagree and still get along on most issues, but when faced with the incessant clucking from someone who seeks to disenfranchise me of my civil rights, Katy bar the door. "Courtesy" is not synonymous with "civility." Courtesy implies respect. I do not respect the opinion of someone who does not respect my civil liberty of self-defense. My civil liberties are not up for their attempt at debate. A liberty trumps a right trumps their feelings. Feelings can be restored. Liberties, once fallen to lack of recognition, are never recovered.

There are times I've received a small bit of criticism when I am on television opposite a progressive strategist who also doubles as an anti–Second Amendment advocate, because I will interrupt them midsentence the moment they attempt to frame a debate with idiocy. Allow me to defend myself: It is a rare thing that occurs only when the person against whom I am debating has such a lack of respect for me, the viewing audience, and for the topic that they consider outright lies or uninformed opinion to serve as fact. Presenting false information researched for you by a producer is an affront to the viewing audience as much as it is to the people with whom one is debating. It is discourteous and will be met with equal discourtesy in the form of me interrupting them as often as necessary. I am civil. I do not raise my voice. I do not substitute vulgarity or name calling for wit and fact. However, I will absolutely interrupt and railroad misleading opposition with substantive fact until they drive on up out of the ditch and back onto the pavement of reality.

I spoke with a young woman activist at CPAC one year who

confided that this part of the debate always made her nervous. She didn't want to be viewed as "mean" because she corrected someone midsentence.

"No," I told her. "You're the one actually speaking up for yourself and your audience for the offense of lying about a premise. If someone wants to discuss offenses with you, explain to them cause and effect."

These are our rights and liberties we're discussing. If you won't get angry and insist on accuracy while less informed people talk about limiting your freedom, when will you get angry? After they're gone? That's too late for me.

THEY, NOT YOU, ARE THE EXTREMISTS

At some point during the gun control debate exercising your Second Amendment liberty became "extreme." "Pro-gun extremists" was the term bandied about on left-leaning websites and in the talking points of gun control lobbyists on MSNBC. Never has it been said that those who think a free speech is one without restrictions are also "extremists"; no one is told that if they assemble too much, or practice too free a press, that they are "extremists." Somehow, that distinction is only applicable to firearms. Pro–Second Amendment, law-abiding gun owners are not the fringe, the minority, or the exception; they are the rule in the country.

Support for the Second Amendment has never dissipated. The harsh reaction in Colorado to anti-gun legislation and the thousands who refused to register their firearms in Connecticut, among other examples, have proven that. Those who dispute such liberty are best defined as the fringe, the extremists who think it taboo for women to defend themselves with a firearm if attacked for fear of harming the attacker, those who put their full faith and trust for their family's security in the state. These people are the extremists. Public opinion is on our side, despite the best effort of anti-gun lobbyist push polls, which is why gun control lobbyists are trying so desperately to change this with the perception of momentum with groups like Moms Demand Action. It's time to label their motives for what they are and accurately call out the fringe. They are anti–Second Amendment, gun control extremists. They've earned the title, so make it stick.

IT'S "TO KEEP AND TO BEAR," THANKS

The Second Amendment doesn't just guarantee our right to possess arms; it guarantees our right to bear them, to carry them on our person and in our vehicles, too. The Founders didn't suggest and the Constitution doesn't say, "You have the right to bear arms and keep them only in the privacy of your own home as deemed appropriate by your government." The Founders were drafting a document in the wake of challenging the British crown and the crown's attempt to retain the colonies as an unrepresented part of the kingdom would have been made possible by a disarmed populace. That brings us to the other part of the Second Amendment:

A well regulated Militia, being necessary to the security of a free State, the right of the people to keep and bear Arms, shall not be infringed.

It isn't a happy accident that an elective, citizen organization of armed, nonmilitary participants leads this amendment. Progressives cringe at the word and have at every opportunity sought to disparage it and poison the well with the idea that militia members are extremists. By saying that militias are extreme, progressives are casting their lots against the Founders. The very idea of government regulation neutralizes the ability of a free citizen to form a militia against the same government that has turned to tyranny over liberty. A militia is a check and balance. A "well regulated militia" is a militia comprised of free men and women who have refined a level of preparedness and are ready to act to preserve their free state. Regulation, if viewing earlier drafts of the Second Amendment and Alexander Hamilton's *Federalist* 29, from which our Bill of Rights originated, is not an explanation or invitation of government intrusion by way of oversight.

This is a liberty inherent to American citizens that was not formed by the state, or granted, given, or gifted to the citizen. It is a liberty with which they are born, the privilege of free citizens belonging to a free state. Free men and women do not ask for permission. Free men and women do not carry a plastic, government-issued permission slip to carry what they are already allowed to carry. Free women do not seek the state's blessing on their right to defend themselves from rapists. Free men do not seek the state's approval to protect themselves and their families. A free, law-abiding, educated people do not acquiesce to a group of overinflated, undereducated bureaucrats who believe the color black makes guns shootier.

Government has no say in the discussion—at least, it's not supposed to have one, yet it tries to insert itself into the equation by installing itself as the arbitrator. Sure, you can have your right, but first we have to conduct a background check. Yes, the government, where more crimes are committed every day in the name of bureaucracy (what they view as "liberty") than just about anywhere else. They conduct a background check as a means to catch criminals who don't submit to background checks. Sure, you can have your right, but first we must issue you a license. Adorable! Free men don't have to ask the government's permission to carry the guns they are afforded to carry by their Constitution. Sure, you can carry that handgun, but you have to conceal it behind cloth, oh, and you have to get a license to do that.

My only disappointment upon moving to Texas was discovering the absolutely *heinous* state of their gun laws. Vermont has more freedom than Texans do when it concerns bearing arms. I can open-carry my rifle in Texas without hassle; I can't open-carry my handgun, but I can carry concealed, so long as I submit to a more-rigorous-than-Missouri's CCW course and get a piece of laminate that says the government allows it. The idea of my husband, who range-bosses for fun, or myself, who is an avid shooter, having to take beginner handgun courses, and pay to do so, just to carry is ludicrous.

All of these are infringements upon our Second Amendment civil liberties.

YELLING "FIRE!" IN A CROWDED THEATER

I hear this argument ad nauseum from the uninformed as a way to negate the liberties of a law-abiding American. Never accept this phrase even in passing. It's simply historically ignorant to use in this context. The phrase was part of a judicial ruling with an opinion by Oliver Wendell Holmes from *Schenck v. United States*, in which he famously concluded:

> *The most stringent protection of free speech would not protect a man in falsely shouting fire in a theater and causing a panic. [...] The question in every case is whether the words are used in such circumstances and are of such a nature as to create a clear and present danger that they will bring about the substantive evils that Congress has a right to prevent. It is a question of proximity and degree. When a nation is at war, many things that might be said in time of peace are such a hindrance to its effort that their utterance will not be endured so long as men fight, and that no Court could regard them as protected by any constitutional right.*

And to what was this opinion in response? A socialist named Charles Schneck was outspoken in his opposition to the draft during World War I and passed out leaflets to draft-aged men to encourage them to refuse to serve. Note that last line:

"It is a question of proximity and degree. when a nation is at war, many things that might be said in time of peace [...] will not be endured so long as men fight."

Speech which may harm the nation's fortune in the war won't be tolerated as it would be during times of peace. It was situational. Furthermore, you can still yell "fire" in a crowded theater. You can still "carry" your words. Any language said with the intention to harm, language which proves libelous, slanderous, or injurious to a party is punishable, but you don't lose your right to speak it.

Using this analogy, anti–Second Amendment advocates are suggesting that the mere ownership of a firearm presents intent to harm. Anti–Second Amendment advocates invalidate their own argument by citing this phrasing. Irresponsibly using a firearm with malicious intent is the only action remotely analogous to yelling "fire" in a crowded theater. Yelling "fire" to protect yourself and others in the event of a real fire is constitutionally protected. Using a firearm to defend the lives of yourself or another is protected. Yelling "fire" to have someone trampled and cause injury, and using a firearm to cause injury where there is no need for defense, is not protected. By citing this phrase, anti–Second Amendment advocates are stating that the intent to harm is standard, yet we know for fact that purchasing a firearm is not a confession of future malicious action, especially as more lives are saved than not (which we will later explore) with firearms. By attempting to analogize this phrase, anti–Second Amendment advocates are also inadvertently suggesting that perhaps the First Amendment be subjected to the same regulation and oversight which they're demanding for the Second.

WE ARE TRULY PRO-CHOICE

Progressives like to say that they're "pro-choice" for lots of things—abortion, for instance—but pro-choice isn't so much support for many choices as it is agreement with their belief, their choice. I like to give that phrase new meaning when discussing my choice of self-defense. There are many choices when it comes to self-defense. Revolver or semiauto? Which Glock?

Shotgun or .22? There are so many choices. I'm for all of these choices, which means that I am for a woman's right to choose her manner of self-defense. Anti–Second Amendment advocates argue that because violent criminals have black market access to firearms, law-abiding innocents should not. They argue that because rapists and murderers may illegally possess firearms the law-abiding, innocent women and men should not carry them. They don't defend your constitutionally protected choice and instead better enable the choice of a criminal to make you a statistic. They want to be able to have a choice as to what to do after you've been raped but want to restrict your choices of how to prevent your rape. As Colorado lawmakers Joe Salazar and Paul Rosenthal said, maybe use a rape whistle to hurt your attacker's ears or employ the buddy system. The University of Colorado released the helpful suggestion of further enabling your prospective attacker's lust for power through rape by encouraging women to urinate on themselves to ward off attacks. These are the so-called choices that anti–Second Amendment advocates want to leave women.

THE UNITED STATES LEADS THE WORLD IN GUN DEATHS DUE TO ITS GUN CULTURE

Misleading. Graham Noble observed in the parts of the United States with the strictest anti-gun laws: "If one were to exclude figures for Illinois, California, New Jersey and Washington, DC, the homicide rate in the United States would be in line with any other country."[1] The study was based upon a detailed map created by Zara Matheson of the Martin Prosperity Institute, and it compared the rate of violence from illegally used firearms in major cities to those of foreign countries.

THE "STAND YOUR GROUND" ILLOGIC

In the wake of the Trayvon Martin shooting—which was not a Stand Your Ground case, as the defense was never used in court—this manner of self-defense came under fire. One newspaper in Virginia led with the headline "How 'Stand Your Ground' Is Killing Black People."[2] Because Zimmerman claimed self-defense and didn't invoke SYG during defense, suddenly it's an indictment of a law that wasn't cited in a case, because we are dealing with emotionally charged anti–Second Amendment advocates. Progressives are now arguing for the repeal of a law which disproportionately protects black Americans, especially in Florida, where it has successfully been used in the defense of black Floridians at a rate of 55 percent. According to the *Tampa Bay Times*, SYG claims constitute one-third of the defenses in cases with a fatality—fatalities of predominately white victims. The newspaper calls its interactive way to search SYG cases online "the most comprehensive list of 'stand your ground' cases ever created."[3]

It begs the question that the disenfranchisement of an individual's ability to stand their ground in case of attack would see a much higher conviction rate in the black community. Progressives have discovered a way to walk back gun liberties for black Americans not seen since Southern Democrats attempted to disarm free black men and women during Reconstruction. In "The Second Amendment: Toward an Afro-

Americanist Reconsideration," Robert Cottrol and Raymond Diamond write:

> *The Ohio Supreme Court in 1920 construed the state's constitutional right of the people "to bear arms for their defense and security" not to forbid a statute outlawing the carrying of a concealed weapon. In so doing, the court followed the lead of sister courts in Alabama, Arkansas, Georgia, and Kentucky, over the objections of a dissenting judge who recognized that "the race issue [in Southern states] has intensified a decisive purpose to entirely disarm the negro, and this policy is evident upon reading the opinions."[4]*

Black codes during Reconstruction was a de facto way to perpetuate slavery. It has been described as "the Klan's favorite law":

> *After the Civil War, the defeated Southern states aimed to preserve slavery in fact if not in law. The states enacted Black Codes which barred the black freedmen from exercising basic civil rights, including the right to bear arms. Mississippi's provision was typical: No freedman "shall keep or carry firearms of any kind, or any ammunition."[5]*

As we explored earlier, Democrats largely opposed free black Americans possessing firearms, because it was much easier to control and intimidate them when their defenses were unequal to what white Americans were allowed. Stand Your Ground isn't a law for black Americans; it's a law used in certain states that exonerates black Americans from unfair convictions and subsequent incarceration.

MORE GUNS EQUALS MORE SAFETY, INCREASED DEFENSE, NOT MORE CRIME

I look at guns as tools of defense. Anti–Second Amendment advocates look at them as tools of murder. Therein lies the difference: their projection.

The Second Amendment advocate would argue from the statistical perspective that more guns in fact decrease crimes. This isn't an illogical argument to make, but it is a clumsy one. First it begins with the presupposition that firearm ownership is predicated on whether or not gun ownership makes for a safer society. It's irrelevant and a distraction from the real debate. First, a free society is a double-edged sword. People make good decisions with freedom and bad decisions with freedom. It's a drawback of freedom, if there is to be a drawback.

Thomas Jefferson once observed in a letter to his friend Archibald Stuart that he would "rather be exposed to the inconveniences attending too much liberty than to those attending too small a degree of it." I agree. With this freedom comes the expectation that sometimes people make bad choices and we are free to react to those choices. There are many things which endanger society: drunk driving (which takes more lives than firearms), prescription drug abuse, and so forth, but alcohol is still legal, driving cars is still a legal activity, and prescription drugs are still available. Yes, the more law-abiding citizens who own guns reinforces the statistically true trope "an armed society is a polite society," but that's not the litmus test for why we have them. We have them because they are liberties. Focusing on this argument only criminalizes inanimate objects rather than the motivation with which they are used.

IT'S THE LAW. PERIOD.

After the passage of Obamacare we heard ad infinitum that the Affordable Care Act was "the law, period." Whenever anyone was to criticize the incessant delays, the numerous waivers, the bungled website, or in any manner objected to its passage, the criticism were met with *"It's the law. Period"*—even by our own president.

Well, guess what? We have other laws. And one of those other laws is the right of the people to keep and bear arms.

It's the law, period.

BUT REAGAN SUPPORTED THE BRADY BILL

Progressives like to bring out Ronald Reagan, *Weekend at Bernie's* style, as a trump card to shut down conservative debate. If Reagan believed something, that nullifies your ability to disagree, they argue. Try as I might, I've been unable to find mention of a second, infallible god in Scripture, one who was born in California and never made any mistakes such as nominating Sandra Day O'Connor to the bench, amnesty, or supporting an abridgment on Second Amendment rights. Reagan wasn't perfect, but he's a hell of a lot better than anyone the Democrats have got. When anti–Second Amendment advocates point out that Reagan supported the Brady Bill, my response is "So?"

Ronald Reagan's support for the Brady Bill was obviously driven by his great sympathy for Jim and Sarah Brady personally after the 1981 assassination attempt that almost cost the president his life. Brady, Reagan's press secretary, was standing in the line of fire when John Hinckley fired—and he suffered irreversible brain damage as a result. In other words, Reagan clearly knew and believed that the Bradys' lives were changed forever simply because Jim Brady had chosen to work for him. Maybe Reagan would have always supported the elements of the Brady Bill, but that seems unlikely.

Reagan's 1991 *New York Times* op-ed focused on handguns and states' rights in determining background checks, as opposed to focusing on all firearms and a massive federal authority overseeing gun rights. Reagan specifically gave preference to states' rights:

> *While the Brady bill would not apply to states that already have waiting periods of at least seven days or that already require background checks, it would automatically cover the states that don't.*[6]

Still, I disagree, especially considering that our federal government barely prosecutes cases of submitted false information on Form 4473s:

> *Jim Baker, the NRA representative…recalled the vice president's words during an interview with the* Daily Caller: *"And to your point, Mr. Baker, regarding the lack of prosecutions on lying on Form 4473s, we simply don't have the time or manpower to prosecute everybody who lies on a form, that checks a wrong box, that answers a question inaccurately."*[7]

Criminals intent on malicious activity will not be deterred by a background check. John Hinckley, Reagan's would-be assassin, was insane, or so his lawyers argued. An insane person will find a way to get a gun, background check or no. They'll simply go around it, just as they do now. And just like Sarah Brady herself apparently did. As the New York *Daily News* reported in 2002, Mrs. Brady may have "skirted" Delaware background check requirements in buying a rifle for her son, James Brady Jr. Mrs. Brady wrote about the gun purchase in her memoir, "I can't describe how I felt when I picked up that rifle, loaded it into my little car and drove home," she writes. "It seemed so incredibly strange: Sarah Brady, of all people, packing heat."

It is a poor argument to say that because a criminal may illegally obtain and use a firearm against an innocent, an innocent should be restricted from legally obtaining and using a firearm in their own defense. As president, Reagan had security to jump in front of him and carry firearms to protect him, whereas average Americans do not. Do not be foolish and interpret my remarks as being those from someone who dislikes President Reagan; to the contrary. He's one of the best presidents we've had, but he was a man, like all presidents are, and not infallible. Furthermore, unlike progressives, conservatives don't believe in hive mind. We're all right with not agreeing on 20 percent of things, so long as we accomplish the 80 percent. If progressives want to seize upon something in which Reagan believed, I'm all for it. Let's help them by starting with his economic policy or stance on nationalized health care. Their fascination with Reagan will disappear as quickly as it surfaced.

NOT NUTS, JUST EVIL

There is a difference between being mentally ill and being evil. People with mental problems aren't bad people, and it's unfair to those who struggle with mental illness to attribute every crime committed as a result of mental illness, as was done with the Santa Barbara murderer, Elliot Rodger. Some people, like Rodger, who opened fire on passersby from his parent-provided black Mercedes, are just evil. Evil exists in this world. It's real. We risk our own safety by pretending it's only a symptom of mental illness and conflating the two. This isn't to say that one cannot exacerbate the other—it can—but too often society seeks to absolve evil from responsibility by blaming it on something beyond evil's control. Mental illness doesn't necessarily mean an inability to distinguish right from wrong.

Chapter 11

The Fourteen Biggest Anti-Gun Lies, Debunked

It's not a lie if you believe it.
—George Costanza, *Seinfeld*

The scientific theory holds that you fit the theory to the facts, but it's applied backward in the world of gun control advocates. They modify or omit the facts to fit the theory.

My own personal experience from the past five years is that those who want to abridge our Second Amendment civil liberties know the least about firearms. For example, they want to ban so-called assault weapons, but they can't explain why a semiautomatic rifle is an assault weapon when a semiautomatic pistol isn't. In most cases, they've never seen the gun they want to ban. It's a case of having more zeal than knowledge, and when knowledge fails, gun grabbers will fabricate bizarre arguments to support their positions.

Piers Morgan appeared on my radio program at the height of our gun fight, shortly after he said of my defense of the Second Amendment, "It makes me sick." (I had flatly refused to appear on his program anymore until he appeared on mine.) I asked him why he consistently ignored cases like Virginia Tech, where the criminal carried two pistols.

"That happened before I had my show on CNN," he replied.

"So did Columbine," I later remarked, "but you cite that on your program."

Morgan omits Virginia Tech because the criminal didn't use an assault rifle. Though more crimes are committed with handguns, gun grabbers spend most of their energy trying to ban certain kinds of rifles. I almost don't want to educate grabbers on pistols for fear that they will try to regulate those, too.

In this chapter I take the gun grabbers' biggest lies and expose them, one by one.

LIE #1: Guns are only tools of murder.
FACT: Guns are tools of defense.

Fifty-seven-year-old Donna Jackson was alone in her home shortly after midnight when a patio table came flying through her sliding glass door. The stranger who threw it was determined to break into her house, and although Jackson could not be sure of his intentions, she knew they couldn't be good. The police were on their way, but they wouldn't get there in time to protect her. Instead, the only thing between her and the frightening intruder was the sixteen-gauge shotgun in her hands. She pulled the trigger, and with a single blast her nightmare ended, as did the life of her attacker and his long career of crime.

Donna Jackson's story is far from unique. Every year, as many as 250,000 women use a firearm to defend themselves from abuse or a sexual attack.[1] In 2011, sixty-six-year-old

Donna Hopper shot a career criminal who attempted to break into her home through her bedroom window at four o'clock in the morning.[2] In Oklahoma, a twelve-year-old girl who was home alone hid in a closet with the family gun and scared off an intruder by firing through the door.[3] A mother in Alabama used a gun to defend herself and her two young daughters from a home invader.[4]

Gun crime makes the headlines, but although it is far less reported in the media, armed self-defense—like the stories of people like Donna Jackson and Donna Hopper—is far more common. Celebrated criminologist Dr. Gary Kleck, a professor of criminology and criminal justice at Florida State University (and a self-described lifelong Democrat and member of the ACLU) discovered in 1993 that there were 2.5 million cases of guns used for self-defense annually, compared to 0.5 million gun crimes.[5] (The number of gun crimes has significantly decreased since then.) In other words, firearms were used five times more often to defend against crimes than to commit crimes. Far from being "instruments of murder," firearms are tools of defense, and while gun control advocates argue that the tools can amplify evil intent, they ignore that guns amplify good intent and, as studies have shown, do so at a dramatically higher rate.

Kleck's work has weathered attacks from critics and has been vigorously defended by his contemporaries, even those who are staunchly anti-gun, such as fellow criminologist Marvin Wolfgang. He said Kleck provided "an almost clear-cut case of methodologically sound research in support of something I have theoretically opposed for years, namely, the use of a gun in defense against a criminal perpetrator."[6]

More recently, President Obama commissioned the Centers for Disease Control to study the effects of gun control, hoping for an outcome that would support Democrats' push to restrict Second Amendment liberties. When the results came in, however, the President was sorely disappointed.[7] According to the CDC, defensive gun use by crime victims ranges from 0.5 million to 3 million instances per year, and it is at least as common as instances of offensive use, which now peak at about 0.3 million per year. The report also found that 61% of firearm-related deaths are from suicide, not gun crime, and accidental gun deaths account for less than 1% of unintentional fatalities.

LIE #2: Gun control means crime control.
FACT: An armed society is a safer society.

The next time a gun grabber tells you that gun control reduces crime, tell him there's an old saying: You're entitled to your own opinion, but not your own facts.

If the gun grabbers' facts matched their theory, Russia would have much less crime than Finland, because Russia has far fewer guns. Instead, while the rate of gun ownership in Russia is about ten times lower than in Finland, the murder rate in Russia in about ten times higher than in Finland. The rate of gun ownership is more than thirty times lower in Luxembourg than in Germany, but the murder rate in Luxembourg is ten times higher than in Germany.[8]

The fact is this: Study after study has found no link between gun control and crime control. For example, a 2007 article in Harvard Law School's *Journal of Law and Public Policy* titled

"Would Banning Firearms Reduce Murder and Suicide?" concluded that the "assertion that...guns are uniquely available in the United States compared with other modern developed nations" is "false," as is the assertion that "the United States has by far the highest murder rate." Russia's murder rate, for example, is about four times higher than the murder rate in the Unites States, even though gun ownership is far less common in Russia.

Even when U.S. states are compared to one another, the evidence is clear that an armed society is a safer society. It's been clear since at least the early 1990s that crime plummets when states pass laws allowing citizens to carry concealed weapons. As early as 1992, the FBI Uniform Crime Reports showed that states with the most restrictive laws on concealed-carry for self-defense have the highest overall violent crime rates.

Similar results were found in a University of Chicago study from 1996 (highlighted in my friend John R. Lott Jr.'s book *More Guns, Less Crime: Understanding Crime and Gun-Control Laws*). It demonstrated how states that passed concealed-carry laws saw their murder rates drop by over 8 percent, their assault rates drop by 7 percent, and their rate of sexual attacks drop by 5 percent. The study concluded that "allowing citizens to carry concealed weapons deters violent crimes, without increasing accidental deaths. If those states without right-to-carry concealed gun provisions had adopted them in 1992, county- and state-level data indicate that approximately 1,500 murders would have been avoided yearly."[9] The study also found that "rapes would have declined by over 4,000, robbery by over 11,000, and aggravated assaults by over 60,000." According to Lott, "States that adopt right-to-carry laws experience a 60% drop in the rates at which the attacks occur, and a 78% drop in the rates at which people are killed or injured from such attacks."[10]

These statistics shouldn't be surprising. When a state restricts gun ownership and prohibits citizens from carrying concealed weapons, it makes itself a target for crime by guaranteeing criminals that their victims won't be able to fight back. In contrast, when a state allows law-abiding citizens to carry guns, criminals must think twice before they choose to prey on those citizens.

LIE #3: The United States has more guns and thus more gun crime than Britain and Australia.
FACT: Handgun crime has doubled in Britain since its ban, and assaults in Australia increased by 40 percent after its gun control laws were passed.

On a late-spring morning in 2010, a lone gunman went on a shooting rampage. He started by murdering his twin brother and his family's lawyer, then went on to kill ten more innocent people in six small towns before the morning was over. The shooter's name was Derrick Bird, and his mass murders took place in a country where such tragedies cannot take place: Great Britain.

According to the gun grabbers' theory, massacres like the shootings in Newtown and Tucson wouldn't have happened if the United States had gun control like Britain does. But Bird's rampage shows that the facts, once again, don't fit the gun grabbers' theory. In Britain, handguns and semiautomatic weapons are banned, but that didn't stop Derrick Bird from killing twelve people with a shotgun and a bolt-action rifle.

Gun control in Great Britain has not reduced crime. After the country banned handguns in 1998, crime with handguns doubled.[11] According to Joyce Lee Malcolm, a law professor who wrote a book called *Guns and Violence: The English Experience*, "gun crime, not a serious problem in the past, now is."

The results of Australia's gun control are also unhelpful to gun grabbers' theory. After Australia in 1996 banned semiautomatic rifles and certain shotguns, put strict limits on other guns, and required citizens to sell back hundreds of thousands of guns, sexual assaults increased by 20 percent, and other assaults increased by 40 percent. Moreover, while there was a modest decline in gun homicides; the decline had begun years before the new gun regulations.[12]

In short, the two countries that anti–Second Amendment advocates cite as shining examples of gun control have produced no evidence of a link between gun control and crime control.

LIE #4: Gun crime would be lower in Anytown, USA, if neighboring states had stricter gun laws.
FACT: It is already illegal to purchase a gun if you aren't legally allowed to carry it in your home state.

In many big cities with high crime rates, gun control is strict. Not to be deterred, gun grabbers blame the crime on the lack of gun control in neighboring states. Of course, they have little to no proof for their theory.

In order to purchase a firearm, you must be legally able to carry it in your state.[13] The problem, as usual, is not the lack of laws but the refusal of criminals to follow the laws. Just as criminals don't comply with gun-free zones, so will they also refuse to comply with the laws that regulate firearm sales in other states. Progressives tend to believe that just having a gun is tantamount to immorality, that it tempts gun owners to do wicked things, that a innocent can be corrupted simply by an inanimate object. Real life isn't *Lord of the Rings*. A gun in a community doesn't taint the community. A lack of respect for life and a broken familial unit will.

Moreover, gun grabbers inadvertently do you the courtesy of defeating their entire argument for gun control by deploying this myth. If it were true, the crime rate in the areas where said guns are purchased would be astronomically higher than Anytown, USA, because they freely allow the sale of the guns Anytown bans. Grabbers readily admit that Anytown—in this case, let's say Chicago—has a high crime rate, yet blame the crime on neighboring states like Indiana, with little to no proof. Indiana could ban guns, but that won't stop gun crime in Chicago.

LIE #5: The AR-15 is a "military-style assault rifle."
FACT: No, it isn't.

First off, what in the hell is "military-style"? It's a ridiculous adjective created by city mice who think a paint job on a gun can make it shoot magic bullets. Black or camouflage equals scary. If you affix little gadgets and doodads like scopes, lasers, pistol grips, or flash suppressors to a gun, they freak out even more because, OMG SCARIER. Indeed, this was the entire premise behind the 1994 Federal Assault Weapons Ban, which did nothing but limit the number of things one could slap onto a rifle. It's like regulating the flair on a T.G.I. Friday's vest. The rifle itself was legal, but add three or more gadgets to it and suddenly it was a ticking time bomb. One of my kids has a BB gun that, to the uneducated, looks just like an AR-15. I suppose it would qualify as "military style" under the progressive definition, regardless of its capability.

Moreover, the AR-15 is a semiautomatic rifle. That means that only one bullet fires every time the trigger is pulled, and the next bullet can be fired with another pull of the trigger. A semiautomatic rifle is distinct from an automatic rifle, which fires multiple bullets while the trigger is pulled. It is also distinct from a bolt-action rifle, which requires the user to open and close the barrel of the rifle with a small handle in between every shot.

The distinction between semiautomatic and automatic is important. Automatic rifles are machine guns, were developed for the battlefield, and have been regulated by federal law for almost a century. In contrast, semiautomatic rifles are not machine guns, were not developed for the battlefield, and are in widespread use by law-abiding Americans. Most pistols are semiautomatic, and about 40 percent of rifles are semiautomatic.[14] For the purposes of public policy, there is no principled distinction between semiautomatic rifles and other kinds of legal rifles and handguns.

In reality, the AR-15 began as the civilian version of the M16. It's a lightweight, easy-to-fire rifle, and it's the weapon of choice for many women who want an easily manageable firearm for home defense when an intruder breaks into their home. It's also a favorite rifle amongst marksmen at shooting competitions.

LIE #6: *AR-15s are like machine guns capable of firing hundreds of rounds a minute.*
FACT: *This is a superexaggerated claim.*

AR-15s fire forty-five rounds per minute with lower accuracy, around fifteen max for sustained fire. Furthermore, if fired too fast, they overheat and can jam. I've had my own AR-15 jam on me before at the range, and CNN reported that the "rifle used in the Colorado theater killings jammed during the rampage."[15] (The shooter there also used a shotgun and .40-caliber pistol, but the rifle is the only firearm targeted by anti–Second Amendment advocates who want to punish law-abiding Americans for the deeds of criminals.)

LIE #7: *High-capacity magazine clips are dangerous and should be regulated.*
FACT: *What is a "magazine clip"?*

Here's a tip for gun grabbers: Learn the difference between a "clip" and a "magazine" before insisting that either of these completely different inanimate objects is dangerous.

Even if gun grabbers could get their terminology straight, their argument wouldn't make much sense. A ban on what they call "high-capacity magazines"—which are actually standard-capacity magazines—would serve no purpose, because anyone with remedial shop knowledge can fabricate one in his or her garage. Moreover, you can change a magazine in seconds. If you put limits on the number of rounds allowed in a magazine, criminals will just buy multiple magazines. Among all the misguided regulations proposed by gun advocates, it is hard to imagine one that is easier for criminals to bypass.

LIE #8: *We don't have laws in place to address gun ownership and mental illness.*
FACT: *Yes, we do.*

Laws prohibit mentally defective people from owning a gun, but the responsible authorities have to follow the laws for them to work. Take, for example, the tragic shootings in Tucson by Jared Lee Loughner in January 2011.

Loughner had recently been a student at Pima Community College. Officials there observed bizarre behavior by Loughner that terrified students and teachers. In February 2010, he asked in a poetry class, "Why don't we just strap bombs to babies?" In May, his behavior was so worrisome that a teacher asked for, and received, a police guard outside the classroom. In June, a dean told police that students were "afraid of any repercussions that could exist from Loughner being unstable in his actions." In September, Loughner was suspended. Police officers removed him from his biology class and informed the community college that Loughner had mental health issues. According to the *Wall Street Journal*, "Loughner was not allowed back at school without a mental health clearance."[16]

By the time of Loughner's suspension, it was well past the time his mental instability and violent tendencies should have been reported to health officials and the Pima County Sheriff's office. If the threat was serious enough in nature to warrant a police guard outside of the college classroom, it was serious enough for the college to order a mental health evaluation (which it didn't do) and for the sheriff's office to intervene (which it didn't do). Instead, campus police entered information about Loughner into a database, and although the sheriff's office had access to the database, it did not make a practice of investigating reports entered into the system.[17]

In short, laws were in place to prevent psychopaths like Jared Lee Loughner from obtaining a gun, and additional laws have been passed to incentivize faster reporting to the National Instant Criminal Background Check System. The problem in Tucson was not the absence of laws, but the failure to enforce those laws by the very people who could have and should have reported and acted on Loughner's behavior. Perhaps Pima County Sheriff Clarence Dupnik was too busy politicking, much in the way he fear-mongered about the tea party the day of the Tucson tragedy.

LIE #9: Anyone can buy a gun.
FACT: *No, not everyone can buy a gun.*

There are many federal regulations as to who can possess a firearm that has been shipped across state lines (which is almost every firearm).[18] Possession is illegal if you are a felon, a fugitive from justice, or an illegal alien. You can't possess one if you use illegal drugs or were dishonorably discharged from the military. Possession is prohibited if you have been "adjudicated a mental defective," have renounced your citizenship, are subject to a domestic-violence restraining order, or have been convicted of any domestic-violence crime, including a misdemeanor. According to the Justice Department, state and local law enforcement agencies in 1993 made approximately "262,300 arrests in which a weapons offense was the most serious charge."[19]

LIE #10: We need to close those gun show loopholes!
FACT: What loopholes?

First, a little background: Most gun sellers are required to have a Federal Firearms License. Licensees must track inventory and call in a background check for every buyer, or they lose their licenses. The vast majority of guns used in crimes, however, are not obtained through lawful purchases.

Now for some facts about gun shows: Less than 1 percent of guns used in crimes come from gun shows, and many gun shows require sellers to have a Federal Firearms License.[20] It's true that buyers can occasionally purchase from unlicensed collectors selling off pieces here and there, but this represents a fraction of a fraction of gun sales. Moreover, if you cannot legally purchase and carry in your own state, you cannot purchase a gun at a gun show. There exists no exception at gun shows to allow national gun laws to be broken.

LIE #11: Forty percent of gun sales are done without a
background check.
FACT: Unless we're living in the '90s, grunge is still a thing, and Milli Vanilli is still around, then there is no way this is accurate.

President Obama is fond of citing this statistic, but by the White House's own admission, the figure comes from a study[21] of 250 people from the Clinton years taken before the Brady Act went into full effect.[22] Old surveys become outdated when the circumstances have drastically changed after they've been done. Of course, the same people who will freak out at my reference of Kleck's 1992 study—which remains instructive because the relevant circumstances have not significantly changed, and which has been supported by more recent surveys—cling to a statistic on background checks that was taken before the modern era of background checks.

LIE #12: Guns kill more children/people every year than anything else.

FACT: According to the FBI's Uniform Crime Reports from 2007 to 2011, you are more likely to be kicked to death than shot with a "military style" "assault weapon."[23]

According to the National Safety Council's 2011 "Injury Facts" report, firearm accidents accounted for only 1.5 percent of fatal accidents.[24] More fatal accidents were attributed to motor vehicle accidents (47 percent), falls (13.5 percent), poisonings (11.4 percent), drowning (4.8 percent), fires (4.4 percent), and choking on objects (3.0 percent). (I'm getting a Gashlycrumb Tinies vibe here.) President Obama is fond of saying that gun control is justified if it "saves just one life," but if that's the standard, shouldn't we start by banning the swimming pools where kids tragically drown and the cars that kill thirty times more people than guns fired by accident?[25]

LIE #13: Lead bullets are bad for the environment.
FACT: Only if you eat them.

Yet again, when the Environmental Protection Agency decided to declare lead bullets dangerous, it was another example of overreach from the same department that warned us about "cancer" lightbulbs. The department later decided that they lacked the jurisdiction to regulate ammo, especially based on a complete lack of common sense—or research. Gun grabbers believe a flat-earth-esque theory that lead in bullets is the same as the lead in paint, meaning that lead in ammunition isn't inert and can dissolve in water. People who believe that probably shouldn't be allowed to own guns just to keep the rest of us safer.

LIE #14: If you need protection, just call 911.
FACT: Law enforcement is not legally obligated to protect your life.

About thirty miles south of Denver is a picturesque town called Castle Rock. On June 4, 1999, one of its residents, Jessica Gonzales, obtained a permanent restraining order against her ex-husband, requiring him to stay one hundred feet away from her and the couple's three young daughters. Gonzales's husband ignored the order and kidnapped the children eighteen days later from the front yard of the family home. The mother of three called the police all evening and eventually drove to police to beg them to enforce the terms of the TRO, which included a "notice to law enforcement" to "use every reasonable means to enforce this restraining order," including the "arrest of the restrained person when you have information amounting to probable cause that the restrained person has violated or attempted to violate any provision of this order."

In response to Gonzales's calls for help, officers failed to do anything to locate the children. They even refused to issue a bulletin. Then, in the middle of the night, Gonzales's husband drove to the police station and opened fire using a semiautomatic pistol. Police returned fire, killing him, but it was too late. When officers searched the cab of his pickup truck, they discovered the bodies of three murder victims: his daughters Rebecca, Katheryn, and Leslie.

Gonzales sued, and the case made its way to the Supreme Court, where the justices ruled 7–2 that the state has no legal obligation whatsoever to protect life or property. Just as a prior case called *DeShaney v. Winnebago County* had held the state had no responsibility to protect a child from brutal, repeated abuse, the majority in *Castle Rock v. Gonzales* stated that "the creation of a personal entitlement to something as vague and novel as enforcement of restraining orders cannot [as the dissent claimed] 'simply go without saying.' We conclude that Colorado has not created such an entitlement."

A similar issue arose in early 2013 when Milwaukee sheriff David Clarke tangled with Milwaukee mayor Tom Barrett. Due to the lack of financial leadership from Mayor Barrett, the city's police department, according to Clarke, had to lay off forty-two deputies. Sheriff Clarke then made headlines when he recorded a PSA for local radio urging citizens to take a gun safety course because they couldn't expect speedy responses when calling 911. He told citizens they would need to defend themselves "until we get there."

Mayor Barrett chided Sheriff Clarke's assessment, but the sheriff was merely recognizing what the mayor apparently did not: The reduction in the force meant fewer resources for residents, which meant slower responses from the police. If the mayor was going to prevent the police from protecting the citizens of Milwaukee, they would have to protect themselves.

Clarke isn't the only person in law enforcement encouraging citizens to take gun safety courses and assume responsibility for their protection. I spoke with Sheriff Chuck Heiss of Johnson County, Missouri, who, like Clarke, has gone public to encourage citizens to take control of their own safety. He agreed with Clarke: "You are your own first responder."

That's a sentiment the Minutemen of 1776 would have understood and endorsed, and it's a reality that makes the Second Amendment as important today as it was when it was written.

Chapter 12

Victory

I knew it was over nationally for anti–Second Amendment advocates when Dianne Feinstein theatrically assembled her cadre of human props in front of a whiteboard to which a plethora of scary black rifles were affixed.

My grandmother, perhaps the biggest Elvis fan on earth, loved going to Memphis and visiting Graceland with her sister, daughter, and nieces. She had photo albums full of their trips; they'd go and she would take photos of the exact same things trip after trip. It was her mecca. She had a photo of Elvis's headstone in various seasons, and you could watch her daughter and nieces grow up in a series of photos in front the mansion's driveway gate. It was routine.

I've come to regard Dianne Feinstein's "assault weapons" press conferences in the same way. Every few years or so, Senator Feinstein calls a press conference, the D.C. version of theater, and plays Vanna White with guns strapped to whiteboards. You can watch her age through the years at these pressers via Google Images. She begins with a youthful plump to her cheeks, standing tall, holding up a rifle to her chest and as the years go by she takes on the posture of a cocktail shrimp and simply motions to the boards. I give her credit for her dedication to never learning a single thing about the firearms she proposes to ban. It takes devotion to remain ignorant about a topic when you spend decades discussing it.

The scary black rifles included anything that was black. In the minds of people like Senator Feinstein, there are shotguns and then there are "assault weapons." There exist no other kinds of guns. She listed over 150 types of firearms she proposed to ban, including standard-capacity magazines. Nearly every firearm I own is on the list.

Feinstein claimed that it was our country's "weak" gun laws that allowed the Sandy Hook massacre to occur—Sandy Hook, a place that had in effect all the laws she was already proposing and a gun-free school zone, and yet the tragedy *still* happened. To date, Feinstein has never been able to explain why the anti-gun laws failed Sandy Hook. Never mind that Connecticut has had its own "assault weapons" ban since 1993. Feinstein was already successful in Connecticut, as it was one of seven states that banned rifles based on cosmetics, not function ("assault weapons" ban).

The media was so irresponsible in being *first!* with their reporting that they failed to perform their due diligence before running with story developments, marking an equally dark time in media history. For instance, there was confusing and conflicting reports about what type of firearm Adam Lanza used, whether his mother's Bushmaster XM 15 (based on the AR-15 platform) used in the tragedy was left in the car or used (it was used, according to every police officer on the scene and the coroner's report), thereby befuddling all of America and staining their profession.

Here's the thing: The ban didn't affect Adam Lanza because he committed *another crime* to bypass the ban. Connecticut gun laws also allow for law enforcement to seize, sans warrant or order, the firearms of any individual who poses an imminent risk to themselves or others or due to mental instability. This law has been on the books since 1999. Lanza would not have been able to legally purchase a gun anyway, if the reports were true that his mother was in the process of petitioning the court for conservatorship and had begun the process of having him committed to a mental institution.[1] If she was not, then there was nothing in Lanza's record that would have prevented him from purchasing his own firearms—and that is Nancy Lanza's fault. Adam Lanza reportedly only spoke with his mother via email and completely controlled their home life down to whether Nancy Lanza could get a Christmas tree (she couldn't, Adam didn't like holidays), and eschewed human contact. After he created a spread sheet for mass murder Nancy Lanza bought him another gun for Christmas.[2]

Some think that the opposite of abuse is to give your child everything he wants without regard for consequence because that's the easy path. That was Nancy Lanza's choice. (And what about his father, Peter Lanza? I don't think it's fair to mention Mom and not Dad. Where *was* he when his son needed him? *People*'s March 10, 2014, issue quoted Peter Lanza as saying he wished his son would not have been born and added he hadn't seen him since 2010.) She was the gatekeeper and she failed.

I see no need to tiptoe around the dead or anyone else when their irresponsible actions may have contributed to the deaths of twenty schoolchildren, six adults, and the unfair castigation of law-abiding gun owners who keep their guns *responsibly* and the attempt to disarm an innocent populace that police cannot protect 24/7 as a result. If your neighbor crashes her car and tragically kills a family because she's doing ninety on the freeway and texting duckfacing-selfies while driving, does that mean the rest of us should be barred from owning and driving cars? Of course not. Should all bands be barred from playing music because Nickelback exists? No. So it is with 2A.

There is not a single law on the books that would have prevented Sandy Hook, except for *theft*. If Adam Lanza had been my child, my firearms would have been behind a steel door, under lock and key, perhaps not even at my residence. They sure as hell wouldn't have been unlocked in my room or given to him as gifts. Some parents make horrible, life-altering decisions but the majority do not, nor should they be punished by being rendered defenseless because of those who do.

So while anti–Second Amendment advocates crisscrossed the country championing rights restrictions on the backs of slain Newtown children, something interesting happened: Applications for gun permits—in Newtown—began to soar. Newtown police said that gun permits were doubled the year following the Sandy Hook massacre, due to average law-abiding Americans who wanted to protect themselves. According to Newtown police, there were 171 permits in 2012, and double that the following year.[3]

Why the surge? A couple of reasons. First, the Sandy Hook tragedy had the opposite effect on peaceful, law-abiding Americans than anti–Second Amendment advocates had hoped. Something clicked in the minds of Americans that day, when they watched as helpless children were led hand-in-hand from their school by teachers, faces etched in horror. They realized that those children deserved to be protected, that their families deserved to be protected. Americans who were on the fence before about owning a gun did the math and computed the statistics. Regularly they were taking a chance with their lives driving a car, having a drink, taking the family swimming, and so on. Out of all the variables that would take their children's lives, firearms are the least of these yet there is more attention given to them than anything else for a purpose other than safety, it's for a purpose of wresting control.

Americans aren't stupid, and the anti–Second Amendment lobby would do well to stop pretending otherwise. They did not expect, in all of the places where they anticipated the least resistance, that so many in Newtown would exercise a different choice. Newtown residents reacted to the massacre by arming themselves. They wanted to be the good guys with the guns because 99 percent of the time the only way to stop a bad guy with a gun is with a good guy with a gun.

Equally armed, good verses evil. After all, it was good guys with guns who showed up to stop Adam Lanza. It was concealed-carry Second Amendment practitioner Nick Meli who drew his pistol on a criminal illegally using a firearm in the Clackamas Town Center in December 2012. Meli and a friend heard three shots in close proximity. Meli saw the shooter, drew his concealed-carry handgun, positioned himself behind a pillar, and put the criminal in his crosshairs. When the criminal saw Meli he squeezed the trigger one more time—on himself.

In May 2010 Abraham Dickan walked into an AT&T store in New York Mills with a kill list of six names and shot a store clerk. He was aiming for more when he was taken out by off-duty officer Donald J. Moore, who was there as a customer.

Moore's boss, Chief Kevin Breach said that it's the personal choice of officers to carry and that they are encouraged to do so.[4]

In 1998 a kid named Andrew Wurst came to his junior high school dance with a handgun, killed a teacher, and shot at other students. He was disarmed by the location's (a banquet hall) owner, who brandished his shotgun and told Wurst to get on the ground.

There are a number of stories of armed citizens who defend themselves, their families, off-duty officers, good guys with guns who stop evil guys with guns. The same people who ignore the cases of trained citizens and instead focus on off-duty officers so as to make a case for skill or training, anti–Second Amendment advocates have shown that it doesn't matter how much training an citizen has, they won't even allow for our men and women in uniform—our trained military—to carry firearms on bases, even with multiple shootings at Fort Hood and the Navy Yard just in the last year. Make no mistake: Whenever criminals bent on massacre realize that good guys with guns are on their six, they either give up or take themselves out. That's exactly what happened with Adam Lanza. When first responders made it to the scene, he shot himself.

Connecticut hastily passed stringent new gun-control laws, among the new rules was massive registration, the other factor fueling the surge in permit applications. In the year following the Sandy Hook shooting, Connecticut governor Dannel Mallory signed into law new restrictions on firearms and expanded the definition of "assault weapon" to include nearly one hundred kinds of semiautomatic firearms. Connecticut gun owners in possession of rifles based on the AR-15 platform could keep them but would be required to register them with the state. Law-abiding Americans who did nothing to provoke such action from their government would be rendered felons if they did not declare their firearms.

Connecticut residents refused to comply. Said State Senator Tony Guglielmo, "I honestly thought that from my own standpoint that the vast majority would register. If you pass laws that people have no respect for and they don't follow them, then you have a real problem."[5]

Connecticut gun owners informed the state rep that they would engage in civil disobedience. "He made the analogy to prohibition," said Guglielmo. Law enforcement said they wouldn't aggressively hunt down gun owners—or even send out letters—but rather focus on outreach and awareness. As little as 15 percent of the estimated "assault weapons" were registered with the state. The *Courant* estimated that as many as 350,000 gun owners are refusing to comply.

While this action played out in Connecticut's legislature, Dianne Feinstein failed to secure any momentum or support for her Assault Weapons Ban. Even though Feinstein angrily demanded that her colleagues "show some guts," Senate Majority Leader Harry Reid failed to include her ban in gun safety legislation he championed on the Senate floor. Only forty of her colleagues even voted to attach the ban to the Senate's gun bill, a decline from the fifty-two votes she received in 2004 to reanimate her ban after its sunset in 1994. Reid himself felt that Feinstein's bill was too extreme and would endanger the other anti-gun measures he hoped to pass in the chamber. Feinstein's response was to shame her colleagues with images of the twenty schoolchildren from the Sandy Hook massacre.

Reid knew what Feinstein, Michael Bloomberg, and other anti–Second Amendment advocates secretly know but won't admit: The majority of Americans are against gun control. Anti-gun groups try to obfuscate this by falsely claiming that we don't have background checks or citing poorly sampled polls about gun control, but the bottom line is that if the country supported the extremist measures of Dianne Feinstein, Michael Bloomberg, or others, the Assault Weapons Ban would have passed. Period. The national support isn't there, so it didn't.

It's why Bloomberg groups have to lie about my employment or why they have to completely fabricate stories maligning law-abiding gun owners: They have to create a bogeyman, because the bogeyman *doesn't exist*. Well, not in the way they perceive it to exist. To me the bogeyman is a reality. He's a rich New Yorker with armed, private security, who wants to render me and every other law-abiding mom who simply wants to prevent her family from becoming potential rape/assault victims. That bogeyman *does* exist; he has millions in his war chest and a target on the back of every innocent 2A-practicing American.

In an effort to give momentum to the extremist goal of banning firearms, President Obama presented his gun control agenda in the name of safety. The plan included universal background checks (the Constitutional law scholar never heard of the Brady Bill, apparently), a ban on "high-capacity" (standard-capacity in reality) magazines, an "assault weapons" ban, and an additional twenty-three executive orders, including one that commissioned the Centers for Disease Control to research gun violence. Verbatim: *"14. Issue a Presidential Memorandum di-*

recting the Centers for Disease Control to research the causes and prevention of gun violence."

The president gambled that the CDC's findings would blow away Second Amendment supporters. Anti–Second Amendment advocates were sure that the report would be the death knell for 2A support. Media chatter about firearms ascended into shrieking and then, nothing.

No one said anything further about the CDC report. After months of top stories concerning "gun violence in America" and the simultaneous narratives that fewer Americans owned guns than previously but yet gun crime was at an all-time high, the media went silent on the issue. Then came the news: The CDC report commissioned by President Obama contradicted the White House and anti–Second Amendment advocates' assertions that gun violence was increasing.

The findings in the CDC's latest report echoed the report it issued in 2003 when it was estimated that Americans owned around 193 million firearms, a number that has now more than doubled to around 300 million firearms owned. Among the conclusions of the CDC's 2003 report, "First Reports Evaluating the Effectiveness of Strategies for Preventing Violence: Firearms Laws":

Evidence was insufficient to determine the effectiveness of any of these laws for the following reasons.

1. Bans on specified firearms or ammunition.
2. Restrictions on firearm acquisition.
3. Waiting periods for firearm acquisition.
4. Firearm registration and licensing of owners.

5. "Shall issue" concealed weapon carry laws.
6. Child access prevention laws.
7. Zero tolerance laws for firearms in schools

Furthermore, the study stated: "However, denial of an application does not always stop applicants from acquiring firearms through other means." The report commissioned by the president and published through the Institute of Medicine and National Research Council in June 2013, concluded that the majority of gun deaths from 2000 to 2010 were due to suicides, not crime, with suicides "outnumbering" firearm usage through criminal violence:

Between the years 2000–2010 firearm-related suicides significantly outnumbered homicides for all age groups, annually accounting for 61 percent of the more than 335,600 people who died from firearms related violence in the United States.

The study also found that defensive use of firearms was incredibly common, further validating Dr. Gary Kleck's research on this matter:

Almost all national survey estimates indicate that defensive gun uses by victims are at least as common as offensive uses by criminals, with estimates of annual uses ranging from about 500,000 to more than 3 million per year, in the context of about 300,000 violent crimes involving firearms in 2008.

The *New American* noted that the only mainstream media entity that made mention of this study was the *Washington Post*.

After this, anti–Second Amendment advocates pivoted from any root in logic and amped up the emotional appeals.

———————

Nationally, the fight over gun control is dead. Education remedied a lot of ignorance, thanks to a number of groups such as the National Rifle Association, which emphasizes safety and responsibility. Americans saw that anti-gun groups spend more time attacking innocent Americans, who also happened to be gun owners, than they did actually attacking *the criminals*. For all of their talk, there exists not a single anti–Second Amendment group that puts its vast wealth toward firearm education, safety, or even to putting a safe in every home. Actions say quite a bit, and the nasty actions of extremist groups like Moms Demand Action and others—attacking and smearing innocent 2A moms, who just want to be able to match force with force if ever they or their children were attacked—has been too much for moderate Americans to bear.

Deep down, these anti-gun groups know that they've been defeated nationally, too. They won't have another chance to push forward liberty-curbing restrictions again for a number of years, though it doesn't mean that they won't try. They'll never retreat; give them points for sheer dedication to a losing cause. They've simply moved the battle from the lost front of the national stage to what they believe to be more fertile ground: the states. They're losing there, too, as Democrats have already suffered a setback on this in Colorado.

STATES FIGHT BACK

Colorado has been the testing ground of progressive polices for the past ten years. Democrats began slowly building up resources and momentum from the bottom to the top in a bid to take over the state legislature. The process was chronicled in the book *The Blueprint: How the Democrats Won Colorado (and Why Republicans EVERYWHERE Should Care)*. Soon Democrats assumed majority control and then began proposing and passing restrictive gun laws—laws so restrictive that the standard shotgun would be banned. Magazines holding more than fifteen rounds were banned. After the tragedy of Sandy Hook and the Aurora Theater (both gun-free zones), anti–Second Amendment advocates assumed that the fight would be an easy one.

Not a single proposal was put to the ballot for a vote. It was the restriction of gun rights that finally propelled Victor Head, a twenty-eight-year-old plumber from Pueblo, to act. Plain-spoken with a no BS demeanor, Head recruited some fed-up friends and they made state history. "Me and my friends, we're plumbers and HVAC guys. We fix problems. We see a problem and we fix it," Head said matter-of-factly of his motivation when I spoke with him in Dallas early in 2014.

The year before I was in Colorado on the ground for their Farewell to Arms event, organized by a plethora of grassroots groups and gun parts manufacturer Magpul, whose standard-capacity magazine, its biggest product, was just outlawed by the state. The event took place in Glendale, a suburb of Denver, ground zero for libertarian activism in the state (also, coincidentally smack next door to Aurora, the site of the theater massacre). Not a single volunteer was over the age of thirty, and hundreds of them swarmed the Glendale rugby field setting up hours before the event.

Those attending were angry at the national narrative circulating about their state. "They say 'nice priorities, stoners. You passed pot legalization but failed to do anything to save your gun rights.' That's because they put pot on the ballot, but they didn't with the gun bills! They didn't even want to have any public dialogue about their gun laws!" said one young woman, the anger in her voice matching her fiery dyed-red hair. She was loading boxes of T-shirts and other swag for event attendees. Every grassroots group in the state would later attend, including Head's group, Pueblo Freedom and Rights.

The night before the event, my husband and I dined at the Bull and the Bush with libertarian members of Glendale's government. The restaurant, known in Glendale for its good food and equally good scotch list, is a dimly lit revolutionary's paradise. The owner came over to introduce himself and soon heartily joined in the political conversation.

Everyone in Glendale is mad, damn mad, mad enough to spend every evening and every weekend door-to-door politicking in their area and surrounding neighborhoods. Head and his group quietly went about the business of setting Colorado right again and collected nearly thirteen thousand signatures to recall his state senator, Angela Giron, who proudly supported, and voted for, the anti-gun bills that the Democrat majority passed into law. One day Head walked in and dropped the stack of signatures on the secretary of state's desk. Pueblo Freedom and Rights caught Colorado Democrats off guard. As a result, they were unable to discredit Head *before* he secured the recall. They had to go into overdrive, relying heavily upon friendlies in Denver media and party surrogates on social media to do speed-shaming for them.

Head was declared a racist. "I know it's partially about me being a Latina and being in this position of authority," said Giron.[6] Except that Republican Latina Clarice Navarro opposed the gun bill and wasn't recalled. Democrat Latinos Ed Vigil and Leroy Garcia opposed the ban on magazine restrictions and the expansion on background checks, respectively.[7] No effort was made to recall any of these three. So wouldn't it then be racist for Giron to disarm these Latinos?

Giron was successfully recalled along with Senate President John Morse, an enthusiastic supporter of the anti-gun bills. Giron was recalled by a wide margin, 56 to 43 percent, and Morse lost his seat 50 to 49 percent. Morse was replaced by George Rivera, a Republican, who scored over 88 percent of the successor vote.[8]

Evie Hudak, that senator who looked rape survivor Amanda Collins in the eye and told her that she was too helpless and stupid to carry a firearm, was next on the grass roots' recall list, but she quickly resigned the seat because of the inevitability—and for strategy. Under Colorado law, if the grass roots had successfully recalled her, they could have replaced her with a Republican and gained control of the state senate by one seat. As it was, she resigned, meaning that her successor had to be a member of her own party.

But, due to the successful recalls of Giron and Morse, as of July 2014 Democrats have a one-seat majority over Republicans, and the grassroots stand to take even more in the next election cycle. Meanwhile, grassroots rock star Head is running for Pueblo County clerk.

Democrats fought hard to win this war in Colorado. They outspent grassroots 2–1, and Giron claimed before the recall that if she didn't win "[MAIG] might as well fold up." Everyone from Vice President Biden to Mike Bloomberg visited the state to raise money and garner support—all for laws that were never put to a vote of the people. Why? Because they needed a national narrative. Joe Biden said as much on a call with three Colorado Democrat legislators: Dominick Moreno, Tony Exum, and Mike McLachlan.[9] Said Exum: "He said it would send a strong message to the rest of the country that a Western state had passed anti-gun control bills."

And what a powerful narrative, indeed. It was a victory that Democrats needed to maintain momentum in the wake of Sandy Hook. They gained in the short term, but once a Republican majority is elected, restrictive gun laws will be repealed. The grass roots are in a political war right now with a list of lawmakers and grassroots is winning. Colorado isn't used in national talking points anymore, because pro–Second Amendment Colorado grass roots completely derailed the momentum of the anti-gun movement and robbed them of their national narrative with the overwhelmingly successful recall of three lawmakers—one of which was the figurehead Senate president.

EVERYTOWN TAKES A HIT

When former Pennsylvania governor Tom Ridge announced that he was stepping down from his positions as a board member and advisor of Michael Bloomberg's rebranded anti–Second Amendment effort, Everytown, observers murmured that it had only been a matter of time. Ridge told the *Daily Caller*: "When I signed on as an advisor to Everytown, I looked forward to a thoughtful and provocative discussion about the toll gun violence takes on Americans. I have decided that I am uncomfortable with their expected electoral work, therefore, we have decided that we will pursue this issue in our separate spheres."

If you look at this statement in its raw form, before Ridge fed it to the Political BS Filter, it shows Ridge was uncomfortable underwriting Everytown's credibility. Instead, he bailed the weekend of the NRA convention just as Bloomberg's Moms Demand Action group was hoping to hijack the headlines from the thousands of moms at the NRA to cover their coterie of a hundred or so lobbyists, PR flacks, and professional activists lured by boxed lunches and a free happy-hour post-rally.

Ridge stomped all over their anti-gun parade with his announcement. Even though he supported an "assault weapons" ban, his faculties hadn't completely failed him. He realized that this wasn't a group about background checks or "military-style" firearms; this was a group so hopped up on hoplophobia and so publicly hysterical that Ridge stood to have his image tarnished by association.

And Bloomberg worked to hard to rebrand it. Since the creation of his Mayors Against Illegal Guns group, nearly fifty mayors jumped ship. Bloomberg rounded up mayors from across the country to sign a statement petitioning Congress for more gun control laws at the federal level.

The first scandal involved James Schiliro, former mayor of Marcus Hook, Pennsylvania, who enthusiastically supported anti–Second Amendment policies. Schiliro was sentenced to twenty months in jail early in 2014 after he was convicted of being a giant gun-wielding pervert. He had a squad car bring his twenty-year-old former neighbor, to whom he was attracted. He got him drunk on wine and held him hostage for over three hours. The man resisted Schiliro's sexual advances, and when he tried to leave, Schiliro took his gun and shot a stack of papers. The neighbor, now captive and victim, talked Schiliro, a mayor against "illegal guns," out of further violence by reminding him that his daughter was sleeping upstairs. Schiliro was convicted of reckless endangerment, unlawful restraint, false imprisonment, official oppression, and giving alcohol to a minor. He was sentenced to five years probation, fifty hours of community service, and a $1,300 fine.[10]

Michael Bloomberg thought that the best representation for his gun control was a community figure who held a minor prisoner, got him drunk, came on to him, and threatened to kill him after discharging his gun. Four words: *Gun Control Poster Child*. Bloomberg hastily scrubbed Schiliro's name from their MAIG website, fingers crossed that Americans wouldn't notice that gun control is being repped by a reckless perv who threatens minors with guns.

That wasn't the only offense from an MAIG member—the group is rife with them, as seen earlier. Things got even worse for MAIG after that. The *New York Post* reported that Bloomberg had a city employee lobby for gun control in Nevada, and that MAIG's website was registered by the New York Department of Information and Technology.

It got worse from there. Bloomberg's next item of business was to release bitter clinger ads. The ads, called "Family" and "Responsible," featured a perfectly manscaped farmer-actor on his borrowed truck bed, wearing J.Crew flannel while awkwardly handling a shotgun. I was terrified the entire time thinking that ol' Rent-a-Redneck was going to shoot a gaffer or cameraman. He haphazardly pointed the shotgun at everything (either point it up in the air or at the ground for safety) and fingered the trigger (zero trigger discipline) while jawing about how he was just an average American because he was wearing flannel, so you should hate guns like he does, or something to that effect.

I love how big-city anti–Second Amendment advocates view firearm owners, and how self-exalted they are to think that lecturing responsible, gun-owning Americans about their 2A rights with some doucher video would convince anyone. Watching this actor handle a shotgun was like watching a kid who can't catch a football.

Bloomberg is nothing if not persistent. He went back to his Wile E. Coyote Acme box and came back to hold a press conference to lecture New York City about gun crime. Next to his podium stood two tables on which were displayed countless pistols, every single one of them pointed at the assembled media.[11]

Then came the story that Bloomberg sent a New York City employee, special counsel to the office of the mayor, Christopher Kocher, to register as a lobbyist representing MAIG on gun issues in…Nevada. The *New York Post* reported that Kocher tried to hide the connection by scrubbing his City Hall e-mail address from Nevada's lobbyist registry. Sources also told the *Post* that MAIG staffers were using the ninth floor of the mayor's office for group purposes.[12]

After this, blogger John Ekdahl noticed that the MAIG website was being hosted on New York city servers and that the city's Department of Information and Technology was listed as the registrant of the MAIG URL. *Judicial Watch* FOIA'd more evidence showing the closeness of the association between the mayoral office and MAIG. E-mails showed that one week following the Sandy Hook massacre, Katherine Oliver, commissioner of the mayor's media and entertainment office, coordinated tweets with celebrities and others to direct traffic to his new project, DemandAPlan.org.

Bloomberg's surrogate, John McCarthy, defended the scandal. "With 85 percent of guns used in crimes here coming from out of state, gun policy everywhere has an impact on the safety of New Yorkers," he told the *Post*. "The mayor's top priority is keeping New Yorkers safe, and that includes seeking sane gun laws in other states to help reduce the flow of illegal guns to New York." So gun crime in New York City is carried out with firearms from Nevada?

Even if in a cracked-out reality this were remotely true, there are already laws on the book to prevent this: If a purchaser is prohibited by law from legally owning in the state in which they live, they may not purchase a firearm in another state.

The Bloomberg MAIG slow-mo train wreck continued. In June 2013 MAIG held a demonstration against guns in Concord and read off a list of names belonging to victims of gun violence and included the name of Boston bomber Tamerlan Tsarnaev in their commemoration. Outrage ensued. MAIG was forced to apologize and claimed that they relied on a list compiled by the functionally illiterate website Slate.com for their information, and Tsarnaev's name was on the list. Oops.

E-mails also showed that MAIG and the Brady Campaign had an ego-fueled turf war over celebrities and anti-gun tweets, mostly between MAIG executive director Mark Glaze and

Brady Campaign president Daniel Gross. Said one e-mail: "Dan—if true that you are attempting to intervene in the work we are doing with celebrities on Demand A Plan and drive them toward Brady: don't."[13]

The group incurred the wrath of Sen. Chuck Schumer when they began targeting any Democrat who was not on board with their anti–Second Amendment agenda. MAIG went after embattled Arkansas Senator Mark Pryor, nearly making him a sympathetic figure, whose first campaign ad had to be against his own side, MAIG.[14] In his ad, Pryor stated: "The mayor of New York City is running ads against me because I opposed President Obama's gun-control legislation. I approve this message because no one from New York or Washington tells me what to do."

Bloomberg threatened to target other Democrats, which put Schumer and other senior Democratic leaders on edge. They saw how MAIG reportedly infuriated Colorado governor John Hickenlooper with their involvement, and he feared they could cost him the Democrat-controlled state senate. Said Schumer to *Time*: "I am trying to persuade—in whatever way I'm allowed to—the gun groups to put out different ads. Frankly, I don't think Bloomberg's ads are effective. The mayor of New York City putting ads against people in red states is not going to be effective."

Nor was it effective in putting its own membership at ease.

MAIG began hemorrhaging members after the Pryor debacle. Capital Research Center quoted a number of the almost fifty mayors' reasons for leaving:

Mayor Lawrence Morrissey: "The reason why I joined the group in the first place is because I took the name for what it said, against 'illegal' guns. I thought it was about enforcement of existing gun laws. As the original mission swayed, that's when I decided that it was no longer in line with my beliefs."

Said Sioux City, Iowa, mayor Bob Scott upon leaving MAIG: "They're not just against illegal guns, they're against all guns."

Mayor Donnalee Lozeau upped stakes and left when MAIG began haphazardly targeting anyone not for disarmament: "I said, 'Wait a minute. I don't want to be part of something like that. I told them, 'You're Mayors Against Illegal Guns; you're not Mayors for Gun Control.'"[15]

It wasn't going any better for Bloomberg's Moms Demand Action group, either. Instead of making informed, compelling arguments in an effort to persuade people to consider their stance, they chose instead the verbal equivalent of flailing their arms wildly and screaming at anyone who threw them some side-eye. First was Shannon Troughton-Watts's insistence that any firearm that fires ten rounds a minute should be classified as an "assault weapon" and banned, which includes virtually *all* firearms, save for historical relics like maybe muskets. Anything can fire ten rounds a minute, and skill and machine capability aren't considered, which makes the demand silly on its face. Bloomberg was cruel in setting up his corporate PR mom group to be mocked for that, but they trudged ahead.

Then came their campaign to have me booted from ABC's *The View* when it was announced that I would be a guest cohost. Troughton-Watts fired up her Internet Outrage Machine and launched e-mail and Facebook petitions plus a Twitter onslaught campaign to try to inflate their numbers, exaggerate their influence, and force *The View* to drop me. Troughton-

Watts tweeted about me 24/7 in a freaky, Hedra Carlson way for over a week to no avail.

While in makeup with the other ladies, Whoopi Goldberg remarked how annoying it was that her time was filled up by the same people screaming at her over me for days on end. "It's called *The View*," she said. "We will bring on the other side." Jenny McCarthy nodded in agreement and remarked that the Bloomberg "moms" campaign against me was "over the top."

The ladies were funny and engaging and made it fun to join. While there were things on which we did not agree, there were things on which we *did* agree. "It's about finding common ground," I told Whoopi backstage as the show wrapped. "Exactly," she replied.

After that blistering defeat for Bloomberg's mom group, a couple of members continued to whine about me for a few days after, and then they found their new squirrel: Staples, the office supply store. Fresh off of one failure, Troughton-Watts kicked her PR gears into action and called forth the Internet Outrage Machine to Staples. Since their inception, Bloomberg Moms have been working to force Staples to disregard the gun laws of whichever locality they're established and ban them outright, even concealed firearms carried by law-abiding folks. Bloomberg Moms! Changing the world, one office supply store at a time! A few Bloomberg Moms called the press and then staged a dramatic delivery at Staples's headquarters in March 2014 to deliver another one of their famous petitions, but Staples wasn't having any of it. The store kicked them off the property. Another fail.

At this point, people who understand strategy might scratch their heads and think "People—other mothers—are mocking us and kicking us off property for being extremists. Maybe we should rethink our tactics." I can tell that Bloomberg's calling the shots with this group, because I can't imagine Shannon Troughton-Watts, onetime bigwig PR executive for Monsanto, agreeing to a campaign of nagging. *Irrelevant!* Fire up ye ol' Internet Outrage Machine!

The next target was Starbucks. Once again, the coffee giant followed local gun laws. If an area in which a Starbucks was located prohibited firearms, that Starbucks also prohibited firearms. If an area in which a Starbucks was located allowed for CCW, that Starbucks allowed for CCW. And there you see the Bloomberg Moms goal: They're incapable of meaningful action or effecting change legislatively, so when state legislatures and city councils fail to cower to these anti-gun extremists, they aim at area businesses. It's a cruel thing to do, to threaten a business and their employees in this age of unemployment. Starbucks's CEO, Howard Schultz, issued a response in light of the Bloomberg Moms. Excerpted, with emphasis added:

We appreciate that there is a highly sensitive balance of rights and responsibilities surrounding America's gun laws, and we recognize the deep passion for and against the "open carry" laws adopted by many states. (In the United States, "open carry" is the term used for openly carrying a firearm in public.) For years we have listened carefully to input from our customers, partners, community leaders and voices on both sides of this complicated, highly charged issue.

Our company's longstanding approach to "open carry" has been to follow local laws: we permit it in states where allowed and we prohibit it in states where these laws don't exist. We have chosen this approach because we believe our store partners should not be put in the uncomfortable position of requiring customers to disarm or leave our stores. *We believe that gun policy should be addressed by government and law enforcement—not by Starbucks and our store partners.*

For these reasons, today we are respectfully requesting that customers no longer bring firearms into our stores or outdoor seating areas—even in states where "open carry" is permitted—unless they are authorized law enforcement personnel.

I would like to clarify two points. First, this is a request and not an outright ban. *Why? Because we want to give responsible gun owners the chance to respect our request—and also because enforcing a ban would potentially require our partners to confront armed customers, and that is not a role I am comfortable asking Starbucks partners to take on. Second, we know we cannot satisfy everyone.* For those who oppose "open carry," we believe the legislative and policy-making process is the proper arena for this debate, not our stores.

Starbucks's explicitly stated that it's "not a ban." Bloomberg's moms would have no idea if a concealed carrier was sitting next to them or not, sipping her caramel macchiato. Another fail. McDonald's and Chipotle said the same thing, with Chipotle telling one of my listeners via e-mail: "this is not a ban."[16]

Meanwhile, back at Crazytown Headquarters, Michael Bloomberg sat down with his Monsanto Moms and his remaining coterie of mayors who hadn't been arrested for kidnapping minors, possession of kiddie porn, shooting at things, DUIs, or bribery, and tried to figure out how they could spin all these fails into something positive. Someone of their crew had the brilliant idea of simply labeling all these failures as successes and praying—no, not praying, that's too *bitter clinger*, thinking positively that no one in America was smart enough to notice. *The View* ignored their tantrums? Success! Staples throws you out of their headquarters? Success! Starbucks, McDonald's, Chipotle says this is not a ban? Success!

Now, some of my pro–Second Amendment brethren wanted to denounce these businesses and claim that they caved to Bloomberg's Moms. Why would you give Bloomberg a victory he hasn't earned? These companies simply released requests but refused to infringe on our rights by banning firearms where they were allowed legally and thus disarming us. Bloomberg did not earn this victory; do not give it to him. It's asinine for Michael "Big Gulp" Bloomberg to bully business owners with his extreme agenda by exploiting mothers and motherhood. Bloomberg is a failure at policy, even within his own party. He's relevant only because he's a rich 1 percenter who buys it.

His moms continued the string of embarrassments with the scrubbing of Leland Yee from their pages. Before Yee was discovered to be an alleged gunrunner and a proponent of disarming women so that there are more guns and easier prey for criminals, he was a Moms Demand poster child. They lauded him for his efforts against the Second Amendment as he was one of the leading voices against it. Said Paul Song, executive chairman of the anti-gun group Courage Campaign: "Ironically, while he's being charged with gun trafficking, next to Dianne Feinstein he was probably the second most outspoken gun control advocate. This really leaves us scrambling for someone to pick up that mantle. If it wasn't so sad it would be comical. But what we're really worried about is that this will further destroy the momentum for gun control here in California."[17] Moms Demand scrubbed all compliments about Lee from their website and refused to acknowledge that while they were supporting Lee (who was arrested in the middle of his California secretary of state campaign), he was arming criminals. They never denounced him, either. Sometimes the enemy of my enemy is my friend, I suppose, but where does that leave them on principle?

While in Indianapolis to counter the annual NRA Convention with Bloomberg's Moms, anti–Second Amendment advocate Jennifer Longdon told far-left website *Mother Jones*, that she was repeatedly assaulted by pro-gun people for a piece that *Mother Jones* peddled to *Glamour* magazine and later to MSNBC. The incidents involved just Longdon and some man, no witnesses and no police reports, either, apparently. One incident occurred at the Indianapolis airport following the rally:

> *As Longdon sat waiting for her flight, a screen in the concourse showed footage of the press conference. A tall, thin man standing nearby stared at Longdon, then back at the screen. Then he walked up to Longdon and spat in her face. No one else blinked.*
>
> *Longdon was shocked and embarrassed, she told me, but she didn't falter. "Wow, aren't you a big man," she said as he turned and walked away. Instead of calling for security, she wheeled herself to a restroom to clean herself off. She was tired—she lives with constant physical pain—and didn't want to miss her flight.*

Initially I saw this piece on *Glamour*'s website and when I asked the author, Tanya Edwards, if she vetted the piece, she reacted angrily and called me a "troll," for which she later apologized. I asked because I genuinely wanted to know. If there is someone in our pro–Second Amendment community who is treating women in such a manner, I'd like to know so I could beat him senseless myself. People such as that make my fight harder as a woman who would not like to be disarmed and left as easy prey for a rapist.

The story struck me as odd because we're talking about people who flip out if kids eat Pop Tarts in the shape of a gun so that they wouldn't flip more when *assaulted*—in a public place where witnesses abound and cameras are everywhere, it seems odd. Plus, I was at that same airport that same day. I flew in that Saturday morning and left that evening. It was crowded the entire time. You're telling me no one said anything? It disturbs me that if such a thing occurred no one would speak up in her defense.

But ProgressivesToday.com discovered something that answered the question. They wrote on May 19, 2014:

Hmm. So this incident reportedly occurred on April 25 at the Indianapolis airport after the concourse television aired a report on the Everytown for Gun Safety protest outside the NRA convention?

That's odd—the TV report never made it on the Everytown for Gun Safety website.

And, since the Indianapolis airport airs CNN on their TV screens you'd think you could find their report on the protest on their website, right?

Nope. It's not there.

CNN has no record of the protest.

TV Eyes also has no record of Jennifer Lo on on cable
news on April 25.

It looks like Mother Jones *was just caught in* e.

They really ought to do better research next tim

Jim Hoft, a proprietor of the website, searched telev   ion ar-
chives and LexisNexis, and never found anything to corr orate
Mother Jones's reporting. It was the tea-party-spitting strategy
from 2010 that was disproven when six-figure rewards couldn't
obtain proof. I offered *Mother Jones* $100 to obtain airport se-
curity camera footage of the alleged incident (I don't have
Bloomberg bucks, so $100 was it), but the site's senior editor
proceeded to deflect and whine and incited a virtual riot against
me. One of the site's readers even told me, of which I saved a
screencap: "You are a filthy bible-humping whore bag. I hope
someone shoots you in the cunt with one of those guns you love
so much."

This is what desperation looks like. Now you see why I carry
in the event I have to defend myself or my family.

MCDONALD V. CHICAGO

In 2008 we were one vote away from having our Second
Amendment rights stripped from us and a dangerous precedent
established in a court case involving anti-firearms regulations in
Washington, D.C. The 5-4 decision in the *District of Columbia v.
Heller* overturned the restrictions of the Firearms Control Regu-

lations Act pa͠ by D.C. in 1975, which barred D.C. residents from carryin͠ay firearms and required them to keep registered firearm͠ and inform law enforcement where they would be located͠ their homes unloaded, unassembled, and with a trigger lo͠ In D.C., residents were forced to politely ask home invaders͠ give them a bit of time to unlock their firearms, assemble͠em, and load them for self-defense if the criminals were ͠nning on raping or assaulting them.

D͠pite the law, gun crime committed by criminals barred fro͠ illegally possessing a firearm (but did anyway, laws be damned) soared (even with Operation Ceasefire, wherein law enforcement collected 282 handguns to no avail, crime still rose) and residents lived in fear. After the Act was passed, D.C. saw a 97 percent increase in crime from 1976 to 1993. Home Rule is still subject to the restraints of the Constitution, the Court affirmed in *Heller*.

The Supreme Court decided that the Second Amendment also applied to individual firearm ownership, that they need not be affiliated with a militia, and be free to *keep and to bear* within their own homes and legally outside of them. The *District of Columbia v. Heller* laid the groundwork that reaffirmed the Second Amendment isn't just for law enforcement, the military, or the militia—it's also for the individual.

The victory of *Heller* paved the way for *McDonald v. Chicago*, involving seventy-seven-year-old Otis McDonald from Morgan Park, Chicago, who history will remember as the man who took on and brought down Chicago's gun ban. Spring-boarding off of *Heller*, this case examined whether states could prohibit the possession of handguns in the home, since it was decided that the federal government cannot. McDonald

was tired of the gangs and drug crime ravaging his neighborhood, and he feared for his own life and that of his family's.
According to McDonald, Chicago's gun ban was the equivalent
of the slave codes from the south, codes enacted by states after
the abolishment of slavery to keep free men and women from
owning firearms due to their skin color. There was a wrong
done a long time ago that dates back to slavery time. I could
feel the spirit of those people running through me as I sat in the
Supreme Court," he said.[18]

McDonald wasn't just a Second Amendment hero, he was a
civil rights hero. He died on April 4, 2014, just two years after
his victory. Just days before McDonald passed away, Chicago
posted their lowest homicide totals since 1958. Numerous studies and statistics (listed in previous chapters) show that this is
the natural conclusion of allowing law-abiding Americans to
defend themselves as constitutionally allowed.

Since the *Heller* and *McDonald* petitions for certiorari requests have received more media attention, these two victories
have given momentum to pro–Second Amendment advocates
in these cases. The Supreme Court declined to hear *NRA v.
BATFE* and also refused *Drake v. Jerejian*, which would have decided who can legally possess and carry guns and where you can
take and use your gun, respectively.

Wilson v. Cook County is a case currently making its way
through the Illinois judicial system. Three Cook County residents challenged the county's ordinance which banned vaguely
detailed "assault weapons" based solely on cosmetics and not
on firearm capability, and to challenge the ordinance's lack of
a grandfather clause, making all previously owned firearms of
the sort illegal and owners criminals unless they turned them

in, sent them out of the state, or modified them into compliance.

STATE BY STATE

Around the same time of *McDonald* a Chicago federal appeals court ruled that citizens's right to carry a firearm in public for the purpose of self-defense is protected by the Second Amendment. Commonly known as *Moore v. Madigan*, the case is actually a pair of court battles (the other being *Shepard v. Madigan*) that challenged Illinois's ban on carrying firearms. In 2009, sixty-nine-year-old Mary Shepard was volunteering at her Baptist church along with seventy-six-year-old Leona Mount when Willis Bates discovered them during a burglary attempt. He beat them within an inch of their lives and left them for dead. Bates fractured Shepard's skull, broke her cheekbone and nose, fractured her jaw, and gave her a concussion after viciously stomping on and kicking her head. Shepard, who holds two concealed-carry permits in two different states and has undergone rigorous firearms training, had been disarmed by the state of Illinois's gun ban and made a victim. Gun bans protect only criminals. Shepard sought to change that, and won with the help of the NRA.

Earlier I mentioned that the battle for the Second Amendment has moved to the states. So far this has been about as successful as the national effort to disarm America, but it doesn't mean that we can be lax in our vigilance. My home state has few restrictions on Second Amendment liberties but in the wake of Sandy Hook lawmakers took to solving the problem of protecting state schoolchildren on a limited budget for many districts. SB 656, a bill that would allow teachers and school officials to become protection officers and each carry a firearm for defense against a possible Adam Lanza, with police vetting and training. The measure was soundly approved by the Republican controlled Senate, 111–28.

Earlier, on July 1, 2013, South Dakota passed a low to allow for the supervised arming of teachers with its "School Sentinel" law. Teachers who want to carry would seek permission from the school district and undergo training before being permitted. In May 2013 Alabama passed a similar measure to allow teachers to carry in HB 116, so long as teachers passed scrutiny and were trained by the local sheriff.

Anti–Second Amendment groups claim that armed teachers will cause casualties, demonstrating their lack of faith in educators to not only educate our children but protect them, and ignoring that every tragedy on a campus was done by an outside individual, not armed personnel. They ignore the success of this plan, which is the Israelification of school security.

In 1974 members of the Democratic Front for the Liberation of Palestine invaded the Netiv Meir Elemenraty School and took more than 115 people hostage, 102 of which were children, in a two-day standoff. Terrorists killed twenty-five children. An IDF special forces unit ended the standoff. Israel didn't play; after the massacre they implemented a policy in which school personnel comprised of parents, grandparents, and other school administrators were trained by the civil guard and stationed in the schools conceal carrying semiautomatic handguns. That was the last massacre at an Israeli school. Any later attempts were quickly defused.

Americans are seeing now that the lives of their children are more important than political correctness, and the Israeli method is further proof that allowing schools to protect our children *works*.

Texas, so often portrayed as the Wild West, where gun laws are the least restrictive, actually has some of the more restrictive gun laws in the country and more bureaucratic CHL courses. It's a massive drawback that reduces the state's appeal—a shame, considering the state's financial appeal. Grassroots groups are pushing for a more conservative Republican majority, with emphasis on prospective elected leaders strong on Second Amendment issues. Meanwhile, Bloomberg's millions are going toward pushing anti–Second Amendment policies in state legislatures all across the country. It's taken him this long, but he's finally got it, although he realizes how unsuccessful that effort would be after the Colorado disaster. It's one reason he's poured resources into targeting fast food joints: It's the perception of impact without teeth.

Granted, there have been Second Amendment losses, too, mostly in states with extreme gun control laws already in effect such as New Jersey, Connecticut, or New York, with their restrictive SAFE Act that reduces magazine capacity to seven bullets—but there was a win on that for Second Amendment supporters. In December 2013 Federal District Court judge William Skretny ruled that the seven-bullet limit on magazine capacity violated the Second Amendment and thus was unconstitutional. You can't find a magazine for a semiautomatic handgun—*the* firearm of choice for self-defense by civilians.

Sure, you could load seven bullets into a standard-capacity ten-round magazine but, as *Legal Insurrection*'s Andrew Branca notes: "One could use a large capacity magazine and only load it to 7-rounds; if, that is, one were willing to risk a felony conviction based on a police officer's honest ability to accurately count to seven. Not me, thanks."[19]

Why are states' rights so important? There is the ongoing argument if whether it is Constitutionally allowable for states to enact limitations on Second Amendment liberties in the name of regulating said liberties. In many ways, it's what *Moore v. Madigan* was all about. Note this from Justice Antonin Scalia in his majority opinion on *Heller*:

> *The Second Amendment right is not unlimited. It is not a right to keep and carry any weapon whatsoever in any manner whatsoever and for whatever purpose. For example: concealed weapons prohibitions have been upheld under the Amendment or state analogues. The Court's opinion should not be taken to cast doubt on longstanding prohibitions on the possession of firearms by felons and the mentally ill, or laws forbidding the carrying of firearms in sensitive places such as schools and government buildings, or laws imposing conditions and qualifications on the commercial sale of arms.*

Some states allow concealed-carry with a permit, and of those states some are shall issue or may issue. States like Alaska, Arizona, Vermont, and Wyoming have unrestricted, or constitutional carry. No permit is required to carry concealed. You can also legally open-carry in these states sans permit. To contrast:

You cannot open-carry a handgun. Concealed-carry requires a permit, and permitting between states differs in testing and reciprocity.[20]

Scalia was appealing to states' rights in determining Second Amendment liberties. He's a Supreme Court justice, and I am not, yet I still disagree with him because I believe constitutional rights such as speech and bearing arms to be preeminent over state sovereignty. These are liberties derived from God, unpolluted by the state with exceptions for mental stability and criminal record. Scalia's interview with Chris Wallace in July 2012 on the issue of *Heller* revealed more of his thought process. The justice remarked:

> *What the opinion* Heller *said is that it will have to be decided in future cases. What limitations upon the right to bear arms are permissible. Some undoubtedly are, because there were some that were acknowledged at the time. For example, there was a tort called affrighting, which if you carried around a really horrible weapon just to scare people, like a head ax or something, that was I believe a misdemeanor…My starting point and ending point probably will be what limitations are within the understood limitations that the society had at the time. They had some limitation on the nature of arms that could be born. So, we'll see what those limitations are as applied to modern weapons.*

Two things: First, Scalia specifically mentioned unusual weapons (and he says that the Second Amendment is inapplicable to "arms that cannot be hand-carried") uncommonly owned by the populace; second, he refers to *motive*. Anti–Second

Amendment advocates aren't arguing for "unusual" weapons, they're arguing against the most common and widely owned firearms in the country. Secondly, law-abiding Second Amendment owners don't engage in affrighting. These laws are already on the books.

Regardless, it is Scalia's opinion that anti–Second Amendment advocates are hoping to bastardize while shifting the battle over right to bear arms to the states and localities. Perhaps, they figure, by starting with city councils and moving on up, they can effect strict anti-gun policies and from that momentum change the national sentiment. In other words, retail politicking the Second Amendment from the Constitution. Fortunately for us, the vast majority of anti–Second Amendment advocates are terrifyingly angry people prone to hypocrisies and hysterical outbursts. They do the job for us of persuading people *against* their platform. Don't be apathetic, however. The entire reason, for instance, that Bloomberg groups have received national attention and are edging the Brady Campaign out of some of its turf is because they are pretentiously, annoyingly relentless with their nagging. Fast food restaurants are being forced to issue nonstatements on issues of policy just to shut them up.

Despite the best efforts of Bloomberg to hijack the female sex with his porn-titled Moms Demand Action group to exploit mothers and make them the face of gun control, most mothers disagree. At the NRA Convention in Indianapolis in 2014, thousands upon thousands of mothers roamed the exhibitor hall looking at the latest and greatest in firearms. The surge of female firearms enthusiasts even caught the attention of the *New York Times*, which profiled the new face of gun ownership in a February 2013 article titled "Rising Voice of Gun Ownership Is Female." The *Times*[21] profiled a number of female gun groups and noted:

> *Women's participation in shooting sports has surged over the last decade, increasing by 51.5 percent for target shooting from 2001 to 2011, to just over 5 million women, and by 41.8 percent for hunting, according to the National Sporting Goods Association.*
>
> *Gun sales to women have risen in concert. In a survey last year by the National Shooting Sports Foundation, 73 percent of gun dealers said the number of female customers had gone up in 2011, as had a majority of retailers surveyed in the two previous years.*

Anti–Second Amendment advocates have insisted that women are simply adopting firearms to appropriate a Dirty Harriet persona when, in reality, female firearm ownership disputes their prejudiced association of masculinity, the patriarchy, and firearms. The left fetishizes men and guns and ignores women except to inaccurately lecture us about falling victim to firearms at the hands of men—which is *precisely* why so many women opt to empower themselves with this ultimate equalizer.

Beyond this, women enjoy hunting and communing with nature and more women are entering competitive shooting. Competitive shooting Olympians like Amanda Furrer and Sarah Scherer are becoming the norm, not the exception. According Gallup's annual poll on firearm ownership, the number of female gun owners is at an all-time high. Gallup in 2005 concluded that 13 percent of women were gun owners. In 2010, 36 percent reported a gun in their home or on their property. As of 2011, 43 percent of women reported a gun in their home and 23 percent said they personally owned at least one gun.[22]

It is empowering for a woman to know that if need be, she can handle her family's security and she can hunt. I once visited the home of my friends Ted and Shemane Nugent in Waco, Texas. Walking through the front door, I made the mistake of assuming that their amazing predator wall—what I call a trophy wall, because they remind me of the trophy room in *Predator*—was to showcase most of Ted's kills. Shemane quickly corrected me and pointed out that more than half of the mounted heads on the wall and the zebra rug on which we were standing were courtesy of her, the legit Queen of the Forest. Shemane features on her own television show with Ted, *Spirit of the Wild*, carried on the Outdoor Channel. I view her as somewhat of a pioneer in women's hunting. I watched her when my boys were very small and seeing her expertly handle her firearm or bow and kill meat for her family did a lot to dispel the myths I had in my own mind about women and hunting. I imagine it did the same for many other women. The same with Sarah Palin and her reality show, which showcased her beautiful state of Alaska and the Palins' dependence on hunting for meat during winter. We need more television shows featuring women and hunting.

This is a trend, a victory for Second Amendment advocates, and firearms manufacturers have moved to capitalize on it, giving women what they want—and we're not just talking pink pistols. Magpul is introducing slimmer, more streamline furniture like slenderer grips; other manufacturers are creating thinner, lighter profiles and smaller frames for female customers. Nemesis Firearms has a collapsable rifle perfect for hunting.

It's not just the firearms themselves—accessories are flooding the market. Personally, I find most concealed-carry handbags to be aesthetically vomit-inducing, but thank heavens for capitalists, because every week I see a new line of bags that serve two purposes and look great while doing so. Concealed-carry has gone further in fashion than just accessories like bags, it's gone *firearms couture*. Chicago-based fashion designer Sarah Church launched a line of concealed carry dresses because she believes women shouldn't have to sacrifice. In Church's home state of Illinois more than 8,300 concealed carry licenses were issued to women, 20 percent of the total.[23] Church makes concealed carry dresses, garters, and in 2014 participated in the second annual Firearms and Fashion show in Chicago, hosted by retailers Marilyn Smolenski and Karen Bartuch (also a former police officer) who told the *Tribune* that "we're girly girls who like fashion, but we like guns, too."

———

Support for the Second Amendment has always been mainstream and the effort to turn Americans against their own self interests on this issue has proven a difficult hill to climb for anti-gun advocates. Tragedies are rare and they are awful, but they don't trump my right to legally and peacefully carry a firearm. I'm not going to be persuaded to give up my rifle or my pistol simply because a criminal may have one. I want to match or outmatch the skill and firearms resources of any perp who threatens to harm my family or make me into a statistic. I will not be disarmed by the state under the guise of safety regulations.

No, Michael Bloomberg. The face of gun control isn't a wealthy PR executive from Monsanto that you lured into fronting an extremist [hate] group against law-abiding moms. The faces of gun control are rapists. Drug dealers. Gang members. Car jackers. Muggers. Abusers. By working to disarm women—and men—you're encouraging them.

———

My commitment to protecting my Second Amendment civil liberties shouldn't pose any threat to anyone except those who seek to exert control over a vulnerable target. That I carry a firearm doesn't mean a firearm will magically appear in the hands of one who chooses *not* to carry. It is a choice. The Second Amendment ensures that we have that choice, a choice not given to us by a government but a choice protected *from* government. That which government gives can be taken away, which is precisely why the Founders never enshrined the authority over gun rights within the often weak, easily influenced dominion of man. That authority, the authority to choose to lawfully carry or not to carry, is an individual choice. My holster, my choice. Let's protect it.

Notes

CHAPTER 1: THE TRAGEDY CAUCUS

1 The video is widely available on the Internet.
2 The ban was overturned by a court of appeals in late 2012, but the city was given 180 days to apply the ruling.

CHAPTER 2: OBAMA'S WAR ON GUNS

1 "United States—Gun Facts, Figures and the Law," Gun Policy.org, http://www.gunpolicy.org/firearms/region /united-states.
2 The questionnaire went on to say: "If so, provide complete ownership and registration information. Has the registration ever lapsed? Please also describe how and by whom it is used and whether it has been the cause of any personal injuries or property damage."

CHAPTER 3: THE ANTI-GUN LOBBY

1 Alex Pappas, "Exclusive: Gov. Tom Ridge Resigns From Bloomberg's New Gun Control Group," *Daily Caller*, April

25, 2014, http://dailycaller.com/2014/04/25/exclusive-gov-tom-ridge-resigns-from-bloombergs-new-gun-control-organization/.

2   John R. Lott, "Typical Misinformation Put Out by Bloomberg's Moms Demand Action: The Claim That US Accounts for '84% of Female Firearm Homicides in 25 Countries Are in US,'" Crime Prevention Research Center, May 25, 2014, http://crimepreventionresearchcenter.org/2014/05/typical-misinformation-put-out-by-bloombergs-moms-demand-action/.

3   "Suspect Arrested in Fatal Shooting near Morehouse College," myfoxatlanta.com, June 20, 2013, updated November 7, 2013, http://www.myfoxatlanta.com/story/22648057/suspect-arrested-in-fatal-shooting-near-morehouse-college.

4   Laura Anthony and Lilian Kim, "Friends, Family Gather at School to Mourn Teen," ABC 7 News, February 14, 2013, http://abc7news.com/archive/8992648/.

5   "2 Teens Charged in Shooting of Elizabeth City State Univ. Student," WVEC.com, August 30, 2013, http://www.wvec.com/news/escu-221819011.html.

6   Tachana Johnson, "Fight over Money Leads to Shooting at Stillman College," ABC3340.com, April 17, 2013, http://www.abc3340.com/story/22003093/fight-over-money-leads-to-shooting-at-stillman-college

7   "Schools React to Asst. Principal's Shooting Death," Newschannel5.com, July 25, 2007, http://www.newschannel5.com/story/6834915/schools-react-to-asst-principals-shooting-death.

8   Andrew Ford and Stacey Barchenger, "Shooting on Fla.

campus May Have Been Self-Defense," *USA Today*, January 30, 2014, http://www.usatoday.com/story/news/nation/2014/01/30/florida-state-college-shooting/5059041/.

9 Seth Koenig, "Police Release Name of Teen Who Shot Himself During Homecoming Festivities in Gray," *Bangor Daily News*, September 30, 2013, http://bangordailynews.com/2013/09/30/news/lewiston-auburn/police-release-name-of-teen-who-allegedly-shot-himself-during-homecoming-festivities-in-gray/.

10 Adam Ferrise, "Police: Two Boys Charged in Brush High School Shooting May Have Fired Shots at Man over Girl," cleveland.com, February 12, 2014, http://www.cleveland.com/metro/index.ssf/2014/02/police_two_boys_charged_in_bru.html.

CHAPTER 4: FLYOVER BIGOTRY

1 FBI Uniform Crime Reports 2010.

2 FBI Uniform Crime Reports 1992.

3 John R. Lott Jr., *More Guns, Less Crime: Understanding Crime and Gun Control Laws* (Chicago: University of Chicago Press, 1998).

4 Clayton E. Cramer and David B. Kopel, "'Shall Issue': The New Wave of Concealed Handgun Permit Laws," *Tennessee Law Review* 62, no. 3 (Spring 1995), pp. 679–757.

5 FBI Uniform Crime Reports 2012.

6 FBI Uniform Crime Reports 2007.

7 Kim Bellware, "Chicago Posts Lowest First Quarter Homi-

cide Totals Since 1958," *Huffington Post*, April 1, 2014, http://www.huffingtonpost.com/2014/04/01/chicago-homicide-rate-2014_n_5070438.html.

8   2012 CDC death and mortality data.

CHAPTER 5: GUNS FOR THEM, BUT NOT FOR YOU

1   "Crazed Eco-Terrorist Shot Dead After Taking Hostages at Discovery Channel HQ After They 'Ignored His Ideas for a TV Show'," *Mail Online*, September 2, 2010, http://www.dailymail.co.uk/news/article-1308138/Eco-terrorist-James-Jay-Lee-shot-dead-Discovery-Channel-HQ.html.

2   Victor Medina, "Fact Check: Columbine High's Armed Guard Saved Student Lives," *Examiner.com*, December 24, 2012, http://www.examiner.com/article/fact-check-columbine-high-s-armed-guard-saved-student-lives.

3   Jessica Montoya Coggins, "Woman, 86, Defends Herself with a Gun During Home Invasion (But Only Shoots a Wall)," *Mail Online*, February 7, 2013, http://www.dailymail.co.uk/news/article-2275142/Woman-86-defends-gun-home-intrusion.html.

4   Anna Chan, "Chris Rock, Jim Carrey, Bruce Willis Take Fresh Aim in Gun Control Debate," NBC News, February 6, 2013, http://entertainment.nbcnews.com/_news/2013/02/06/16872099-chris-rock-jim-carrey-bruce-willis-take-fresh-aim-in-gun-control-debate?lite.

CHAPTER 6: GUN CONTROL, A RAPIST'S BEST FRIEND

1 "Media Cites Convicted Rapist As Anti-Gun Source," January 30, 2013, The Dana Show, January 30, 2013, http://danaloeschradio.com/media-cites-convicted-rapist-as-anti-gun-source/.

2 Crisis Connection, National College Health Risk Behavior Survey, Fisher, Cullen, and Turner, 2000.

3 One In Four USA Sexual Assault Statistics; NY State Coalition Against Sexual Assault; CDC SV Data Sheet 2012.

4 National Crime Victimization Survey, 2001

5 Robin Warshaw, *I Never Called It Rape: The* Ms. *Report on Recognizing, Fighting, and Surviving Date and Acquaintance Rape* (New York: HarperPerennial, 1994).

6 U.S. Department of Justice, Bureau of Justic Statistics, "Sex Offenses and Offenders: An Analysis of Data on Rape and Sexual Assault," January 1, 1997.

7 Don B. Kates et al., "Guns and Public Health: Epidemic of Violence or Pandemic of Propaganda?" *Tennessee Law Review* 62 (1994).

8 Kendall Brunette, "Young Women Help Grow Colorado Gun-Ownership Numbers," *Coloradoan.com*, November 24, 2013, http://archive.coloradoan.com/article/20131124/NEWS01/311240067/Young-women-help-grow-Colorado-gun-ownership-numbers.

9 Dana Hunsinger Benbow, "Well Armed: Gun Permits for Indiana Women Up 42 Percent," *Indy Star*, April 25, 2014, http://www.indystar.com/story/life/2014/04/24/armed-gun-permits-indiana-women-percent/8095055/.

10 Carol Marin, "Firearms and Fashion—How Chic!" *Chicago*

Sun-Times, May 2, 2014, http://www.suntimes.com/news
/marin/27199359-452/firearms-fashion-how-chic.html#
.U5ZMWZSwL19.

CHAPTER 7: THE LEFT-WING LYNCHING

1   David B. Kopel, "Trust the People: The Case Against Gun
    Control," CATO Institute, July 11, 1988, http://www.cato
    .org/pubs/pas/pa109.html.

CHAPTER 9: VIOLENT EUROPEANS

1   Quoted in Glenn Beck, *Control* (New York: Simon and
    Schuster/Threshhold Editions, 2013), p. 16.
2   Quoted in Beck, *Control*, p. 18.
3   Don B. Kates and Gary Mauser, "Would Banning Firearms
    Reduce Murder and Suicide? A Review of International
    and Some Domestic Evidence," *Harvard Journal of Law
    and Public Policy* 30, no. 2 (2006), pp. 649–694.
4   Beck, *Control*, p. 16.
5   Chart from Beck, *Control*, p. 17.
6   Olga Khazan, "Here's How U.S. Gun Violence Compares
    with the Rest of the World," WorldViews (blog), Washing-
    ton Post, December 24, 2012,
    http://www.washingtonpost.com/blogs/worldviews/wp/
    2012/12/14/schoo-shooting-how-do-u-s-gun-homicides-
    compare-with-the-rest-of-the-world/.
7   Ibid.

8 Dr. John R. Lott Jr., "Think Tough Gun Laws Keep Euro-
    peans Safe? Think Again...," Fox News, June 10, 2010,
    http://www.foxnews.com/opinion/2010/06/10/john-lott-
    america-gun-ban-murders-multiple-victim-public-
    shootings-europe/.

9 Ibid.

10 Beck, *Control*, pp. 29–30.

11 Lott, *More Guns, Less Crime*, p. 316.

12 Joyce Lee Malcolm, "Two Cautionary Tales of Gun Con-
    trol," *Wall Street Journal*, December 26, 2012,
    http://online.wsj.com/news/articles/
    SB10001424127887323777204578195470446855466.

13 Quoted in Beck, *Control*, p. 18.

14 Beck, *Control*, p. 19.

15 Malcolm, "Two Cautionary Tales of Gun Control."

16 Ibid.

17 Beck, *Control*, p. 23.

18 Malcolm, "Two Cautionary Tales of Gun Control."

19 Lott, *More Guns, Less Crime*, pp. 316–319.

20 Beck, *Control*, pp. 37–39.

21 Lott, *More Guns, Less Crime*, p. 325.

CHAPTER 10: RECLAIMING THE LANGUAGE

1 Graham Noble, "Gun Violence Facts in New Report Con-
    tradict Anti-Gun Narrative," Liberty Voice, June 26, 2013,
    http://guardianlv.com/2013/06/gun-violence-facts-in-
    new-report-contradict-anti-gun-narrative//

2 Tonya Weathersbee, "How 'Stand Your Ground' Is Killing

Black People," *Roanoke Times*, March 17, 2014,
http://www.roanoke.com/opinion/commentary/
weathersbee-how-stand-your-ground-is-killing-black-
people/article_d738013c-abcc-11e3-8640-0017a43b2370
.html.

3 "Florida's Stand Your Ground Law," *Tampa Bay Times*, updated December 21, 2013, http://www.tampabay.com
/stand-your-ground-law/fatal-cases.

4 Robert J. Cottrol and Raymond T. Diamond, "The Second
Amendment: Toward an Afro-Americanist Reconsideration," *Georgetown Law Review* 80 (1991).

5 David B. Kopel, "The Klan's Favorite Law," *Reason*, February 15, 2005, http://reason.com/archives/2005/02/15/the-
klans-favorite-law.

6 Ronald Reagan, "Why I'm for the Brady Bill," *New York
Times*, March 29, 1991, http://www.nytimes.com/1991/03/
29/opinion/why-i-m-for-the-brady-bill.html.

7 Caroline May, "Biden to NRA: We 'Don't Have the Time' to
Prosecute Gun Buyers Who Lie on Background Checks,"
Daily Caller, January 18, 2013, http://dailycaller.com/
2013/01/18/biden-to-nra-we-dont-have-the-time-to-
prosecute-people-who-lie-on-background-checks/.

CHAPTER 11: THE FOURTEEN BIGGEST ANTI-GUN LIES, DEBUNKED

1 Gary Kleck and Marc Gertz, "Armed Resistance to Crime:
The Prevalence and Nature of Self-Defense with a Gun,"
Journal of Criminal Law and Criminology 86, no. 1 (Fall
1995), pp. 150–187.

Notes

2 KGO-TV, San Francisco, Calif., December 7, 2011, available at https://archive.org/details/KGO_20111208_070000_ABC_7_News_at_11PM.

3 News9, October 2012.

4 WVTM-TV, August 2012.

5 Kleck and Gertz, "Armed Resistance to Crime."

6 Marvin E. Wolfgang, "A Tribute to a View I Have Opposed," *Journal of Criminal Law and Criminology* 86, no. 1 (Fall 1995), p. 188.

7 Institute of Medicine of the National Academies, "Priorities for Research to Reduce the Threat of Firearm-Related Violence" June 2013, available at http://www.iom.edu/~/media/Files/Report%20Files/2013/Firearm-Violence/FirearmViolence_RB.pdf.

8 Kates and Mauser, "Would Banning Firearms Reduce Murder and Suicide?"

9 John R. Lott Jr. and David B. Mustard, "Crime, Deterrence, and Right-to-Carry Concealed Handguns" (John M. Olin Law and Economics Working Paper No. 41 [2nd series], University of Chicago Law School, Chicago, IL, 1996).

10 John R. Lott Jr., "Letting Teachers Pack Guns Will Make America's Schools Safer," Los Angeles Times, July 13, 2003, http://articles.latimes.com/2003/jul/13/opinion/oe-lott13.

11 Malcolm, "Two Cautionary Tales of Gun Control."

12 Ibid.

13 18 U.S.C. § 922.

14 Nicholas J. Johnson et al., *Firearms Law and the Second Amendment: Regulation, Rights, and Policy* (Frederick, MD: Wolters Kluwer Law and Business, 2012), chap. 1.

15 Susan Candiotti, "Source: Colorado Shooter's Rifle

Jammed During Rampage," CNN U.S., July 22, 2012, http://www.cnn.com/2012/07/22/us/colorado-shooting-investigation/.

16 Leslie Eaton, Daniel Gilbert, and Ann Zimmerman, "Suspect's Downward Spiral," *Wall Street Journal*, January 13, 2011, http://online.wsj.com/news/articles/SB10001424052748703889204576078331279621622.

17 "9OYS Investigates: college cites "errors" in Loughner reporting," June 2011.

18 18 U.S.C. § 922(g) and (n), 27 CFR 478.32.

19 U.S. Department of Justice, Office of Justice Programs, *Bureau of Justice Statistics: Selected Findings*, November 1995, http://bjs.gov/content/pub/pdf/woofccj.pdf.

20 U.S. Department of Justice, Office of Justice Programs, "Guns Used in Crime," *Bureau of Justice Statistics: Selected Findings*, July 1995, http://www.bjs.gov/content/pub/pdf/GUIC.PDF.

21 Philip J. Cook and Jens Ludwig, "Guns in America: National Survey on Private Ownership and Use of Firearms," *National Institute of Justice Research in Brief*, May 1997, https://www.ncjrs.gov/pdffiles/165476.pdf.

22 Glenn Kessler, "Obama's Continued Use of the Claim That 40 Percent of Gun Sales Lack Background Checks," *Fact Checker* (blog), *Washington Post*, April 2, 2013, http://www.washingtonpost.com/blogs/fact-checker/post/obamas-continued-use-of-the-claim-that-40-percent-of-gun-sales-lack-background-checks/2013/04/01/002e06ce-9b0f-11e2-a941-a19bce7af755_blog.html.

23 Federal Bureau of Investigation, "Crime in the U.S.," table 8, FBI.gov.

24 National Safety Council, "Injury Facts," 2011 Edition, http://www.nsc.org/Documents/Injury_Facts/Injury_Facts_2011_w.pdf.

25 "Car Crashes Are Number One Killer of Children in the U.S.," ABC2, August 9, 2012, http://www.abc2news.com/news/health/car-crashes-are-number-one-killer-of-children-in-the-us; Gary Kleck, *Targeting Guns: Firearms and Their Control* (Piscataway, NJ: Transaction, 1997); National Safety Council, "Injury Facts," 2001 Edition.

CHAPTER 12: VICTORY

1 "Adam Lanza's Motive: Did Fear of Being Committed Lead to Sandy Hook Elementary Shooting?" *Huffington Post*, December 21, 2012, http://www.huffingtonpost.com/2012/12/19/adam-lanza-motive_n_2329508.html.

2 Robert Miller and Dick Perrefort, "Report: Mother Said Adam Lanza Had 'No Feelings,'" *Stamford Advocate*, November 25, 2013, http://www.stamfordadvocate.com/local/article/Report-Mother-said-Adam-Lanza-had-no-feelings-5011614.php.

3 Edgar Sandoval and Corky Siemaszko, "Request for Gun Permits in Newtown Set to Double Last Year's Numbers: Police," *New York Daily News*, August 15, 2013, http://www.nydailynews.com/news/national/request-gun-permits-double-newtown-connecticut-article-1.1426754.

4 "Shooter with Hit-List Shot Dead in AT&T Store," WKTV.com, May 27, 2010 (updated November 24, 2013),

http://www.wktv.com/news/crime-reports/
95032689.html.

5   Dan Haar, "Untold Thousands Flout Gun Registration
    Law," *Courant*, February 10, 2014, http://articles
    .courant.com/2014-02-10/business/hc-haar-gun-
    registration-felons-20140210_1_assault-weapons-rifles-
    gun-registration-law.

6   Dana Loesch, "Colorado Senator Claims Democracy Is
    Racist," *RedState,* June 11, 2013, http://www.redstate.com
    /diary/dloesch/2013/06/11/colorado-senator-claims-
    democracy-is-racist/.

7   "Save the Race Bait: Giron Plays the Race Card," *Colorado
    Peak Politics*, June 11, 2013, http://coloradopeakpolitics
    .com/2013/06/11/save-the-race-bait-giron-plays-the-
    race-card-ignoring-that-3-other-hispanics-opposed-gun-
    grab/.

8   Kirk Woundy, "Giron, Like Morse, Defeated in Recall,"
    Colorado Springs Independent, September 10, 2013,
    http://www.csindy.com/IndyBlog/archives/2013/09/10
    /early-results-have-morse-in-danger.

9   Lynn Bartels, Kurtis Lee, and Tim Hoover, "Joe Biden
    Calls Four Colorado Democrats On Gun Bills, GOP
    Smells a Rat," *Denver Post*, February 18, 2013,
    http://www.denverpost.com/ci_22601723/colorado-
    republicans-democrats-butt-head-gun-debate-drags.

10 Mari A. Schaefer, "Ex–Marcus Hook Mayor Sentenced to
    10–20 months," *Philly.com*, January 15, 2014,
    http://articles.philly.com/2014-01-15/news/
    46188759_1_schiliro-nicholas-dorsam-false-
    imprisonment.

11 Dana Loesch, "Bloomberg Fail: Mayor's Presser Aims Guns at Audience, Literally," *RedState*, August 19, 2013, http://www.redstate.com/diary/dloesch/2013/08/19 /bloomberg-fail-mayors-presser-aims-guns-at-audience-literally/.

12 Tara Palmeri, "Bloomberg Spending NYC Cash, Resources on Nevada Trip as Part of Push for Tougher Gun Laws," *New York Post*, June 25, 2013, http://nypost.com/2013/06 /25/bloomberg-spending-nyc-cash-resources-on-nevada-trip-as-part-of-push-for-tougher-gun-laws/.

13 "Dubious Mayors Against Legal Guns: The Not So Pretty Story Behind Michael Bloomberg's Mayors Against Illegal Guns," Capital Research Center, March 5, 2014, http://capitalresearch.org/2014/03/dubious-mayors-against-legal-guns-the-not-so-pretty-story-behind-michael-bloombergs-mayors-against-illegal-guns/.

14 Michael Scherer, "Bloomberg's Gamble: Risking the Democratic Senate Majority for Gun Control," *Time*, May 28, 2013, http://swampland.time.com/2013/05/28/ bloombergs-gamble-risking-the-democratic-senate-majority-for-gun-control/.

15 "Mayors Misled: Gun Group Needs a New Name," *New Hampshire Union Leader*, July 22, 2013, http://www .unionleader.com/article/20130723/OPINION01/ 130729794.

16 "Chipotle to Customer: 'Not A Ban' on Guns," The Dana Show, May 22, 2014, http://danaloeschradio.com/ chipotle-to-customer-not-a-ban-on-guns/.

17 Don Thompson, "Gun Control Advocates: Lawmaker Arrest Is Setback," Associated Press, March 27, 2014,

available at http://news.yahoo.com/gun-control-advocates-lawmaker-arrest-setback-220631790.html.

18   Dahleen Glanton, "Otis McDonald, 1933–2014: Fought Chicago's Gun Ban," *Chicago Tribune*, April 6, 2014, http://articles.chicagotribune.com/2014-04-06/news/ct-otis-mcdonald-obituary-met-20140406_1_gun-ban-illinois-state-rifle-association-gun-rights.

19   Andrew Branca, "Federal Court Voids 7-Round Mag Limit of NY's SAFE Act, Allows Rest," *Legal Insurrection*, December 31, 2013, http://legalinsurrection.com/2013/12/federal-court-voids-7-round-mag-limit-of-nys-safe-act-allows-rest/.

20   Jazz Shaw, "NJ 'Gun Control' Law Would Ban Small Bore Hunting Rifles," hotair.com, May 25, 2014, http://hotair.com/archives/2014/05/25/nj-gun-control-law-would-ban-small-bore-hunting-rifles/.

21   Erica Goode, "Rising Voice of Gun Ownership Is Female," *New York Times*, February 10, 2013 http://www.nytimes.com/2013/02/11/us/rising-voice-of-gun-ownership-is-female.html?pagewanted=all&_r=0.

22   Deborah Netburn, "The Number of U.S. Women Who Say Household Has a Gun Hits Record High," *Los Angeles Times*, October 26, 2011, http://latimesblogs.latimes.com/nationnow/2011/10/gallup-poll-record-43-of-us-women-have-gun-in-house.html.

23   Dahleen Glanton, "Mixing Guns and Fashion," *Chicago Tribune*, May 10, 2014, http://articles.chicagotribune.com/2014-05-10/news/ct-concealed-carry-fashion-met-20140509_1_gun-owners-holster-dress.

Index

Index

Index

Index

Index